Hart Crane's Queer Modernist Aesthetic

Hart Crane's Queer Modernist Aesthetic

Niall Munro

© Niall Munro 2015

All rights reserved. No reproduction, copy or transmission of this publication may be made without written permission.

No portion of this publication may be reproduced, copied or transmitted save with written permission or in accordance with the provisions of the Copyright, Designs and Patents Act 1988, or under the terms of any licence permitting limited copying issued by the Copyright Licensing Agency, Saffron House, 6–10 Kirby Street, London EC1N 8TS.

Any person who does any unauthorized act in relation to this publication may be liable to criminal prosecution and civil claims for damages.

The author has asserted his right to be identified as the author of this work in accordance with the Copyright, Designs and Patents Act 1988.

First published 2015 by
PALGRAVE MACMILLAN

Palgrave Macmillan in the UK is an imprint of Macmillan Publishers Limited, registered in England, company number 785998, of Houndsmills, Basingstoke, Hampshire, RG21 6XS.

Palgrave Macmillan in the US is a division of St Martin's Press LLC, 175 Fifth Avenue, New York, NY 10010.

Palgrave is the global academic imprint of the above companies and has companies and representatives throughout the world.

Palgrave® and Macmillan® are registered trademarks in the United States, the United Kingdom, Europe and other countries.

ISBN 978–1–137–40775–7

This book is printed on paper suitable for recycling and made from fully managed and sustained forest sources. Logging, pulping and manufacturing processes are expected to conform to the environmental regulations of the country of origin.

A catalogue record for this book is available from the British Library.

Library of Congress Cataloging-in-Publication Data

Munro, Niall, 1979–
 Hart Crane's queer modernist aesthetic / Niall Munro.
   pages cm
 Includes bibliographical references and index.
 ISBN 978–1–137–40775–7 (hardback)
 1. Crane, Hart, 1899–1932—Criticism and interpretation.
 2. Homosexuality and literature—United States.   3. Modernism (Literature)—United States.   I. Title.
 PS3505.R272Z754 2015
 811'.52—dc23   2014038554

Typeset by MPS Limited, Chennai, India.

To Nadia and Frieda

Contents

List of Figures	ix
Acknowledgments	x
Abbreviations and Notes on Sources	xiv
Introduction: Relationality	**1**
Writing about "the activity of living"	2
Crane's modernism	3
Difficulty and queerness	7
Following "different paths to queerness": interpreting Crane's aesthetic	11
1 American Decadence and the Creation of a Queer Modernist Aesthetic	**16**
(American) Decadence	17
Crane's Decadence: The outsider and aesthetics	19
Crane's Wilde and "song of minor, broken strain"	25
Crane's defence of Decadence	28
Forming an aesthetic vocabulary	30
Impressionism and Imagism	32
Hellenism and Walter Pater	35
2 Abstraction and Intersubjectivity in *White Buildings*	**41**
Visual influences and the language of art	42
Ekphrasis: An alternative form of literary modernism	44
The challenge to artistic and heteronormative reproduction	48
The further challenge: abstraction	50
Doubleness and the crisis of perception	52
Reality	53
Looking and touching	57
3 Spatiality, Movement, and the Logic of Metaphor	**63**
Enclosed spaces	65
Utopian spaces?	67
Atopias	71
The queer flâneur	73
The conflicts of cruising	75
A poetics of transgression	79

viii Contents

	Space deregulated	83
	The logic of metaphor, space, and the phatic aspect	85
4	**Temporality, Futurity, and the Body**	**91**
	Out of time and out of history	91
	The "Moment"	97
	Negation and futurity	99
	The body and temporal gaps	104
	Temporal blur	110
	Recurrence and sameness	112
	Self-consciousness	115
	Completion	118
	Death and ecstasy	120
	Beyond time	123
5	**Empiricism, Mysticism, and a Queer Form of Knowledge**	**125**
	The difficulties of experience and knowledge	127
	Radical empiricism	132
	The new materiality	136
	A crisis of materiality, sexuality, and language	142
	"Hauntology" of the body	147
6	**Queer Technology, Failure, and a Return to the Hand**	**150**
	Technology and failure	154
	Failed technology and queer community	157
	Language and difference	161
	Technology's threat	163
	Nature and the primitive	165
	Making things: The ordinary and a return to craft	167
Conclusion: Towards a Queer Community		**172**
	Unexpected interest	172
	Queer reading	174
	Reading strategies	176
	Embracing surprise	177
	A queer modernist community: Crane, H.D., and the reader	178

Notes 183

Bibliography 198

Index 211

List of Figures

I.1 Walker Evans, [*Hart Crane's Hands*], 1929–30, printed ca. 1970, The Metropolitan Museum of Art, Gift of Arnold H. Crane, 1972 (1972.742.11) © Walker Evans Archive, The Metropolitan Museum of Art.   xvi

Acknowledgments

I have been very fortunate, particularly so in the current climate, to have worked for a number of years now in various roles in the English and Modern Languages Department at Oxford Brookes University, and there I have also been extremely lucky to be part of a team that consists of exceptional scholars and teachers. There can be no better environment in which to work.

My first acknowledgement must be to Alex Goody. Her advice, knowledge, and expertise were essential in getting the project started and sustaining it in its original incarnation, and I owe her a great debt.

Other former and present colleagues at Oxford Brookes have been tremendously supportive, particularly Steven Matthews, who kindly offered the benefit of his experience and unfailing eye for detail at crucial moments, and Eóin Flannery, who has been a fantastic colleague in the Poetry Centre, and invited me to deliver a paper about Crane as part of the research seminar series at Brookes. Eric White has been a model of enthusiasm, intellectual commitment, and good academic sense, and his generosity in looking over and commenting thoroughly upon my work and ideas has always been much appreciated.

Mark Whalan took an interest in the project early on, answered questions that I had about Crane and Jean Toomer, and was generally encouraging. I am much indebted also to Nick Selby for his constructive and incisive comments on an original draft of parts of the book.

I also owe thanks to Richard Sales of the Camden Library Service, who made a number of enquiries on my behalf to dredge up obscure volumes from Camden's holdings.

At Palgrave Macmillan, Paula Kennedy and Peter Cary were very supportive of the book from beginning to end, and have been a pleasure to work with. The manuscript also benefited a good deal from the constructive comments of an anonymous reviewer, and I am very grateful to them.

My friend Néstor Cerdá offered great encouragement throughout the writing of the book, and his commitment to his own academic work has been an inspiration.

I should also like to put on record my thanks to TLM, LA, and TTK.

A substantial portion of the book deals with Crane's manuscripts, and if it had not been for the generosity of Gerry and Daoud Arbach, I would not have been able to visit the Crane archive at Columbia University in order to do the research which this project demanded. They have always shown interest in the book, and I am thoroughly grateful to them.

As they always have, my Mum, Dad, and my brother supported (and cajoled) me throughout the writing of this book, and I will always be thankful for everything that they have done – whether they realise it or not – in preparing me to write it. Their support has been essential.

I could not have written this book without Nadia Arbach. On a practical level she helped enormously with editing and referencing, which happen to be things she is exceptional at doing, but she also willingly gave an extraordinary amount of time and energy to the project and encouragement to me when I really needed it. Her importance in the book's creation truly was "[b]eyond all sesames of science."

Frieda should probably start her study of literature by reading *The Snowy Day* or *I Want My Hat Back*. But one day, perhaps, she might look this book over. It is dedicated to her and her mother.

Permissions and copyrights

I am grateful to Carl Schmitt Jr. for sending me documents about his father and for answering questions about Carl Schmitt's relationship with Crane, and to Professor Langdon Hammer for kindly sending me, and generously allowing me to quote from, his unpublished essay about Crane's interest in photography.

I should like to thank Jane Siegel and all the amiable staff at the Rare Book and Manuscript Library, Butler Library, Columbia University, where I spent a very enjoyable couple of weeks in the Crane archives in May and June, 2008. I am most grateful to Tara C. Craig, Reference Services Supervisor there, for allowing me to quote from the following selections from the Hart Crane Papers: "Notes for / VOYAGES," 27 September 1924, Hart Crane Papers, Rare Book & Manuscript Library, Columbia University in the City of New York, "Voyages II," ca. Autumn 1924, "Voyages II," ca. Autumn 1924, "Voyages II," ca. Autumn 1924, "Voyages – II," ca. Autumn 1924, "VOYAGES II," ca. Autumn 1924, Untitled, ca. Autumn 1924, "*CAPE HATTERAS*," ca. 1927-August 1929, "NOTES | *Cape Hatteras section – (the forge)*," ca. 1927.

I am grateful also to Nancy M. Shawcross, Curator of Manuscripts at the Kislak Center for Special Collections, Rare Books, and Manuscripts, University of Pennsylvania, Philadelphia, for permitting me to quote part of a letter from Crane to Waldo Frank from April 21, 1924: "SONNET," April 1924.

xii *Acknowledgments*

I am happy to acknowledge Jean Cannon at the Harry Ransom Center, The University of Texas at Austin, who was a great help in tracking down Crane manuscripts, and Natalia Sciarini at the Beinecke Rare Book and Manuscript Library, Yale, who also provided a number of copies of Crane documents.

I am very grateful indeed to Eileen Sullivan of the Digital Media Department at The Metropolitan Museum of Art in New York City for kindly granting me the rights to reproduce Walker Evans's photograph [*Hart Crane's Hands*], 1929–30, printed ca. 1970, The Metropolitan Museum of Art, Gift of Arnold H. Crane, 1972 (1972.742.11) © Walker Evans Archive, The Metropolitan Museum of Art.

Thanks are also due to Melissa Malone, Digital Licensing and Permissions Associate at Perseus Books for allowing me to quote from the following of Hart Crane's letters (the page references refer to the pages of my book on which these quotations appear): quotation from Ezra Pound, 30, "To Carl Zigrosser [late Feb 1919]," 32, "To Gorham Munson, Nov 22, 1919," 32, "To Gorham Munson, Dec 27, 1919," 32, "To Gorham Munson [mid-Feb 1920]," 31, "To Gorham Munson, Dec 13, 1919," 32, "To Gorham Munson, April 10 [1921]," 43, "To Gorham Munson [prob early July 1921]," 43, "To Gorham Munson, October 1, 1921," 100, "To Gorham Munson, Nov 26, 1921," 43–4, "To Gorham Munson, Dec 10, 1921," 185, "To Sherwood Anderson, Jan 10 [1922]," 44, quotation from Crane to Munson, 153, "To Allen Tate, May 16 1922," 100, "To Allen Tate, June 12 [1922]," 100, "To Gorham Munson, Sunday midnight [June 18 1922]," 136–7, "To Gorham Munson, Friday night [late Aug 1922]," 44, "To Wilbur Underwood, Dec 10, 1922," 187, "To Gorham Munson, Jan 5, 1923," 45, "To Louis Untermeyer, Jan 19, 1923," 83, "To Waldo Frank, Feb 7, 1923," 140, "To Gorham Munson, Feb 9, 1923," 77, "To Allen Tate, Feb 15 1923," 137–8, "To Gorham Munson, Feb 18, 1923," 127, "To Waldo Frank, Feb 27, 1923," 78, "To Gorham Munson, Mar 2, 1923," 193, "To Alfred Stieglitz, April 15, 1923," 60, "To Alfred Stieglitz, Fourth of July, 1923," 79, "To Jean Toomer, Sun Aug 19 [1923]," 51, "To Alfred Stieglitz, Sun Aug 25, 1923," 54, "To Jean Toomer, Sep 28 1923," 76, quotation from "Possessions," 77–8, "To Allen Tate, Mar 1, 1924," 55, "To Waldo Frank, April 21, 1924," 62, "To Jean Toomer, Mon June 16, 1924," 119, "To Waldo Frank, Aug 19 [1925]," 52–3, "To Charlotte and Richard Rychtarik, Mar 2, 1926," 156, "To Gorham Munson, Mar 17, 1926," 56, "To Wilbur Underwood, [July 1? 1926]," 192, "To Waldo Frank, Aug 19, 1926," 164, "To Yvor Winters, May 29, 1927," 35, "To Caresse Crosby, Dec 26, 1929," 159, "To Yvor Winters, June 4, 1930," 92–3, "To Wilbur Underwood, Feb 14, 1932," 143–4 from *O, My Land, My Friends: The Selected Letters of Hart Crane* by Langdon Hammer and Brom Weber, copyright © 1997. Reprinted by permission of Da Capo Press, a member of The Perseus Books Group.

I would also like to thank Elizabeth Clementson, Permissions Manager at W.W. Norton & Company, Inc for her assistance in arranging for the following permissions to quote from Hart Crane's poetry and prose: "Legend," "Black Tambourine," "My Grandmother's Love Letters," "Garden Abstract," "Stark Major," "Sunday Morning Apples," "Possessions," "Lachrymae Christi," "Passage," "The Wine Menagerie," "Recitative," "For the Marriage of Faustus and Helen," "At Melville's Tomb," "Voyages I," "Voyages II," "Voyages III," "Voyages VI," "To Brooklyn Bridge," "Ave Maria," "Van Winkle," "The River," "The Dance," "Indiana," "Cutty Sark," "Cape Hatteras," "Quaker Hill," "The Tunnel," "Atlantis," "C33," "October-November," "The Hive," "Fear," "Annunciations," "Modern Craft," "Porphyro in Akron," "Interludium," "The Broken Tower," "The Moth that God Made Blind," "Episode of Hands," "The Bridge of Estador," and "Hieroglyphic," from *The Complete Poems of Hart Crane* by Hart Crane, edited by Marc Simon. Copyright 1933, 1958, 1966 by Liveright Publishing Corporation. Copyright © 1986 by Marc Simon. Used by permission of Liveright Publishing Corporation.

"Joyce and Ethics," "Sherwood Anderson," "A Letter to Harriet Monroe," "General Aims and Theories," and "Modern Poetry," from *The Complete Poems and Selected Letters and Prose of Hart Crane* by Hart Crane, edited by Brom Weber. Copyright 1933, 1958, 1966 by Liveright Publishing Corporation. Copyright 1952 by Brom Weber. Used by permission of Liveright Publishing Corporation.

A short section of Chapter 1, "American Decadence and the Creation of a Queer Modernist Aesthetic," first appeared in the chapter "Hart Crane's American Decadence," published in *American Modernism: Cultural Transactions*, edited by Catherine Morley and Alex Goody in 2009. It is published with the permission of Cambridge Scholars Publishing, and I am grateful to Konstantinos Peslis and Chris Humphrey for granting that permission.

Abbreviations and Notes on Sources

I. Abbreviations

CP: Crane, Hart. *The Complete Poems of Hart Crane.* Ed. Marc Simon. New York: Liveright Publishing Corporation, 1986.

CPSL: Crane, Hart. *The Complete Poems and Selected Letters and Prose of Hart Crane.* Ed. Brom Weber. New York: Liveright Publishing Corporation, 1968.

OML: Crane, Hart. *O My Land, My Friends: The Selected Letters of Hart Crane.* Eds. Langdon Hammer and Brom Weber. London: Four Walls Eight Windows, 1997.

WUD: Webster, Noah, ed. *Webster's Unabridged Dictionary: An American Dictionary of the English Language.* Rev. Chauncey A. Goodrich and Noah Porter. Albany: J.B. Lyon, 1909.

LM: Lohf, Kenneth A. *The Literary Manuscripts of Hart Crane.* Columbus: Ohio State University Press, 1967.

II. Hart Crane – original manuscripts

The manuscripts cited are catalogued in Kenneth A. Lohf, ed., *The Literary Manuscripts of Hart Crane* ([Columbus]: Ohio State University Press, 1967).

"Voyages I"

A31a, "THE BOTTOM OF THE SEA IS CRUEL," October 1, 1921, Ohio State University, Columbus.

"Voyages II"

A32, "Notes for / VOYAGES," September 27, 1924, Hart Crane Papers, Rare Book & Manuscript Library, Columbia University in the City of New York.

A33, "Voyages II," ca. Autumn 1924, Hart Crane Papers, Rare Book & Manuscript Library, Columbia University in the City of New York.

A35, "Voyages II," ca. Autumn 1924, Hart Crane Papers, Rare Book & Manuscript Library, Columbia University in the City of New York.

A36, "Voyages II," ca. Autumn 1924, Hart Crane Papers, Rare Book & Manuscript Library, Columbia University in the City of New York.

A37, "Voyages – II," ca. Autumn 1924, Hart Crane Papers, Rare Book & Manuscript Library, Columbia University in the City of New York.

A39, "VOYAGES II," ca. Autumn 1924, Hart Crane Papers, Rare Book & Manuscript Library, Columbia University in the City of New York.

A42, Untitled, ca. Autumn 1924, Hart Crane Papers, Rare Book & Manuscript Library, Columbia University in the City of New York.

The Bridge

B24, "*CAPE HATTERAS*," ca. 1927-August 1929, Hart Crane Papers, Rare Book & Manuscript Library, Columbia University in the City of New York.

B29, "NOTES | *Cape Hatteras section – (the forge),*" ca. 1927, Hart Crane Papers, Rare Book & Manuscript Library, Columbia University in the City of New York.

"The Broken Tower"

C45, "The Broken Tower," March 14, 1932, University of Virginia, Charlottesville. "What miles I gather up and unto you"

D102, "SONNET," April 1924, University of Pennsylvania, Philadelphia. Incorporated into letter from Crane to Waldo Frank, April 21, 1924.

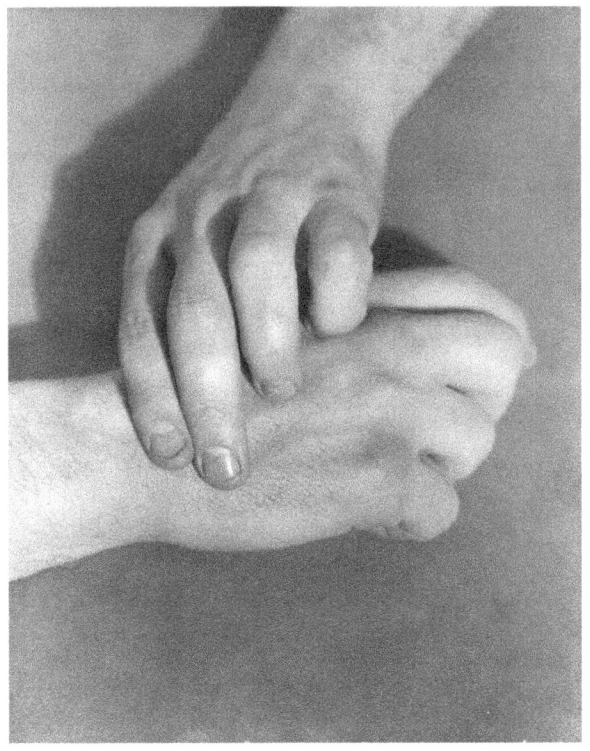

Figure I.1 Walker Evans, [*Hart Crane's Hands*], 1929–30, printed ca. 1970, The Metropolitan Museum of Art, Gift of Arnold H. Crane, 1972 (1972.742.11) © Walker Evans Archive, The Metropolitan Museum of Art.

Introduction: Relationality

With his right hand on the table, fingers bent to show only the first finger and knuckles, and his left hand placed on top of the right, Hart Crane posed for Walker Evans's camera in 1929–1930 (Figure I.1). Evans took a number of other photographs of Crane at the time this untitled picture was taken, but in photographing the poet's hands he emphasized Crane's identity as a writer. The pose itself might even suggest something of Crane's style: self-referential, unexpected, complicated. Yet these aestheticized objects are also instantly recognizable *as* hands. The arrangement of them draws a viewer to the image and to the hands, either to try and pose their own hands in a similar fashion, with the thumb invisible but the first four fingers in various stages of being bent, or simply to acknowledge that such a gesture could be an affective one of comfort or certainty. The hands therefore suggest something relational, of tactile possibility.

Crane's poem "Episode of Hands" (1920/unpublished) (*CP* 173)[1] is a verbal correlative for Evans's photograph. It too offers an "unexpected" presentation, as "unexpected interest" gives way to unexpected metaphor, a transformative moment of homoerotic contact (hands become butterflies and "knots and notches" are "like the marks of wild ponies' play") set against the unlikely background of modern technology such as wheels, factory sounds, and factory thoughts. Such contact, born of one moment of daring and surrender ("Suddenly he [...]/Consented, – and held out/One finger from the others"), even suggests the illicit ("the thick bed"), and culminates in the creation of a wordless erotic understanding, as "[t]he two men smiled into each other's eyes."

Writing about "the activity of living"

Like Evans's photograph, this poem presents a moment of aesthetic contemplation. It takes its place in a tradition of homoerotic writing, a tradition in which Robert K. Martin gave Crane a significant place in his 1979 book *The Homosexual Tradition in American Poetry*, and for a young writer (Crane was twenty-one when he wrote "Episode of Hands"), the poem is also legitimized by such literary connections. These are most obvious in the poem's allusions to the "wound dresser" Walt Whitman, whose work is also metonymically represented in the "[b]unches of new green breaking a hard turf," a phrase reminiscent of Ezra Pound's message to Whitman: "It was you that broke the new wood,/Now is a time for carving" ("A Pact" 269). But Crane's aesthetic is also formed out of this sometimes contradictory environment, indeed it consists of it: the homosexual attraction, the unexpected content and style, the sometimes oppressive modern conditions. Here is a newness ("new green breaking a hard turf") derived from sexuality, an alternative modernist aesthetic that is developed from conflicting elements and which instead of being guided by an Eliotic "impersonality," emphasizes the personal and relational.

If this too is "unexpected," it may be because in the past modernism has been dominated by heterosexual and mainly male modes of discourse and desire, represented by Pound and T. S. Eliot, though Eliot's sexuality and its effect upon his writing has been the subject of considerable discussion. Whilst the reading of Crane's work through the lens of sexuality is the basis for this book, the notion of "queerness" offers a theoretical and intellectual engagement with modernism that goes beyond sexuality and offers another way of reading modernist texts that sometimes endorses, sometimes challenges modernist formulations. Robert K. Martin has written that "Episode of Hands" represents "a strong statement of social and political unity founded on sexual bonds" (*The Homosexual Tradition in American Poetry* 139), and I argue that such striving for unity, or relationality, can be found throughout Crane's oeuvre. As his career progressed, it became clear to Crane that a form of relationality was always necessary, since readers consistently misread or claimed that they could not read his work. Yet even before this became a serious concern for Crane, I argue that relationality – creating an intimate connection with his reader – was always an essential part of his aesthetic. In her recent book-length discussion with Lee Edelman, the queer theorist Lauren Berlant has suggested ways of understanding relationality that suggest some of what is to be gained by reading Crane in this way.

In sex, in politics, in theory – in any infrastructure that we can call intimate or invested with the activity of living – we cannot banish the strangeness in ourselves or of anything in the world. While we can point to the impossibility of staying reliable to one's self- and other-directed relations and to the impact of the ways we fail them, though, these contacts can spark new forms of life, of being in the scene of relationality, whose effects are always being calculated yet are beyond calculation (*Sex, or the Unbearable* 116).

Whilst Berlant's discussion captures some of the most important recent lines of interrogation within queer theory (and some of these concerns, such as negativity, futurity, and failure I engage with in this book), it also indicates that relationality is as much about "strangeness" as it is about familiarity; recognizing the other as Other, and accepting that certain forms of failure, whether in terms of personal relations, aesthetic choices, or interactions with the world, can actually form positive or constructive modes of expression. The unexpectedness of Crane's writing, which describes "the activity of living" in ways that many readers – both in his own time and now – can find obscure, "beyond calculation," is often precisely what makes those readers turn back to Crane, and encounter in his poetry certain indefinable effects – whether they see the poetry critiquing the American modernity about which Crane wrote, or whether they perceive it in relation to the "intimate" levels of our "activity of living" now.

Crane's modernism

An analysis of Crane's queer relational aesthetic can thus help to destabilize prevailing beliefs and prejudices about Crane's work and about modernist writing in general, and in this way the book aims to take up Laura Doan and Jane Garrity's fundamental question: "how can we productively engage queer theory in a rereading of both canonical and non-canonical modernist texts while simultaneously interrogating the foundational assumptions of modernism itself?" (549). Addressing this question also allows me to examine Crane's place within modernism, a contested position that has lead Christopher Nealon to claim that "[Crane] is not, in the central accounts, a modernist, despite his chronological placement at the beginning of the twentieth century" (*Foundlings* 25). Although I disagree with Nealon's premise, his suggestion is indicative of the way in which Crane's work can be seen to sit uneasily at times within the modernist canon, and this unease or unexpectedness can, I argue, be traced to his particular, queer form of modernism.

Despite Nealon's suggestion, in one kind of reading Crane's modernism is plain. In his poetry, prose, and letters he deals with a number of themes that we might term "modernist" preoccupations, such as urban space, technology, new modes of perception, and the creation and subversions of myths, and he does so by challenging linguistic expression, frequently through a "difficult" style. Both Crane's poem "For the Marriage of Faustus and Helen" (1921–1923/1923–1924) and *The Bridge* (1923–1930/ 1927–1930) are often seen as entering into a dialogue with Eliot's *The Waste Land*, even being "positive" American responses to a "negative" postwar European poem, and some of these assertions are based upon Crane's own explanations about his work. This straightforward "modernist" reading of Crane would go on to show how his exposure to New York City and the group of writers and artists he met there, such as William Carlos Williams, Jean Toomer, Waldo Frank, and Alfred Stieglitz, sought to form a nativist American modernism that was to be based on the myths and soil of America, and whose leader, the artist, "is the bringer of a new religion, [...] the maker of multitudes" (Frank, *Our America* 230). As one of the "Young Americans," with, amongst others, Frank, Toomer, Van Wyck Brooks, and Gorham Munson, Crane pursued a particular kind of modernism, subscribing to the idea that America, corrupted by materialism, needed its writers to recreate the country as a "mystic Word" (Frank, *Our America* 10). Such pronouncements and attempts to create were evident in a number of the little magazines that these artists founded and edited, and to which they contributed.[2]

But such a narrative of Crane's modernism, even inflected by Frank's influence, gives only a limited view of the poet's complexity. Crane was certainly inspired early on by the kind of writers championed by Frank, such as Walt Whitman and Sherwood Anderson, but at this time he also embraced a transatlantic connection, reading widely within the work of Oscar Wilde, Walter Pater, and poets such as Algernon Charles Swinburne and Lionel Johnson. As I indicate in my first chapter, Crane's work can be seen to bridge the gap between these decadent writers of the 1880s and 1890s and nascent modernism. Indeed, Crane's work is representative, I argue, of a particular kind of decadent modernism that fused together different forms of experimentation in terms of language and content. This was also in part an attitude, fostered by the kind of people Crane met in the bohemian environment of Greenwich Village during his first forays into New York literary culture in the 1910s. It was represented by Guido Bruno, who took Crane's poem about Oscar

Wilde, "C33," and published it in his magazine *Bruno's Weekly* in 1916, and Joseph Kling, the editor of the *Pagan*, a magazine to which Crane contributed a number of poems and reviews, and of which he became an editor. Crane read widely amongst these little magazines and found that the kinds of publications that his friends and associates created, such as *Others*, edited by Alfred Kreymborg and William Carlos Williams, the *Little Review*, edited by Margaret Anderson and Jane Heap, and *Broom*, edited by Matthew Josephson and Gorham Munson, all contained within their covers not just the "new" work, but also published the "old," decadent material.[3] Even as late as 1922, Munson was still celebrating the work of Edgar Saltus in *Others*, a writer whom Crane admired, but who was often perceived as a lost soul from the era of French decadence (Weir, *Decadent Culture* 157).

Crane himself asserted that the American Renaissance to which he aspired could be derived from the kind of European writing that he was absorbing, but the contrast at this time with Eliot and Pound's embrace of Charles Baudelaire and the French Symbolists such as Jules Laforgue is striking. Whilst the examination of this early period in Crane's career can, as Brian M. Reed has written, "offer a corrective to the common, lingering stereotype of Crane as a belated romantic" (42), an assumption that is frequently based upon his association with Whitman and a charge of sentimentality, it also draws attention to certain contradictions that can be perceived within modernist writing. In his criticism and even in his creation of Imagism, Pound attempted to discredit the value and standing of nineties verse, accusing the writers of being too vague in their use of language, and of being Hellenists, an unofficial school of influence he associated with effeminacy. However, such commentary does not fit with Pound's own recommendations to readers and writers that they should seek out and study Sappho's lyrics, and nor does it fit with his promotion of Hilda Doolittle (H.D.), whom he even placed at the center of his new poetic movement, Imagism. As I describe in the first chapter of this book, these kinds of oppositions, which in Pound are clear contradictions, are part of the substance of Crane's queer modernism. Crane destabilizes certain of the "foundational assumptions" of modernism that Doan and Garrity discuss (549), blurring the boundaries of Impressionist writing and Imagism, and adopting the vocabulary of Pound, Eliot, and their proto-Imagist forebear, T. E. Hulme, whilst at the same time maintaining a style and attitude towards sexuality that Pound would have seen as alien to the aggressively masculine, heterosexual content and style of writing that he favored.

Crane's simultaneous rejection and acceptance of these contemporaries indicates that he was interested in writing an alternative modernism based upon his sexuality. Academic study has often sought to uncover examples of what has come to be called "lesbian modernism" in work by writers such as Dorothy Richardson, Virginia Woolf, and Willa Cather, with scholars such as Cassandra Laity and Diana Collecott drawing attention to a "Sapphic modernism" in the work of H.D., whom, they both argue, uses Hellenism as a code to express sexual desire. Yet study of "Sapphism" in respect to modernism poses two difficulties. Firstly, such analysis rarely takes into account writing of male homosexuality, and tends to examine work in which lesbianism is, in Elizabeth Meese's words, "written in invisible ink" (18) and requires decoding – a problematic issue in respect to Crane, since, as I argue throughout the book, Crane employs queer strategies that challenge modernist difficulty, and adopts a relational position in respect to his reader. Secondly, as Suzanne Raitt observes, Sapphic modernism has become such a prominent part of modernist studies – Doan and Garrity suggest it may even have become a literary subgenre – that connections between a Sapphic style and a modernist aesthetic can be made almost immediately. Not only is the kind of perverse reading of key authors done in the 1990s no longer such a revelation, but there is a correlation drawn between the kind of formal and linguistic strategies employed by lesbian writers in order to hide or express their sexuality, and the kind of strategies that have been regarded as typical of modernist writers more generally. Suzanne Raitt therefore asks: "[i]s there an inevitable link between lesbianism and modernity? Or have we imagined such a link – or at least exaggerated it – as a way of rescuing our sense of our own radicalism in a rapidly reconfiguring postmodern world?" (120). As I demonstrate in this book, Crane certainly employs techniques that might be considered modernist, such as his use of spatial and temporal gaps, his creation of neologisms, and an emphasis upon a lack of closure, but if, as Langdon Hammer has suggested, modernism "institutes and enforces its own monopolies of cultural prestige, reasserts hierarchies of sexual and racial difference, and reconstructs traditional authority in restrictive ways" (*Hart Crane and Allen Tate* 9), then complete subscription to such an authority, whether in terms of ideas or techniques, would be damaging for Crane's subversive poetics. Instead, as I will go on to discuss, Crane frequently seeks to challenge existing modernist strategies and concepts rather than merely replicate or adhere to them, whether this is in his refusal to locate himself in space and time, or in his resistance to a certain kind of knowledge and knowledge-making that he felt was being imposed upon him by the aesthetic concerns of his modernist contemporaries. Such questioning allows Crane not only to define a position for himself that is outside the modernist mainstream, but also to suggest gaps in modernist meaning and ways in which the preoccupations of modernism can exclude certain groups. In "Episode of Hands," Crane's introduction of a non-conformist relationship into the factory introduces an "unexpected" element into an otherwise precise, money-oriented environment, setting at risk the progress of modern technology within the capitalist society. This queer moment threatens to retard the progress of "the wheels" of the machines and to curtail efficiency, and at the same time makes a stand against the Taylorist principles of the factory ("factory sounds and factory thoughts/Were banished from him") by emphasizing individuality.

The bond forged across a class divide in "Episode of Hands" – the factory owner's son and the factory worker – together with this concentration upon the individual as opposed to the mass, calls attention to the democratic strain of intersubjectivity that runs through Crane's work. Here too, Crane can be seen to be writing in a way that contradicts certain assumptions about modernism's élitist sensibility, and the joining of hands demonstrates relationality, that part of Crane's aesthetic that I regard as fundamental to a definition of its queerness.

Difficulty and queerness

In its examination of modernist writing, and the presentation of new understandings of it through a reading informed by queer theory, this book attempts to "interrogate" anew what Doan and Gerrity call those "foundational assumptions of modernism." It does so by focusing upon four key areas of the modernist aesthetic: the visual (in Chapters 1 and 2), the spatial (in Chapter 3), the temporal (Chapter 4), and the material (Chapters 5 and 6). Joseph Allen Boone has remarked that "[t]o the degree that a major project of the modernist aesthetic was to reconceive the spatial-temporal coordinates of written and visual art, the queering of narrative movement in the modernist texts provides a particularly salient instance of the degree to which the more general modernist revolution in conceiving space and time was accompanied by a specific if largely unacknowledged subcultural politics of sexuality" (211). The following pages demonstrate not only that Boone's discussion of narrative can apply to modernist poetry, but that queerness fundamentally underlies some modernist writing. My argument goes further, however, to demonstrate that Crane himself conceptualized the modernist aesthetic by aspiring to what I am terming a dimensional aesthetic that was based not only on the ways in which the "subcultural politics of sexuality" recasts the spatial and temporal, but how these politics within Crane's modernism also affected the visual and material in an attempt to create an absolute aesthetic experience. As he wrote in 1925,

> it seems evident that certain aesthetic experience (and this may for a time engross the total faculties of the spectator) can be called absolute, inasmuch as it approximates a formally convincing statement of a conception or apprehension of life that gains our unquestioning assent, and under the conditions of which our imagination is unable to suggest a further detail consistent with the design of the aesthetic whole ("General Aims and Theories," *CPSL* 219).

As I have already suggested, Crane's queer modernism is characterized by an impulse towards relationality, quite unlike many of his contemporaries, and an exploration of Crane's attempts to "engross the total faculties of the spectator" naturally leads to an examination of one of the aspects of Crane's work that is most frequently discussed: difficulty. My argument is based on the ways in which Crane's work queerly contests this charge, and in doing so also negotiates certain aspects of modernist expression.

This reading challenges a number of critics of Crane who have sought to affirm Crane's difficulty or obscurity. Critics have tended to describe Crane in these terms for one of three reasons. They have determined it as a necessary mark of his modernism, perhaps subscribing to Eliot's assertion in his review of Herbert Grierson's anthology of the metaphysical poets that modern poetry had to be "difficult" ("The Metaphysical Poets" 247). They have also simply been unable to understand Crane's writing. For R. P. Blackmur, in an early and influential essay, Crane showed "the distraught but exciting splendor of a great failure" (316), and Blackmur warned readers that they must "supply or overlook what does not appear in the poems, and [...] agree to forgive or guess blindly at those parts of the poems which are unintelligible" (308). In his description of a poetics for which the reader must "supply or overlook what does not appear," Blackmur provides a wrongheaded summary of Crane's logic of metaphor, which rather than limiting his expression, seeks to extend it – an idea I explore in my third chapter. But critics, most prominent amongst them Thomas E. Yingling and Tim Dean, have also argued that Crane deliberately makes himself obscure in order to conceal his sexuality. Comparing Crane's early poetry such as "Episode of Hands" with later work of the mid-1920s, Yingling claims "not that homosexuality disappears from his work [...], but that it becomes textually obscure, hidden in a multitude of oblique references that encode it as the authorizing secret of the text" (110). I do not argue that Crane elided discussion of "difficulty" in his poetry, but Yingling's analysis neither takes into account Malcolm Cowley's reports that Crane made great efforts to render his writing less obscure through an extensive drafting process, nor does it recognize his repeated attempts to clarify his work for his readers: in the famous letter to Harriet Monroe published in *Poetry* in 1926, in "General Aims and Theories" (1925) that he wrote to assist Eugene O'Neill in his writing of a foreword to Crane's *White Buildings*, or in his essay "Modern Poetry" (1930). More specifically, Crane's "deliberate obscurity" cannot be reconciled with the attempts that Crane makes to relate to his reader with a dimensional aesthetic through which he seeks to appeal on several levels; or the intersubjective relationship that he sets up with a reader in order to acknowledge the shared difficulty in perceiving the world; or in his attempts through ekphrasis to bring his readers as close as possible to the tactile experience of an artwork.

Dean disputes Yingling's claim that Crane's work becomes encoded, and instead argues that it is created "according to the logic of a radical privacy that attempts to circumvent the very possibility-condition of such a code by constructing a form of privacy alternate to that of the closet" (101), and that "[the] [i]ntensity [of Crane's poetry] eliminates inviolate identity and produces instead a second order of substantive privacy – that of inviolate experience – which the poems preserve for their readers. Crane's reader is asked not to identify with a textually generated subject position (homosexual or otherwise) but to reexperience a *jouissance* that eliminates every subject position" (105). I concur with Dean's suggestion that Crane prioritizes experience and the re-encountering of experience in his writing. However, the kind of experience that results from the "radical privacy" that Dean describes is not representative of the queer aesthetic that Crane created in his work. Even if Dean offers an alternative to closet logic, he still suggests that Crane seeks to keep his experience sealed off in its privacy. The "inviolate experience" that "the poems preserve" is pure, untouched, and untouchable, and once encountered by his readers, is presumably left behind for future readers to experience in exactly the same way. It is an experience contrary to Crane's own desire for his writing, which he intended to grant "an orbit or predetermined direction of its own" ("General Aims and Theories," *CPSL* 220). The poem Crane describes may have its own genetic information, but it then shapes and reshapes that material as it develops and evolves: "[i]t is as though a poem gave the reader as he left it a single, new *word*, never before spoken and impossible to actually enunciate, but self-evident as an active principle in the reader's consciousness henceforward." This is a word that the reader is able to *change*, it is "active," and they incorporate it into themselves. When Yingling suggests that homosexuality is "the authorizing secret of the text," he too suggests that the experience of reading a poem by Crane results in the revealing of a stable and fixed solution. Such a proposal also implies that the sexual currents that exist to shape the queerness of Crane's aesthetic are similarly stable and fixed, but as I continue to argue in the rest of the book, queerness cannot be forced to remain static in this way.

In his queer readings of modernist drama, Nick Salvato has treated queerness "not so much [as] a category as a border-crossing between categories, if not the contestation of categorization altogether" (9). Salvato would seem to suggest that queer texts do not just break the rules but deny they ever existed, and such a position seems contrary to what I perceive as one of the strengths of queerness: its capacity to unsettle the normative. His initial premise however, that queer occupies a space in the borders, suggests a resistance to the normative might take place whilst retaining a place within that normative structure. As I argue, Crane adopts such a position between, which is not just one of resistance but also one of authority. The space occupied by Crane's queer aesthetic allows him to contest the power held over sexuality, which Michel Foucault has described as taking "the general form of limit and lack" (*The Will to Knowledge* 83). In so doing, it points once again towards Crane's unsettled and unsettling place within modernism. Later in my discussion I offer ways in which Crane's language can be perceived as a bridge, being open both to normative and non-normative forms of expression, and by occupying this space, the speaker of the poems asserts a certain authority. Thus, examining Salvato's attention to the space between is pertinent for the book, since it draws attention to those frequent moments where Crane's aesthetic contests "foundational assumptions," whether normative or modernist.

A number of my chapters directly examine this contestation. The first chapter of this book, "American Decadence and the Creation of a Queer Modernist Aesthetic," considers the poetry through Pater's notion of the "impression" ("unstable, flickering, inconsistent" (*The Renaissance* 153)), and examines how aesthetic engagement with an object allows for movement beyond that object. In the third chapter,

"Spatiality, Movement, and the Logic of Metaphor," queerness is seen to act on space, deregulating it and leading to forms of linguistic and physical transgression, whilst in the fourth chapter, "Temporality, Futurity, and the Body," Crane's queering of modernist time causes slippages and spaces to appear in which queerness can exist. In the final chapter, "Queer Technology, Failure, and a Return to the Hand," I show how Crane adopts modern technology in *The Bridge* to reveal a queerness that extends beyond the normative, material world. Crane's queer modernism therefore embraces but also contradicts and challenges modernist features of style, language, and content. Basing his work upon unfixed currents of sexuality, Crane also adopts queerness as an intellectual strategy and position of authority and validity to resist what he sees as those parts of modernist culture that restrict alternative forms of expression and instances of Otherness. Crane's work thereby opens up modernist writing for analysis of its contrasts and contradictions.

Following "different paths to queerness": interpreting Crane's aesthetic

In addition to the employment of various queer theorists, the book also reads Crane's work alongside a number of philosophers and cultural critics such as Martin Heidegger, Maurice Merleau-Ponty, Henri Lefebvre, and Michel de Certeau. In his own discussion of his use of theorists not usually associated with queer criticism José Esteban Muñoz comments that his choices were made in order to offer "different paths to queerness" (15). This is also an apt description of my approach to using philosophers and critics. Rather than restrict the focus to queer criticism of Crane, the argument seeks to open up his work by examining the ways in which Crane's queerness intersected with the heteronormative world, whether in terms of the way he looked at visual culture, the way he moved through the city, or the way in which he considered his (queer or straight) reader. Such discussion is therefore aligned with Crane's own concern that he might retain his queer identity, but still speak within – or in the gaps between – a normative framework. Furthermore, after many years of criticism that described Crane as lacking intelligence, a charge often tied into his "failure" as a poet and a man, which was itself linked to his alternative sexuality, the book also attempts to show that the intellectual density of Crane's work can sustain such inflected readings, and that it can again be seen to "reek[…] with brains," as Harriet Monroe once described it (40). In this I agree with Daniel Gabriel's claim that Crane "was an astute letter writer and theorizer about poetry and more of a 'thinker' than he has been recognized for" (5). This also means that I have frequently taken Crane at his word, and offered arguments for why he made certain choices rather than merely assume, again like past critics, that his technique or even his temperament was somehow lacking. This debate comes to its culmination in the fifth chapter, "Empiricism, Mysticism, and a Queer Form of Knowledge," in which I show how Crane's decision to ground his poetry in experience conflicted with the desires of his friends that he situate it first of all in knowledge. Setting Crane's work alongside phenomenology is a way of gesturing out from Crane's work towards the modernist world at large, an especially valuable approach since so much of Crane's poetry has been discussed as if there were no context for it whatsoever.

As I have intimated, Crane's work can contain and sustain a multiplicity of meanings and readings. Gordon A. Tapper has observed the double duty of Crane scholars when he explains that "[t]easing out these alternatives is a necessary component of reading Crane, but rather than coming to rest in a normative paraphrase, which would betray the spirit in which Crane created these enigmas, it is more important to ask why these enigmas were created in the first place" (19). In order to do so, I have used a mode of genetic criticism to chart the changes within Crane's manuscripts for "Voyages" (1921–1926/1923–1926).[4] "Voyages" is particularly apt for genetic criticism since there are numerous extant drafts for this six-part sequence (as many as fifteen for "Voyages II" alone). Malcolm Cowley has described how Crane's revision process was unusual for his time, since "[t]here were many poets of the 1920s who worked hard to be obscure, veiling a simple idea in phrases that grew more labored and opaque with each revision of a poem. With Crane it was the original meaning that was complicated and difficult; his revisions brought it out more clearly" (*Exile's Return* 230). Crane's poetry remains complex however, and a genetic approach can help to open a wider field for interpretation of Crane's work and offer new possibilities and directions for the reading of poems, the meaning of which might previously have seemed difficult to discern. Recent scholarship, such as Lawrence Kramer's annotated edition of *The Bridge* and John T. Irwin's extensive treatment of Crane's poetry (both published in 2011) have done much to suggest the scope and ambition of Crane; Irwin in particular providing a remarkable tapestry of Crane's possible and actual influences in a way that allows readers to reassess the intellectual content of his work. Irwin's method is to provide a reading of *The Bridge* first, arguing that "the best entry to the shorter poems in Crane's first volume [...] and to his last poem, 'The Broken Tower' is through his epic" (xi). Whilst I often admire his reading of Crane's poems, my discussion implicitly disagrees with this approach: *The Bridge* has always received extensive attention in criticism, and to present it in this way marginalizes the poems of *White Buildings* (not to mention Crane's other unpublished poetry), thereby encouraging readers to think of them as somehow less significant. Whilst I give due attention to *The Bridge*, I also show how it is important to demonstrate how Crane's aesthetic was shaped, and how his queer form of craft came about.

As Paul Giles has observed (5, 17), Crane spent a good deal of time developing his craft by searching through a dictionary when in the process of composition, and his notebooks are full of words and definitions that later appear in poems.[5] Malcolm Cowley recalled "his frantic searches through Webster's *Unabridged* and the big *Standard*, his trips to the library – on office time – and his reports of consultations with old sailors in South Street speakeasies" (*Exile's Return* 230).[6] Given Crane's attention to the sounds and meanings of words, my use of a contemporary Webster's dictionary is intended to approach the definitions of words as Crane would have understood them in the 1920s and 1930s.

In the course of my discussion, I range widely throughout Crane's oeuvre in an attempt to give a sense of his development as a queer modernist. I look at work that was published in his own lifetime, primarily poems collected in *White Buildings* and *The Bridge*, and a number of pieces that were only published posthumously. As my introduction has already shown, however, I do not regard Crane's juvenilia necessarily as "minor" poetry, and in the opening chapter I spend some time examining his earliest substantial poem, "The Moth That God Made Blind," as well as other poems from the 1910s such as "Modern Craft" and "C33" in order to draw out from these Crane's significant early influences. I do of course examine a number of the poems more frequently discussed, such as "For the Marriage of Faustus and Helen," "Voyages," and parts of *The Bridge* such as "Cape Hatteras" and "Atlantis," but following recent Crane critics like Christopher Nealon and John Emil Vincent, I also wish to throw light upon poems by Crane that appear infrequently or not at all in critical works about the poet, to argue that these also have a significant amount to say about the intersections between Crane's queerness and modernism.

In my examination of Hart Crane's queer modernist aesthetic I contend that to properly appreciate Crane's work, queerness and modernism must be considered together. The areas of experience that modernist writers sought to destabilize, such as visual perception, space, time, and the material world, were also destabilized by Crane's queerness. The radical energy of Crane's work is derived therefore from this dual aesthetic, and also from the conflicts that Crane generated within it, whether in terms of an approach to modernism like his adversarial attitude to Eliot, or in queer terms, as Crane resisted certain aspects of the dominant heteronormative modernism. Thus, in the first chapter, "American Decadence and the Creation of a Queer Modernist Aesthetic," I explore the influence upon Crane of two queer antecedents, Oscar Wilde and Walter Pater, and consider the extent to which Crane's early interest in Decadence related to prevailing trends in modernism.

The second chapter, "Abstraction and Intersubjectivity in *White Buildings*," investigates the effect of the visual arts upon Crane's work, particularly the work of the Ohio-based painter William Sommer. In his use of ekphrasis to represent Sommer's paintings in language, Crane interrogates the idea of the creative process. The questioning of forms of representation here results in a subjectivity that leads viewers to question their own notions of reality, and thus it opens the way for the creation of queer as well as straight realities. In this and other poems, Crane made use of such uncertainty to posit an intersubjectivity, a crisis of perception, which Crane believed all viewers and readers would share, whether queer or not.

The third chapter, "Spatiality, Movement, and the Logic of Metaphor," argues that Crane's work produces subcultural spaces within modernity that represent active resistance to heteronormativity, and asks whether it was realistic for Crane to create utopias. It shows how Crane adopts certain queer spatial practices within these spaces, such as cruising, and illustrates that a practice of deregulation registers in Crane's work as a kind of democratic impulse, opening his work up to both the normative and non-normative. The chapter analyses Crane's "logic of metaphor" in this context in order to see whether considering the strategy from a spatial perspective can grant a better understanding of its conception.

The following chapter, "Temporality, Futurity, and the Body," seeks to examine what kind of queer strategies Crane employs to address the experimental temporality that appeared in modernist texts. This chapter examines Crane's poetry alongside the work of Nietzsche and Heidegger, and Lee Edelman's queer theoretical writings about futurity are used to read "Voyages I" and *The Bridge*. The chapter adopts a genetic method to read "Voyages," and examines the ways in which Crane asserts the presence of the body and the emphasis which he places upon making history.

In the fifth chapter, "Empiricism, Mysticism, and a Queer Form of Knowledge," Crane's queer theories of knowledge and experience are considered in respect to the relationship between materiality and immateriality. The chapter asks what kind of process Crane used to form experience, and reveals the resistance and restrictions that he met with from friends and critics when he attempted to prioritize a queer experience. It explores the way in which Crane negotiated his pivotal but difficult relationship with T. S. Eliot's work through the language of mysticism and immateriality, and examines "The Broken Tower" (1932/1932) to understand what kind of language Crane considered suitable to describe a queerness that often seemed caught between the materiality of the body and the immateriality of an ideality in which Crane's work could be resistant to categorization.

The final chapter, "Queer Technology, Failure, and a Return to the Hand," analyses the "Cape Hatteras" and "Atlantis" sections of *The Bridge*, suggesting ways in which Crane presents the potential of technology to reveal a queerness that extends beyond the normative world. The chapter argues that just as Heidegger traces technology back to its roots as an art, a "revealing," so too Crane uses technology to realize a queerness that extends outwards beyond the normative, material world. This attitude to the dominant and dominating form of technology is also figured in an emphasis upon a return to "handiness" and forms of craft that actively resist the Machine – an impulse that shows Crane to be in accord with the trend towards a changing aesthetic in the 1930s.

In what follows, I stake a claim for a new reading of Crane's work based on the interaction between his sexuality and key modernist figures, concepts, and spaces. The book engages with several of the areas of debate current within modernist studies, such as geography and spatial form, transatlantic connections, the influence of technology upon writing, and the way in which little magazines shaped modernist culture. It challenges existing readings of Crane as well as existing readings of modernist poetry, and suggests the means by which other queer modernists might be re-read in light of this discussion of Crane's work. In particular, the book argues that Crane was seeking to write an alternative form of modernism, and that an examination of the influences behind his work – the issue to which I now turn – can help to re-think existing assumptions about the languages and motives of modernism.

1
American Decadence and the Creation of a Queer Modernist Aesthetic

Not very many people writing in 1916 would have been so bold as to link the disgraced Oscar Wilde, who had located himself so snugly within English society, to an "American Renaissance." But in his late summer letter of that year to Joseph Kling, editor of the *Pagan* magazine, Hart Crane did precisely that.

> I am interested in your magazine as a new and distinctive chord in the present American Renaissance of literature and art. Let me praise your September cover; it has some suggestion of the exoticism and richness of Wilde's poems (qtd. in Unterecker 46).

This letter, which Kling subsequently published in the October issue, links together two of the key ideas that the following two chapters explore: the extent to which Decadent writing affected Crane's work, and how far and why visual art shaped his queer aesthetic. In this chapter I suggest that, rather than being a youthful dalliance, as many critics have assumed, Decadence was a crucial influence upon not just Crane's early work, but upon poetry that might be considered typically modernist. By examining the juvenilia seriously, a number of important concerns can be discerned that reappear later in Crane's career, such as an affirmation of Otherness and the place of the queer subject in the world.

Although it is clear from the letter to Kling that Crane appreciated Wilde's example, it is also true, I suggest, that he was critical of Wilde's submission to normative authority, and he offered a critique of Wilde's actions in his poem "C33" (1916/1916). At this point in his writing career, critics generally assume that Crane shook off the languor of Decadence, but it continued to be a prominent shaper of Crane's style and content, and he sought to blend together the kind of masculine language that he was absorbing from Ezra Pound and Imagism with a style of Impressionism drawn from Wilde's poetry. In addition, Crane developed a number of unfashionable links with a sexually ambiguous Hellenism through his extensive reading of Walter Pater, and his poem "For the Marriage of Faustus and Helen," seen, together with *The Bridge*, as a rejoinder to Eliot's *The Waste Land*, which contains a significant number of Paterian moments. The positive response to the poem proved to Crane that he could write an alternative modernism and be accepted.

(American) Decadence

As Cassandra Laity observed in a special issue of *Modernism/modernity* (427–30), Charles Baudelaire was identified as the crucial figure of Decadence by T. S. Eliot and Walter Benjamin. This emphasis, Laity explains, together with the association of Baudelaire with perceptions of the urban environment and its inhabitants, particularly the flâneur and flâneuse, has meant that other forms and expressions of Decadence have been neglected. Laity argues that "British Decadence and/or Aestheticism is still understood by many modernists as a 'Baudelairian' derivative or dismissed as blandly 'effeminate,' socially irrelevant, and elitist" (427). Since he was influenced by British decadents such as Oscar Wilde and Lionel Johnson, criticism of Crane's juvenilia has generally followed much the same path, only more so, since Crane's sexuality is considered to be another reason for his attraction to writers perceived at the time to be perverted.[1] Critics such as Thomas E. Yingling, Langdon Hammer, and more recently and in more detail, Brian M. Reed, have granted greater significance to Crane's ties with Decadence, but each provide reasons for Crane's later dismissal of these links. What these critics neglect, and what I want to draw attention to here, are the elements of Decadent thought that continue to appear in Crane's work throughout the 1920s.

Crane discovered many of the little magazines to which he was later to submit work, including the *Pagan*, *Bruno's Weekly*, and the *Little Review*, in Richard Laukhuff's bookstore in Cleveland which, until Crane moved to New York and sought out the publishers of these periodicals in Greenwich Village, proved an invaluable source of the latest work of authors from America and Europe. Many of the issues of these publications from the 1910s featured Decadent European authors.[2] It was from Europe that the definitions of decadence originally came: first in the 1830s through an ongoing debate in French literature and criticism featuring Désiré Nisard, Théophile Gautier, and Paul Bourget, and then in the work of Arthur Symons. Initially, Symons's work appeared in England, but in 1893 he contributed an article entitled "The Decadent Movement in Literature" to *Harper's New Monthly Magazine* in New York. In this he explained that "both Impressionism and Symbolism convey some notion of that new kind of literature which is perhaps more broadly characterized by the word Decadence" (866). Symons claimed that this movement "has all the qualities that mark the end of great periods, the qualities that we find in the Greek, the Latin, decadence: an intense self-consciousness, a restless curiosity in research, an over-subtilizing refinement upon refinement, a spiritual and moral perversity [...] this representative literature of to-day, interesting, beautiful as it is, is really a new and beautiful and interesting disease" (858). Such a description reflects the over-wrought, over-sophisticated, paradoxical state of modern society as many critics saw it, particularly in the cities, but it also suggests Symons's ambiguous attitude to this "new and beautiful and interesting disease." Its "representative" nature and place at "the end of [a] great period" suggests a literature that – whether critics appreciate it or not – is worth their study. If anything he admires certain of its beauties and what he referred to as its "classic qualities" (859). However, by the time he published *The Symbolist Movement in Literature* in 1899, Symons had changed his opinion. Whilst essentially discussing the same authors, he re-branded the movement "Symbolism" and disowned "Decadence." He claimed now that Decadence was no more than an "interlude, half a mock-interlude," which "diverted the attention of the critics while something more serious was in preparation" (4). That "something" was the Symbolist Movement, and Symons proves keen to distinguish Symbolism from Decadence, asserting that Decadence can only be used "when applied to style; to that ingenious deformation of the language, in Mallarmé, for instance" (4).[3] He also observes that "[n]o doubt perversity of form and perversity of matter are often found together, and, among the lesser men especially, experiment was carried far, *not only in the direction of style*" (4, emphasis added). In suggesting that "perversity" went beyond the page, Symons also hints at the need to distance himself from notions of Decadence, for since 1895 the label had been associated with Oscar Wilde, who had been tried and convicted in that year for "acts of gross indecency with other male persons."[4] In the four years between Symons's article on "Decadence" and the publication of his book on "Symbolism," the subsequent public and literary exclamations against Wilde and everything for which he was assumed to have stood, make it clear that we can read "experiment [...] not only in the direction of style" as an attack on those, like Wilde, who carried on queer relations, and that style and sexuality were thus intimately connected.[5] Such attacks were sustained both in Britain and beyond: Neil Miller relates how "in America, some 900 sermons were said to have been preached against Wilde from 1895 to 1900" (48).

So, as David Weir has noted, a rise in decadent culture in the 1910s might have seemed "incompatible with the Puritan, progressive, capitalist values of America," but this might indeed have been what attracted Crane to Decadent work in the first place (*Decadent Culture* 1). It was a reaction against the business culture of his father (Crane would later concur with Waldo Frank's analysis that "American Industrialism is the new Puritanism, the true Puritanism of our day" (Frank, *Our America* 98)), and the limited horizons of an Ohio situation that he always disparaged ("in this town, poetry's a/Bedroom occupation," he wrote in "Porphyro in Akron" (1920-1921/1921)) (*CP* 152). Decadence was an extreme alternative, an Otherness. In *The Mauve Decade: American Life at the End of the Nineteenth Century*, published in 1926, Thomas Beer dates the Decadent revival in American culture to 1916, just as Crane was discovering the little magazines (148). Yet Crane would also have had a general sense of a "decay" within American literature: the *Little Review*'s September number from 1916 contained twelve blank pages, the issue acting as "a Want Ad" for good work. If Crane took this as an indication of a lack of good American literature, he would have felt quite justified in looking abroad to Europe and England for inspiration. In doing so, Crane absorbed the content, style, and form of writers like Oscar Wilde, Lionel Johnson, and Arthur Symons, and faithfully reproduced it in his juvenilia.

Crane's Decadence: The outsider and aesthetics

So faithful were Crane's poems to these writers, that reading them can be like compiling an inventory of typical Decadent features. Matei Calinescu provides a concise summary of such features when he suggests that Decadent art was concerned with "such notions as decline, twilight, autumn, senescence, and exhaustion, and, in its more advanced stages, organic decay and putrescence – along with their automatic antonyms: rise, dawn, spring, youth, germination" (155–56). This kind of imagery is easily located in Crane's early work from 1916–1917: the poem "October-November" (1916/1916) begins with an "Indian-summer-sun" (*CP* 136), "Fear" (1917/1917) describes how "on the window licks the night" (*CP* 138), and "Annunications" (1917/1917) opens by telling of "[t]he anxious milk-blood in the veins of the earth,/That strives long and quiet to sever the girth/Of greenery," and closes with the sounds of "things [...] all heard before dawn" (*CP* 139). Examining two of Crane's earliest poems in detail gives a sense of the kind of decadent influences he was absorbing during this period, and also suggests ways in which that work shows the beginnings of his fascination with modes of perception.

The opening stanza of the early unpublished poem "The Moth That God Made Blind" (c.1915–1917/unpublished), illustrates the kind of exoticism that was prevalent amongst decadent writings in the 1890s and in the revival of the 1910s, with its references to "cocoa-nut palms," "Arabian moons," and "mosaic date-vases" (*CP* 167).[6] The poem describes how one moth, who is born with his eyes covered with a "honey-thick glaze," is led to explore the power of his exceptional wings. The moth flies so high and close to the sun that the glaze on his eyes is burned off, and he can see "what his whole race had shunned" (*CP* 168): the extent and beauty of the world below. In that same moment, though, he is blinded and his wings "atom-withered," (*CP* 169) and he falls back down into the desert.

Integrating decadent concerns, the poem often describes the beauty of the natural world as if it were artifice ("mosaic date-vases"), and it does so in the well-structured form of decadent poetry. Crane's poem is made up of thirteen quatrains, regularly rhymed with a few variations to emphasize key and dramatic moments of the story. Crane also seeks to use a complicated meter, combining a mixture of mostly anapaests and iambs in a way that suggests to R.W.B. Lewis "Swinburnian trappings" (18):

    x   x   / x x   /   x   x   /   x x   / x
That they only can see when their moon limits vision,
   x   / x   x   /   x   x / x x   /
Their mother, the Moon, marks a halo of light
  x   x   /   x x/x x   /   x x / x
On their own small oasis, ray-cut, an incision,
   x   x   / x x   / x x   /   x   x   /
Where are set all the myriad jewelleries of night.

Lewis's comparison is apt, both in terms of Crane's use of such a complex meter (it is unlikely that he would have chosen it if he had not had Swinburne as a model), and in terms of the poem's content, which in its depiction of bitter loss and deep introspection recalls Swinburne's "The Triumph of Time":

>   x   x   /   x   /   x   /   x   x   /
>   I have put my days and dreams out of mind,
>   /   x   x   / x   /   x   x   /
>   Days that are over, dreams that are done.
>   x   x   /   x   /   x   x   /   x   /
>   Though we seek life through, we shall surely find
>   x   x   /   x   x   /   x   x   /   x   /
>   There is none of them clear to us now, not one.
>   x   /   x   /   x   x   /   x   x   /
>   But clear are these things; the grass and the sand,
>   x   /   x   x   /   x   / x   x   /
>   Where, sure as the eyes reach, ever at hand,
>   x   /   x   / x   x   /   x   /
>   With lips wide open and face burnt blind,
>   x   /   x   /   x   /   x   x   /
>   The strong sea-daisies feast on the sun.

The diction used and the sentiments expressed in the second half of this stanza suggest that Crane had this poem in mind when he wrote "The Moth That God Made Blind," since – as shown in the stanza below – it shares images of "sand," the "hand," blindness, and the sun, and an attempt to hopelessly seek solace in the knowledge that has been gained from experience.[7] The fourth line in Swinburne's stanza offers a model for the way in which Crane sought to match style to content: the stunting of the line's anapaests with an iamb to reflect the disillusionment at failed dreams and the understanding of them, is similar to the technique Crane uses in the first and third lines of the stanza quoted above. The addition of an unstressed syllable there to break up the anapaest pattern serves to match the limited nature of the vision described and then suggest the limited space of the moths' existence on the "small oasis." In attempting his own versions of such intricacies of form, Crane showed that he had paid extremely close attention to the structures of late Victorian poetry. Brian Reed has argued that Crane's fascination with Swinburne was still evident as late as 1929, citing a letter that mentioned the English poet's work, and he shows similarities between Swinburne's style and Crane's later work in *The Bridge*. However, he also claims that even though Crane "never cite[d] Swinburne by name as a source or model for *The Bridge* [...] his reticence on this point proves little. Pilloried during his first New York period for his fin de siècle leanings, Crane thereafter had reason to be circumspect" (33). If Crane was "pilloried" during his first New York trip, he continued to meet with people like Joseph Kling, who made Crane an associate editor of the *Pagan* in 1918, and Crane continued to publish work there until 1919. Furthermore, the poem he published in the *Little Review* in 1918, "In Shadow" (1917/1917), contained many similar traits of style and content to those of his earlier pieces. Yet Crane's interest in Victorian poetry and Decadence was certainly not restricted to Swinburne. In fact, the works of Decadent writers such as Wilde, Johnson, and Symons were much more significant for him.[8]

In "The Moth That God Made Blind," Crane presents an image of the outsider who, like Icarus, is also an over-reacher – a description that would have fitted Oscar Wilde, whose use of paradoxes Crane keenly observed and later criticized in "Joyce and Ethics," saying that "after [Wilde's] bundle of paradoxes has been sorted and conned, – very little evidence of intellect remains" (*CPSL* 199). This technique, however, is critical to the meaning of the poem. The moths can only see "when their moon limits vision," and at the very moment of revelation, when the moth gains his sight and understands the great potential of the world, he loses both his sight and his life. The very nature of the paradox as a form suggests a struggle, and a struggle against logical – or normative – behavior. In this sense the poem is allegorical, urging that such a struggle is undertaken against the mainstream or dominant. That message is underlined by the final stanza, which acts as an epilogue, and concludes: "These things I have: – a withered hand; –/Dim eyes; – a tongue that cannot tell." Introducing the first person serves to confirm the truth of the moth's experience: the poem is about sight and about the frustration of the poet to express beauty. Just as the beauty that the moth sees is denied him as the rest of his body fails, so the speaker here explains how what is seen cannot be expressed in language, for it cannot be written or spoken about with any authentic representation. Formally, this frustration with expression reveals itself in the way that Crane's use of the anapaest/iamb combination breaks down in the final two lines. The introduction of the penultimate line with a trochee, and the use of the spondee in the final line bespeak bitter experience that is made even more poignant by the opposition between the form and content in the second halves of the two closing lines, as regular iambs are used to describe the speaker's deficiencies.

Crane's decadent inspiration for this poem was Lionel Johnson's sonnet "Quisque Suos Manes," which opens with the line "What have you seen, eyes of strange fire!" Johnson's sonnet concludes with lines that echo both Crane's images and present the internal hell of postlapsarian man suggested by the sonnet's title, a shortening of a line from Book VI of Virgil's *Aeneid*, that reads: "Quisque suos patimur Manes," which might be understood as "each of us contains our own hell":[9]

> Smitten and purged, you saw the red deeps of your sin:
> You saw there death in life; you will see life in death.
> The sunlight shrank away, the moon came wan and thin,
> Among the summer trees the sweet winds held their breath.
> Now those celestial lights, which you can never win,
> Haunt you, and pierce, and blind. The Will of God so saith
> (qtd. in Rodensky, ed., 131).

But rather than emphasizing the Biblical Fall of Man, as Johnson does, and suggesting that Man is forever bound with the knowledge that he can never be complete again, Crane transforms such terrifying inadequacies into those of the artist, equating the fall of the moth with the inability to describe beauty and aesthetic experience. The sense of the speaker/poet as Other and outsider is evidently one concern of Crane's poem: the moth is literally marked out as being different with "his pinions with signs mystical/And rings macrocosmic." Yet this early sense of Otherness in Crane's work is complicated by its being combined with the aesthetic concerns that are summed up at the end of the poem. It might be possible to read the poem as somehow a triumph in the struggle to express beauty, since the mere presence of the work seems to bear witness to the poet's ability to describe. But the fact that the rest of the poem does not deal directly with the speaker's own experience and instead offers a mythical, oblique version of it, merely confirms the poet's sense of his own inadequacies.

The blending of anxieties over Otherness and aesthetics continues to be of concern in Crane's poem "Modern Craft" (1917/1918) (*CP* 142), published in the January 1918 issue of the *Pagan*.[10] This is another poem with clear Decadent precursors, recalling two of Arthur Symons's poems from his collection *Silhouettes*. The girl's "flesh of moons" and her "tiger-lilies" echo the lines "White girl, your flesh is lilies/Grown 'neath a frozen moon," from "Morbidezza"; whilst the languid atmosphere and descriptions of make-up and luxury are similar to Symons's "Maquillage": "[t]he charm of rouge on fragile cheeks,/Pearl-powder, and, about the eyes,/The dark and lustrous Eastern dyes."[11] Yet, just as Crane complicated the imagery of the fallen decadent figure in

"The Moth That God Made Blind," so here he adds complexity to the image of the fallen woman. This has led the few critics who deal with this poem into diverse interpretations. Sherman Paul asserts that the poem describes "an encounter with a prostitute" (20), whilst Thomas E. Yingling adjudges that the girl in the poem seems to be "an indifferent and sexually jaded female muse who seems to possess a power and authority the poet does not" (113). For Brom Weber, "it is almost impossible to decide whether Crane is viewing a living person or the representation of a woman in sculpture or painting" (*Hart Crane: A Biographical and Critical Study* 46). Weber is really addressing the way in which the speaker is detached from the subject of the poem, but his comment about the visual nature of the poem is nonetheless apposite given the allusion to Ophelia in the final stanza, which seems to suggest the Pre-Raphaelite John Everett Millais's 1851–1852 painting *Ophelia*.

If the character and speaker of "The Moth That God Made Blind" were outsiders in physical terms, the speaker of "Modern Craft" is an outsider in the way that he views the girl in the poem. This peculiar kind of unthreatening voyeurism begins early in the poem at the point where there is clearly sexual disconnection, a mismatch between the desires of the male speaker and the female subject. This sense at the outset, "[t]hough I have touched her flesh of moons,/Still she sits gestureless and mute," bespeaks an acknowledgement that both characters in the poem know they are merely acting out roles, a sense of anti-climax reinforced by the abcb rhyme scheme, which undercuts any energy or momentum that might have accumulated through the rest of the stanza. With this acknowledgment, the speaker can observe the girl in a different way and see through her performance. The language that the speaker employs thereby decodes her, suggesting her unwilling performance through ambiguous imagery or paradox: "[s]he hazards jet; wears tiger-lilies; –/And bolts herself within a jewelled belt." Each of these images suggest her ambivalence, even reluctance, about playing this role: "jet" jewellery might suggest danger, but it is also a "hazard" for her personally; she may appear to be a tiger, but has a sense of herself as a pure, fragile lily; and although she presents herself as desirable with a "jewelled belt," she "bolts herself" securely within it. These contradictions lead Thomas Yingling to suggest that "it may in fact prove more powerfully and certainly more historically accurate to read her as a figure of cross-dressing [...] a female muse only in her ability to masquerade as one" (114). Whilst this reading does not seem to be borne out by the poem as a whole, it is certainly the case that this poem does suggest a complexity of gender. Both she and he are playing roles, and there are certain gendered expectations about the male speaker's behavior to which he refuses to conform.

The final two lines demonstrate this: there is desire here, "[t]his burns," but such desire cannot be (as Crane plays on the imagery of fire) consummated because of these characters' different sexualities. Instead, the poem ends with the reflection that "[m]y modern love were/Charred at a stake in younger times than ours." Whilst the idea that queer people were formerly burned at the stake for their "crimes against nature" is suggested here, a more recent and well-publicized punishment is also implied.[12] During his first criminal trial, from April 26 to May 1, 1895, Oscar Wilde was asked to explain the meaning of a line in the poem by Lord Alfred Douglas, "Two Loves": "the Love that dare not speak its name."[13] As part of his famous response, Wilde said that "[i]t is that deep spiritual affection that is as pure as it is perfect. It dictates and pervades great works of art like those of Shakespeare and Michelangelo [...]. It is in this century misunderstood, so much misunderstood that it may be described as the 'Love that dare not speak its name', and on account of it I am placed where I am now" (qtd. in Hyde 201). Crane therefore appropriates Wilde's conclusion that "[i]t is in this century misunderstood," where "it" is his "modern love," as if he dates his sense of his own sexual love from his reading about that event in 1895. In a similar way, just as the girl's "modern craft" consists in painting herself with make-up and covering herself in the latest fashions (the "cool pearls" are reminiscent of those worn by the "flapper" girls who would become more prominent in the 1920s), so Crane asserts the "modern" nature of his poem in dealing with subject matter that was still current. Indeed, in asserting that to be queer is "modern," Crane seeks to ensure its place in the twentieth-century American world, rather than relegating it to the classical periods with which it had been associated, or restricting it to a short chapter in the latter part of the previous century.

Crane's Wilde and "song of minor, broken strain"

Wilde himself occupied a problematic position of affirmation/relegation for Crane. Ever since his trial (and, as Alan Sinfield has shown, prior to and during it),[14] Wilde had been pitied in different ways. Crane had read about Wilde's trial in an article by Wilde's warder that appeared in *Bruno's Weekly* on January 22, 1916. Crane may also have read the tribute to Wilde by Rose Freeman-Ishill, which appeared as a preface to the warder's recollections in a subsequent pamphlet. Freeman-Ishill's address to Wilde judged that

> [y]our Life is more perfect than your Works, for your life is like a tragedy conceived in the mind of an olden Hellene. You have blended Beauty with Sorrow, and out of this union was born the Music of your Art (11).[15]

There are echoes here of Crane's lines in his 1916 response to Wilde's predicament, "C33," especially in the suggestion that sorrow was a crucial element in Wilde's aesthetic after his imprisonment. This was most plain in his authoring of *De Profundis*, which merely exaggerated his identity as a martyr. For later generations Wilde was a sufferer and a victim; even in Crane's own time, not even two decades after his death, Wilde was referred to – at least in America – as "poor Oscar Wilde," and his death only three years after his release from prison confirmed that identity. Subsequently he has become, as Sinfield suggests, "the apogee of gay experience and expression [...]. For us, he is always-already queer – as that stereotype has prevailed in the twentieth century" (2-3). But as Wilde represents the archetypal gay-man-as-sufferer, so Crane found it essential to set himself against this archetype.

He sought to do so in his poem "C33" (1916/1916), which was published in *Bruno's Weekly* on September 23, 1916. The title is a coded one, a reference to Wilde's identity in prison: block C, floor three, room three, and as such implies that the poem was designed for three types of reader: those who regularly read *Bruno's Weekly* and had seen the article by Wilde's warder earlier that year, and those two groups of readers who took a special interest in Wilde; self-described decadents and, especially – as will become clear – queer readers. Langdon Hammer thus surmises that "'C33' – is in this sense a metonymy for the coded character of gay identity generally – it converts the imposed insignia of state punishment into a badge of male homosexual suffering, connecting Wilde and Crane and certain of Crane's readers" (*Hart Crane and Allen Tate* 128). But I would contest this notion of "homosexual suffering" and suggest that, whilst there is a "code" written into the poem, its message goes far deeper than an acknowledgment of the identity of "C33."

The first stanza of the poem is striking as an adoption of Wilde's own decadent imagery as a eulogy for the man, praising the poet who has "vented his long mellowed wines/Of dreaming on the desert white/With searing sophistry" (*CP* 135).[16] Then, with a gesture towards the status of Wilde as a victim, Crane describes how "he tented with far truths he would form/The transient bosoms from the thorny tree." So Crane acknowledges that in the past (and the whole of this first stanza is in the past tense), Wilde spoke truths. But here the poem shifts, for rather than merely celebrate Wilde in lamenting him, the speaker moves to use him as an example not to be followed.

> O Materna! to enrich thy gold head
> And wavering shoulders with a new light shed
>
> From penitence, must needs bring pain
> And with it song of minor, broken strain.

The stanzaic break between "shed" and "[f]rom" marks the transition from Wilde's past life to his present one. The address "O Materna!" is not a joyful apostrophe to the muse of poetry, for if it were it would be celebrating Wilde's penitence and the "song of minor, broken strain" that goes with it. Instead, Crane uses "Materna" to represent a muse of poetry that reinforces sexual norms.[17] Recalling, perhaps, the notable parts of his criminal trials in which Wilde was condemned by his own writing, Crane proposes that in the face of normative sexuality and authority, Wilde as a poet was forced to repent, and his "transgressive aesthetic," as Jonathan Dollimore has described it, was brought under control (10–17). But hand-in-hand with this penitence, captured in the sober tones of *De Profundis*, is what concerns Crane most of all: the sacrificing of that transgressive art. In other poems of this period, like "Modern Craft," Crane has a tendency to use the final lines of a poem to provide a revelation that changes our perspective on the previous lines. In those poems this revelation can seem forced, but in "C33," perhaps because it is structured more like an argument – indeed, it is nearly a sonnet – the final lines are presented assuredly, as the speaker makes a direct address to his sympathetic (that is to say queer) readers:

> But you who hear the lamp whisper through night
> Can trace paths tear-wet, and forget all blight.

Thomas E. Yingling argues that "[t]he need to 'forget all blight' at the poem's close is clearly the need to forget that one is homosexual, too" (110), but I would argue that, on the contrary, Crane is calling for an affirmation of queerness. This sympathetic audience, the "you" addressed, should, Crane urges, acknowledge the path forged by Wilde up to the point of his failure (his penitence and the "blight"), but return to the scene of Wilde's transgression ("trace paths tear-wet"), and continue transgressing from where Wilde left off. The lamp that represents that transgression is set against the "new light" of penitence, and although it makes itself known only in a whisper, it is notable that its message comes through speech or language, setting up the poetic art as a form of resistance to the repression of anything non-normative.

In his refusal to accept Wilde's capitulation to normative authority, Crane challenges Wilde's own sentiments in *De Profundis*. Wilde wrote:

> Society, as we have constituted it, will have no place for me, has none to offer; but Nature [...] will hang the night with stars so that I may walk abroad in the darkness without stumbling, and send the wind over my footprints so that none may track me to my hurt: she will cleanse me in great waters, and with bitter herbs make me whole (1057).

Such writing uses the language of the guilty outcast, who is able to exist only in the shadows and acknowledge that he is not a "complete" person because of his sexual deviance. But Crane's poem positively encourages his sympathetic readers to "track [Wilde] to [his] hurt." In this sense, Arthur Symons's description of the Decadent movement as having "all the qualities that mark the end of great periods" is also apt to describe Crane's perception of Wilde's trials. Suddenly, those who now identified Decadence with perverse sexuality and moral corruption hoped that Wilde's destruction would also mark the end of Decadence itself. For Crane however, Wilde's imprisonment denoted both the end of a period and its rebirth. It amounted to nothing less than a fundamental shift in the relationship between the queer individual and society. In his darkest moment, the queer individual's identity could be truly fashioned.[18] Wilde was a warning for Crane. But this was not because Crane's own same-sex desire was in danger of being discovered and condemned; Wilde's fate was an aesthetic warning. His identities as writer and individual were *the result* of his queerness, and by being penitent he had denied his sexual identity and his authentic, transgressive aesthetic.

Crane's defense of Decadence

By rejecting Wilde and his new, weakened aesthetic, Crane was not rejecting Decadence. When he read a hostile reader's response to the publication of James Joyce's *Ulysses* in the *Little Review* in May 1918,[19] Crane responded with a letter of his own, which was printed in the

June issue.[20] The discontented reader, R. McM from Los Angeles, made a connection between what they perceived as Joyce's "decadence," and his description of sexuality. In one section of the letter, R. McM averred:

> You are a firm believer in cerise abnormal art, I take it[.] Has art no elasticity, no tolerance, no humor[?] If Joyce is an artist put him beside Turgeniev, Chekhov, Goethe...Even in decadency – anaemic, palely diseased – how do you stack [him] up beside even poor Oscar Wilde, Beaudelaire [sic], possibly Swinburne? They had intellect added to their art ears. [...] We have with us in the world [...] many who have virility, intellect, philosophy and art, – not sexually perverted. The prostitute who paints an already beautiful body may have added unnatural charm, but why call it art? Justify some of Joyce's obsence [sic] commonplaces taken from life neither for power nor beauty nor for any reason but to arrest attention, cheap Bowery vileness (55–56).

Although Crane acknowledged that R. McM had been "adequately answered" by the magazine's co-editor Jane Heap, he said that he felt compelled nevertheless to write since "the temptation to emphasize such illiteracy, indiscrimination, and poverty still pull[ed] a little too strongly for resistance" ("Joyce and Ethics" 65). In that reply, Crane was particularly concerned that R. McM had chosen to "stack up" Wilde, Baudelaire, and Swinburne with Joyce as, Crane said, "rivals in 'decadence' and 'intellect'" (65):

> "Decadence" is something much talked about, and sufficiently misconstrued to arouse interest in the works of any fool. Any change in form, viewpoint, or mannerism can be so abused by the offending party. Sterility is the only "decadence" I recognize. An abortion in art takes the same place as it does in society, – it deserves no recognition whatever, – it is simply outside. A piece of work is art, or it isn't: there is no neutral judgment (65).

R. McM discusses Joyce in the same terms as critics had been describing Decadent writers and texts for years: "abnormal," "sexually perverted," and lacking in "virility."[21] But for Crane "decadence" is a label that critics use "indiscriminat[ely]" to denounce any work that seems to be outside the norms of style and content. If a text makes readers uncomfortable and, as Crane says, constitutes "a thrust which discovers some of their entrails to themselves," it is labelled decadent (65). To R. McM's accusation that Joyce has no "virility" and is "sexually perverted," Crane asserts that "[s]terility is the only 'decadence' I recognize." Instead of associating Decadence with a particular writer or group of writers, Crane treats the idea of a "decadent" work literally in terms of decay: as a failure creatively, as being unable to (re)produce art. But crucially Crane does not dismiss Decadence. Instead he believes it is misunderstood: "[a]ny change in form, viewpoint, or mannerism can be so abused by the offending party," he says. This suggests Crane defined "Decadent" writers as those willing to experiment with form, viewpoint, and mannerism.[22] Any work that does not exemplify fertility of imagination should be ignored: "[a]n abortion in art takes the same place as it does in society,—it deserves no recognition whatever,—it is simply outside." In this respect, Joyce may not be a "decadent" writer in the tradition of Wilde, Baudelaire or Swinburne, but Crane's letter does not dismiss the possibility that they may all share an urge to experiment and, as Ezra Pound put it, "make it new."[23] In addition, Crane's vigorous response to R. McM's outburst suggests that he takes it as a personal attack, and his alarm at the critic's "misconstru[ing]" of "decadence," suggests that he still associates his own work with that movement and its writers, especially if they are Baudelaire and Joyce. In essence, Crane intimates here that his continuing adherence to Decadent traits does not mean that he cannot produce art.

Forming an aesthetic vocabulary

In addition, Crane felt that Decadence did not preclude him either from creating a "modern" art form, or from adopting an aesthetic language derived from the highly masculinized diction of T. E. Hulme, Pound, and Eliot. In December 1918, Crane finally succeeded in being published in the *Little Review* with "In Shadow," a poem which, as mentioned earlier in the chapter, is very similar in its concerns to Crane's decadent poems of 1917. It is set in a garden at twilight and features a mysterious femme fatale. Perhaps recognizing its decadent traits, Ezra Pound, the magazine's foreign editor, disapproved of Margaret Anderson's decision to publish Crane's work and wrote to her, advising her to publish no more. He wrote to Crane about his work, telling him that it "is all very egg: there is perhaps better egg, but you haven't yet the ghost of a setting hen or an incubator about you" (qtd. in *OML* 19). Instead, he told Crane, he should send his work to "that consummate milk pudding *milieu Contemporary Verse*" (qtd. in Fisher 62). This monthly publication, edited by Charles Wharton Stork from Philadelphia, ran from 1918–1929, and offered a wide range of poetry.

A sense of its contents however can be gleaned from the "Maxim for the Month," which was included on the front page of several issues, and was concerned with beauty. In the January 1918 issue, for example, the maxim was: "Truth when 'tis beauty, beauty when 'tis truth." This reworking of John Keats's conclusion to his "Ode on a Grecian Urn" shows how Pound perceived Crane's poetry at this time: as Romantic, even decadent, obsessed with the kind of artificial beauty about which Wilde had written. In his dismissal of Crane and of *Contemporary Verse*, Pound was speaking in the same language with which he had been trying to banish the "effeminacy" of Decadence and Romanticism, and to promote a masculine language associated with the new forms of Imagist poetry. Crane understood this, and he began to adapt his own aesthetic criticism accordingly.

Cassandra Laity has explored the modernists' reactions to the "effeminacy" of Decadence and, further back, Romanticism, through her work on Crane's contemporary, H.D. She shows convincingly how "male theorizers of modernism socially constructed the Decadent past as a ruinous form of feminine writing emblematized by the seductive siren song of the femme fatale or the sexually ambiguous male Aesthete" (*H.D. and the Victorian Fin de Siècle* xii). In particular, Laity draws attention to the modes of vocabulary that T. E. Hulme, Pound, and Eliot used to masculinize criticism and poetic theory, and rescue it from what they saw as the stylistic weaknesses of Decadence and Romanticism. Such a concern is evident throughout the work of each author. For Hulme, "[Romanticism] becomes the expression of sentimentality rather than of *virile* thought" (69, emphasis added); Pound decried "the *softness* of the 'nineties' for which I have different degrees of antipathy or even contempt" ("Lionel Johnson" 362, emphasis added); and for Eliot, Decadent writing was of "a more *feminine* type, [...] also a very sophisticated type, [which] makes its art by feeling and by contemplating the feeling, rather than the object which has excited it or the object into which the feeling might be made" ("London Letter" 217, emphasis added).

Crane read and absorbed these ideas, telling Gorham Munson in late 1919 that "[m]ore and more am I turning toward Pound and Eliot and the minor Elizabethans for values," and he began to adopt the same kind of vocabulary in his aesthetic judgments (*OML* 30). Two months later he was giving Munson Poundian advice: "[t]he modern artist has got to harden himself, and the walls of an ivory tower are too delicate and brittle a coat of mail for substitute. The keen and most sensitive edges will result from this 'hardening' process" (*OML* 33). In other letters too we find the same vocabulary of masculinity. Crane describes poor sections of the *Modernist* magazine as "a confused, indiscriminate, *jelly-like* mass" (*OML* 26, emphasis added), which sounds just like Pound's 1918 description of *Contemporary Verse* as a "milk pudding," regards Matthew Josephson favorably as "class, *hard* and glossy" (*OML* 29, emphasis added), and praises the critics Van Wyck Brooks and Francis Hackett for belonging to "a *harder and more formal* species" (*OML* 30, emphasis added). The "values" which Crane is absorbing from Pound are therefore *aesthetic* values, and Crane repeatedly adopted the imagery of "hardness" used by Hulme, Pound, and Eliot. And yet in his use of this language and imagery, Crane subverted it. In the same letter in which he told Munson "to harden himself," Crane also boasted of a love affair with a man that he had previously called "the most intense and satisfactory one of my whole life" (*OML* 30). Clearly Crane saw no contradiction in endorsing Pound and Eliot's agenda, which suggested an aesthetic based on a language of male virility, whilst celebrating what others would see as his own effeminacy or perversion.[24] Langdon Hammer has suggested that "Crane viewed the modernist break with Aestheticism not as a homophobic maneuver, but as a claim to cultural power and centrality on the part of a new 'generation', a claim in which Crane felt he had a stake *both* as a poet and as a homosexual" (*Hart Crane and Allen Tate* 128). In this respect, despite the anti-effeminate/homophobic sentiments behind Pound's use of a language of masculinity and, as Crane put it, "Mr. Pound's rabid dislike of my things" (*OML* 19), it was possible for Crane to use the same language and not feel himself compromised, and to be an insider and outsider at once.

Impressionism and Imagism

The ability of Crane to adapt his Decadent apprenticeship is clear even from his poetry that predates these letters, for he found a way to blend the impressionist style of Wilde's poetry with the Imagist style and teaching that Pound had been promoting in *Poetry* and the *Little Review*. In his essay on Lionel Johnson, a Decadent writer for whom he actually had considerable respect, Pound explained that "[t]he nineties have chiefly gone out because of their muzziness, because of a softness derived, I think, not from books but from impressionist painting. They riot with half decayed fruit" ("Lionel Johnson" 363). Pound might well have levelled his criticism at a series of poems by Wilde entitled "Impressions," such as "Impression. Le Reveillon."[25]

Wilde's poem exemplifies some of the objections that led Pound to promote Hulme's ideas and conceive Imagism. First, it is inspired by

Impressionism: the subtitle, "Le Reveillon," Karl Beckson and Bobby Fong observe, is "like the Italian term chiaroscuro, [when] a dramatic touch of light in darkness highlights a scene" (64–65). Full of adjectives and sensuous imagery – Wilde uses "laced," for instance, to imply an atmosphere of drugged ecstasy – the poem overwhelms the reader with washes of color. It conjures up a mysterious "white lady" in the femme fatale tradition, and the second stanza contains the kind of abstractions from which Pound would have gone in fear: neither the "jagged brazen arrows" nor "feathers of the night" refer to any concrete thing.[26] As Eliot said of Swinburne: "the object was not there – only the word" ("Swinburne as Poet" 148). The same stanza also features a paradox, the stylistic feature that Crane associated with Wilde: "a long wave of yellow light/*Breaks silently* on tower and hall." For Wilde, surmise Beckson and Fong, "the making of images [...] is presumed to be the poet's art" (65, emphasis added).

Crane's work in this early stage of his career demonstrates affinities with both Wilde's Impressionism and Pound's Imagism, and although Brian Reed has suggested that Crane made a "remarkable decision, while still an adolescent, to ignore [...] the Imagist movement" (19), it is clear in "October-November," written in 1916 and published in the November-December issue of the *Pagan*, that in fact Crane was fusing the language of Impressionism with the techniques and approach of Imagism.[27]

There are clear similarities in diction between "Le Reveillon" and "October-November." Wilde's "fitful red" sky reappears in the "crimson" streaks of the sun in Crane's poem, and the "feathers of the night" in the first poem give way to the "crimson feathers" of the "Indian-summer-sun" in the second. The colors of Crane's poem may be the rich, luxurious ones of decadence (crimson, silver, gold, purple), but they are employed in landscapes where there is far greater energy than in "Le Reveillon." Whereas there the dawn rises "[l]ike a white lady from her bed," and the poem proceeds gloriously yet quite serenely, Crane's work seems at times out of control, as the sun "whips" and "dives," and the trees dance "[i]n delirium." Even the moon appears to usurp the sun as "a mad orange flare."

In terms of form, Crane's poem is indebted to Imagism alone. Whilst Wilde uses iambic tetrameter, filling the poem with a song-like lyricism, Crane adopts *vers libre*. But by doing so, Crane does not lose control of the form; on the contrary, he writes in the best tradition of Imagism. Where Wilde uses predictable end rhymes, Crane follows Pound's advice – "[a] rhyme must have in it some slight element of surprise if it is to give pleasure" (86) – and demonstrates a command of internal rhyme and sound patterning. Thus, amongst many examples, "summer" and "sun" share a vowel sound and the second line has an ongoing repetition of the short "i," as if to mimic the short bursts of movement described. The first three lines of the second stanza seem to be an overdose of alliteration and assonance to culminate in "delirium" – a word chosen for aural effect and suggestive of some kind of decadence in itself – but Crane uses lineation and the Imagist form of his poem to undercut that sense of self-indulgence.

Comparing the conclusion of the poem to work by H.D. makes clear the direction in which Crane's work was heading; towards a poetry concerned with form, intensity, and sensation. Both Crane and Wilde conclude their poems with a moment of natural revelation: the "yellow light" in Wilde's piece "[w]akes into flight some fluttering bird," and in "October-November," "the moon/In a mad orange flare/Floods the grape-hung night." But unlike Wilde's regular and consistent lineation, Crane finishes with a typographical flourish in which the final three lines gradually lengthen and spread across the page as the poem reaches its climax. This visual presentation owes something to H.D.'s architecture of form, exemplified by a stanza from her first published poem, "Hermes of the Ways," which appeared in *Poetry* in January 1913, and also shares similar content to "October-November":

> Apples on the small trees
> are hard
> too small,
> too late ripened
> by a desperate sun
> that struggles through sea-mist (38).

According to Pound, the presentation of the Image (the "intellectual and emotional complex"), "gives the sense of sudden liberation; that sense of freedom from time limits and space limits ..." (84). Crane adheres to the idea of liberation: like H.D. his poem culminates in an epiphany or what William Pratt calls "a moment of revealed truth" (36). Crane also makes use of hyphenation, a technique borrowed from H.D. that he would continue to employ in his later work. Diana Collecott notes that this is a typical feature of H.D.'s verse, explaining that "[s]he delights most in nominal compounds, as a 'gift of Greek' and also as a means to Imagist compression" (*H.D. and Sapphic Modernism: 1910–1950*, 258). Collecott also points out that such compounds in H.D.'s work tend to link together boundaries, like "wood-path" or "field-edge" (258–59).[28] Here too in his title, straddling two months, and in the first line, "Indian-summer-sun," which implies a period at the end of summer and beginning of autumn, Crane suggests liminal spaces in his work. But "October-November" also continues to present the kinds of "abstractions" that feature in Wilde's poem, and of which Pound would have sternly disapproved. This partly explains Pound's rejection of Crane's work. His note to Crane quoted earlier, "you haven't the ghost of a setting hen or an incubator," suggests a need for something concrete, a solid technique that can be relied upon to produce and re-produce good poetry. For Pound believed in "technique as a test of a man's sincerity [...] in the trampling down of every convention that impedes or obscures the determination of the law, or the precise rendering of the impulse" (87). Even in 1927, a full decade later in his writing life, Crane's explanation of his creative process shows how he accepted and also refuted Pound's teachings, and blended Decadent and Imagist tendencies: "I write damned little because I am interested in recording certain sensations, very rigidly chosen, with an eye for what according to my taste and sum of prejudices seems suitable to – or intense enough – for verse" (*OML* 340). The desire for "certain sensations" sounds like the sensuous impulse of the Decadent writers, yet by describing the sensations as "very rigidly chosen," Crane also echoes the methods of the Imagists. The emphasis upon intensity may seem like an emotional choice – what is intense is guided by the emotional reaction to it – but once again it is an aesthetic one, to do with the condensation of imagery.

Hellenism and Walter Pater

As Diana Collecott has explained, Pound's attitude to Greek poetry was complex, and at times, contradictory. A November 1912 issue of *Poetry* described Richard Aldington as "one of the 'Imagistes', a group of ardent Hellenists who are pursuing interesting experiments in *vers libre*," and such a description outraged him because of what he saw as the associations between Hellenism and effeminacy.[29] When he thought that Aldington was pursuing a weak line of thought in 1914, he described it as "Paterine sentimentalesque Hellenism" (qtd. in Collecott, *H.D. and Sapphic Modernism* 117).[30] Nevertheless, Pound recommended Sappho's work as a model for writers, and promoted H.D.'s work, which was influenced by Sappho, extensively. As Helen Carr has argued,

> emotionally and artistically the introduction to Pater, the Pre-Raphaelites and their successors was for some years to be the most

significant to [Pound] in his rejection of the American doctrine of progress and its materialistic present. In particular, Pater's radical apostasy from Victorian values played a vital role in enabling him to escape Philadelphian conformity (19).

Pound's ambiguous relationship with Hellenism was symptomatic of a more general attitude in the little magazines, which could cautiously embrace mention of "Hellas" if it were couched in the right terms, but Collecott has charted how H.D.'s assertion of her own bisexuality and her resistance to Pound's "virile" poetics were made possible by her reading in and use of Sappho's work.[31]

These contradictions within the avant-garde of literary modernism over its uneasy pairing of classicism and decadence also appear in the response to Crane's early published work. In 1922, Louis Untermeyer labelled him one of the "New Patricians" (deriving his term from the name given to the nobility of Rome, and suggesting a certain unwelcome sophistication), holding to

> a new intellectual discipline, for severity of structure, for the subjection of the material to the design [...] It is in essence a patrician attitude that places its emphasis on "style, strangeness, organization." It is primarily a turning away from naturalism – or, as may be contended, a retrogression – to French ideas of a still earlier generation (qtd. in Davison 144, fn. 6).[32]

For Untermeyer, there can be no progress by looking backwards. His great concern is that these writers (and he includes Crane, E. E. Cummings, and John Dos Passos amongst them) risk undermining the hard work of recent American authors by relying upon what he sees as acutely outmoded ("still earlier") foreign influences. It might seem that such a conflict dramatizes modernism's consistently difficult relationship with its own literary heritage, but Untermeyer's nervousness about artifice and his worry about the "strangeness" of writing like Crane's indicates that he is tapping into the language used to describe and warn against an Otherness in writing. This was made clear in Untermeyer's revision of the essay, published a year later, in which he asked: "[w]ill not intellectual subtleties and nuances of form tend toward the very artistic decadence from which we have revolted, the decadence that appraises the values of life chiefly as aesthetic values?" (348). Behind this critique too are those fears of the Other: in the double meaning of "revolted," and a misguided understanding of "the values of life." That kind of style, says Untermeyer, is taking American writing in the wrong direction, and two decades after Wilde's death, it is (at least to an older generation) deeply suspicious.

Nevertheless, Crane continued to maintain the interests of a decadent. Indeed, the links between Decadence, Hellenism, and Crane's own queer identity are explicit in a document from his personal library. This may not have been a public statement, but it is nonetheless telling as an example of Crane's own negotiation of Hellenist influences and, in particular, his relationship with Walter Pater, a crucial figure for modernism and Crane in bridging Decadence and early modernism. In his copy of *The Sonnets of Michael Angelo Buonarroti*, beneath sonnets XXIX and XXX, "Love's Dilemma" and "Love the Light-Giver," Crane copied out Sappho's poem "'Twas this deprived my soul of rest."[33] The three poems all muse on the way in which love, manifest through vision, can incapacitate the body and the soul: Sappho's poem details how "while I gazed in transport tost,/ My breath was gone, my voice was lost," and "the subtle flame/Ran quick thro' all my vital frame/O'er my dim eyes a darkness hung/My ears with hollow murmurs rung." Michelangelo's first sonnet "Love's Dilemma," asks "[i]f then my heart cannot endure the blaze/Of beauties infinite that blind these eyes,/Nor yet can bear to be from our divided,/What fate is mine?," whilst the second, "Love the Light-Giver" (dedicated, in Symonds's edition, "To Tommaso De' Cavalieri"), begins: "With your fair eyes a charming light I see,/For which my own blind eyes would peer in vain." The emphasis that is placed here on the connections between sight and beauty go further than being just typical material for a writer of sonnets. Crane's linking of Sappho and Michelangelo through the means of aesthetic contemplation or gazing reveals not only his ongoing interest in the Hellenic and Renaissance authors favored by the Decadents (Crane dated his copy of Michelangelo's sonnets 1921), but also suggests his continuing apprenticeship to authors writing of same-sex desire. In the background here too, significantly, is Walter Pater's book *The Renaissance: Studies in Art and Poetry*, a copy of which Crane owned, and which he read around 1921–1922.[34] Pater was a key influence upon Crane's poem "For the Marriage of Faustus and Helen" (1921–1923/1923–1924),[35] which both crowned his interest in Hellenism, and also properly launched his own poetic career. In "General Aims and Theories" (an essay unpublished during his lifetime) Crane explained that his intention in "Faustus and Helen" had been to "embody in modern terms (words, symbols, metaphors) a contemporary approximation to an ancient human culture or mythology that seems to have been obscured rather than illumined with the frequency of poetic allusions made to it during the last century"

(*CPSL* 217). As if in response to critics like Untermeyer, Crane makes a case for "retrogression" to "the last century" in order to reinvent classical myth for the modern audience. The poem itself and Crane's commentary upon it owe a great deal to James Joyce's *Ulysses* (which Crane read in a copy smuggled across the Atlantic), and Eliot's essay about the "mythical method" employed by Joyce in his novel.

In Crane's view, "[t]he real evocation of this (to me) very real and absolute conception of beauty seemed to consist in a reconstruction in these modern terms of the basic emotional attitude toward beauty that the Greeks had" (*CPSL* 217). In doing so, Crane's guide to this attitude was Pater's *The Renaissance*, and in his use of it he presented a parallel between classical and modern societies that allowed him to show same-sex desire through aesthetic contemplation. The first section of "Faustus and Helen" blends ancient and modern to situate the legend of Helen in a contemporary urban setting.[36] Crane critiques that contemporary world through his use of Helen and of Pater's reflections upon Greek ideals of beauty. The characterization of the speaker in this part of the poem also suggests Pater's own figures in *The Renaissance*, dislocated from the world because of their queer status within it.

Through his juxtaposition of ancient and modern, Crane warns of the experiential crisis facing the modern self, an idea he adapts directly from Pater. The opening of "Faustus and Helen" claims that "[t]he mind has shown itself at times/Too much the baked and labeled dough/Divided by accepted multitudes" (*CP* 26). The speaker critiques conformity, illustrating that the daily activities of all people in contemporary society (represented by the shaped "dough") do not allow for aesthetic appreciation. Instead, there is a lack of originality and much falsity: "stenographic smiles" suggest a kind of modern emotion by shorthand; "stock quotations" suggests words derived from a standard source and puns on the idea that these might both be about financial matters and "stock" responses that are inauthentic in the moment. The "equivocations" flashed out imply the danger of being deliberately mislead. In preparing the way for Helen's entrance, Crane is also embracing what Pater had taught:

> Certainly, for us of the modern world, with its conflicting claims, its entangled interests, distracted by so many sorrows, with many preoccupations, so bewildering an experience, the problem of unity with ourselves, in blitheness and repose, is far harder than it was for the Greek within the simple terms of antique life. Yet, not less than ever, the intellect demands completeness, centrality (*The Renaissance* 148).[37]

In his use of Helen and classical material, Crane is attempting to follow Pater, whose "turn toward the past," says Heather K. Love, "aim[ed] to transform the present and the future; he explored such moments in an effort to ignite a cultural revolution in the present" (57). Crane draws specific attention to "the problem of unity with ourselves" when he mentions how the "dough" is "[d]ivided by accepted multitudes," and how detritus builds up "[a]cross the stacked partitions of the day." Just as Crane explains the crucial importance of allowing the mind to strive for original thought, so Pater describes how "the intellect demands completeness, centrality."

These multitudes are described in the abstract. Characters in the poem lack proper names (they are merely "[n]umbers"), and they either act as one thing ("[c]onvoying divers dawns"), or lack agency altogether, having things merely done *to* them, rather than acting for themselves ("[t]he mind is brushed"). In his "Conclusion" to *The Renaissance*, Pater described how "[a]t first sight experience seems to bury us under a flood of external objects, pressing upon us with a sharp and importunate reality, calling us out of ourselves in a thousand forms of action" (153). These people seem to occupy precisely this form of reality for Crane: oppressed by worldly experience they can nonetheless find ways of taking advantage of the impulse "calling us out of ourselves." The heat of the man-made asphalt may be oppressive, but they can instead find places to exist on "[t]he margins" where they "accent the curbs," a subtle pun that suggests they can add their own particular slant not just to the marginal space, re-appropriating it, but also resist its implicit power to curb or oppress their individualities. The evening too with its "graduate opacities" offers safe spaces in which their actions will not be seen by the interfering eyes of the normative population. Embracing Pater then allows Crane to present the dilemmas and solutions for the queer individual in the modern urban environment – simultaneously under threat of exposure, but also able to find spaces and times of security.

Crane's description of this "world dimensional for/those untwisted by the love of things/irreconcilable ...," together with the ellipsis, implicitly invites the reader to contemplate its opposite, and in addition, three aspects of that world "*un*dimensional." Firstly, a "love of things" rather than people suggests that one aspect of this world involves aesthetic contemplation. Then the idea that there are things in it which are "irreconcilable" prepares us for the incongruous image of finding Helen in a streetcar, which finally is also an engagement in the modern world with the values and ideals of the classical world. Those who *are* twisted "by the love of things/irreconcilable" describes those who are "queer," which, as Eve Kosofsky Sedgwick has defined it, "comes from the Indo-European root -*twerkw*, which also yields the German *quer* (transverse), Latin *torquere* (to twist), English *athwart*" (*Tendencies* xii). In the new world of experience that is created, the speaker goes on to explore this queer moment that yields Paterian "impressions." Separated from the material world, the speaker "continue[s] to dwell in thought on this world, not of objects in the solidity with which language invests them, but of impressions, unstable, flickering, inconsistent, which burn and are extinguished with our consciousness of them" (*The Renaissance* 153); an idea presented in the fourth stanza of the poem:

> And yet, suppose some evening I forgot
> The fare and transfer, yet got by that way
> Without recall, – lost yet poised in traffic.
> Then I might find your eyes across an aisle,
> Still flickering with those prefigurations –
> Prodigal, yet uncontested now,
> Half-riant before the jerky window frame.

In this moment there is a lack of certainty. The continuous qualification in the thrice-repeated "yet," and the image of the speaker "lost yet poised in traffic," recalls Heather Love's description of Pater's figures in *The Renaissance*: "outside time, suspended in an endless present of indecision" (65). Crane creates a moment in which the foregoing materialism of the poem is rejected ("I forgot/The fare and transfer"), and the focus is entirely on the aesthetic. It requires a Paterian engagement with the intellect, rejecting the "baked and labeled dough/Divided by accepted multitudes," to enter into a realm of impressions, in which the appreciation of beauty makes possible same-sex attraction. In his "Conclusion," Pater notes that "we are all *condamnés*, as Victor Hugo says: we are all under sentence of death but with a sort of indefinite reprieve [...] we have an interval, and then our place knows us no more" (*The Renaissance* 155). The queer moment – the "endless present" – and the moment of aesthetic contemplation are, Crane says, one and the same. Thus, when the speaker "find[s] your eyes across an aisle,/Still flickering with those prefigurations," he sees beauty. What is more, this moment of aesthetic impression situated in "the world undimensional," suggests in miniature the terms through which Crane has negotiated and found ways of articulating his queer desire: Helen stands in for Hellenism.

2
Abstraction and Intersubjectivity in *White Buildings*

Hart Crane could count himself a success when he found himself fêted at a distinguished New York party hosted by the critic Paul Rosenfeld in November 1924. He read "Chaplinesque," "Sunday Morning Apples," "Paraphrase," and then, as an encore, "For the Marriage of Faustus and Helen." His appreciative audience reads now like a roll call of American modernists, and not just literary figures: Alfred Stieglitz, Georgia O'Keeffe, Jean Toomer, Paul Strand, Aaron Copland, Marianne Moore, and Edmund Wilson.[1] The presence of painters and photographers at this party would not have been novel for Crane, since he made a conscious effort to surround himself with visual as well as verbal artists. The strong visual style that he derived from Decadence and Imagism was augmented by his tutelage by visual artists, in particular his Ohio Cézanne, William Sommer, who helped to develop Crane's understanding of aesthetics, and whom Crane must have mentioned at the 1924 party, since "Sunday Morning Apples" is concerned with his work. One of the aims of Crane's queer project is to challenge normative representation, which Crane did through the use of techniques like ekphrasis, and the embrace of abstract presentation which, he hoped, would allow him to connect with his readers. The acknowledgment of mutual difficulties in perceiving the normative world, Crane thought, would allow him and his readers to connect too on a more visceral, embodied level, regardless of their sexuality, an intersubjectivity that Crane sought to achieve through his use of figuration. At the same time as Crane aimed to assert his queerness through language, he also sought to present himself to those readers in a way that would refute any charges of obscurity, and allow them to join the party too.

Visual influences and the language of art

Fusing the language used to describe a verbal aesthetic with that used to comment upon a visual aesthetic became a common feature of Crane's letters and prose as his career developed, and it was enhanced by his relationship with visual artists such as the painters Carl Schmitt and William Sommer, and the sculptor Gaston Lachaise. In 1930, when he wrote his essay "Modern Poetry," Crane summarized the clear – and necessary – relationship between painting and literature:

> Literature has a more tangible relationship to paint [than to modern music]; and it is highly probable that the Symbolist movement in French poetry was a considerable factor in the instigation first, of Impressionism, and later, of Cubism. Both arts have had parallel and somewhat analogous tendencies toward abstract statement and metaphysical representation (*CPSL* 261).[2]

As this section will go on to show, Crane attempted to exploit these "analogous tendencies" and transfigure the plastic arts into the linguistic by adopting certain modes of *abstraction*. In particular, he adopted a technique of ekphrasis to present paintings and drawings by Sommer and a sculpture by Lachaise. In doing so, Crane highlighted the process of creation and echoed other modernists' concerns with *representation* and the limits of language. In his use of "metaphysical," Crane intended to suggest that poetry seeks to represent something beyond our comprehension of reality. It goes beyond physical objects to inhabit an instant that is much more like Pater's impression. Both Schmitt and Sommer broadened Crane's understanding of what poetry could do, for whilst Schmitt advised Crane to avoid creating boundaries between different art forms, Sommer introduced him to philosophical writings about art and a vocabulary that he could use to describe both visual and verbal art forms.

Crane's earliest contact with the physical work of an artist was with Carl Schmitt, a young painter whom Crane had met in Warren, Ohio through the poet's godmother, Zell Hart Deming, one of Schmitt's patrons. Schmitt, who was ten years older than Crane, acted as an unofficial guardian to him on his first stay in New York in 1917. Both Schmitt and, later, William Sommer encouraged Crane to think of the arts in broad terms: that the visual and verbal, or plastic and temporal, as Schmitt described it, overlapped in their influence, and that as an artist it was important to absorb what you could from each kind of medium in order to create your own work. John Unterecker reports that Schmitt's philosophy posed a number of questions:

> How much should [...] "space" arts [such] as painting and sculpture draw on the elements that logically dominate the arts that can only be experienced in time (literature, music, etc.)? How much rhythm – essentially a property of the "time" arts – can be incorporated in a painting before the painter's special concern, vision, becomes distorted? (57).

Schmitt inspired Crane to rethink notions of spatial form and temporality within his work and, in this cross-pollination of ideas between visual art and literature, helped him to challenge what could be represented in language, proposing to Crane the need for a freedom of expression and a disregarding of boundaries, aspirations that the poet would also come to consider in terms of the presentation of transgressive subject matter such as sexuality.

If he drew one strand of his initial interest in experimentation from Schmitt, Crane further developed his aesthetic training under William Sommer, whom he met in 1921. Sommer had been born in Detroit, but trained as a painter in Europe. Ten years before he met Crane, Sommer co-founded the Kokoon Arts Klub in Cleveland, which aimed to introduce the Cleveland public to a number of the modernist artists in whose work Sommer had become interested.[3] His visit to the Armory Show in New York in 1913 proved something of a revelation for him. In a letter to Gorham Munson, Crane described Sommer as "[a] man of 55 or so – works in a lithograph factory – spent most of his life until the last seven years in the rut of conventional forms – liberated suddenly by sparks from Gauguin, Von Gogh [sic], Picasso and Wyndham Lewis etc" (*OML* 61).[4] Crane reported at the time that Sommer's work "seems to carry the most astonishing marks of genius that have passed my eyes in original form – that is – I mean present-day work" (*OML* 61). His tutelage under Sommer, which included an introduction to Cubism and the reading of books by the art critics Clive Bell and Roger Fry, led Crane to discuss both the plastic arts and his own poetry in visual terms. He spoke of "Black Tambourine" (1921/1921) as having value "only [...] in what a painter would call its 'tactile' quality, – an entirely aesthetic feature" (*OML* 64). In a later letter, he discussed how "I believe with Sommer that the 'Ding an sich' method is ultimately the only satisfactory creative principle to follow," and that he reacted against "the current impressionism," which he found exemplified by "the Cocteau poem (trans.) in the *Little Review*" (*OML* 72).[5] In a further letter to Sherwood Anderson, Crane wrote about how he found "the problem of style and form becoming more and more difficult as time goes on" (*OML* 78), and that he sought for an "'interior' form, a form that is so thorough and intense as to dye the words themselves with a peculiarity of meaning, slightly different maybe from the ordinary definition of them separate from the poem" (*OML* 79). Sommer's influence at this early point in Crane's writing career is not only significant for the ways in which he taught Crane to write and think about art, but for the direct impact that this teaching had upon Crane's aesthetic choices about how to represent the world around him. The clearest examples of visual art's influence upon Crane are found in the two ekphrastic poems that Crane composed between 1922–1924, "Sunday Morning Apples" (1922/1924), and "Interludium" (1923–1924/1924). Although they deal with works in different media, Crane's two poems in celebration of artists and art nevertheless result in the expression of similar concerns relating to the experience of encountering an artwork, and the difficulties that a writer faces in seeking to represent it.

Ekphrasis: An alternative form of literary modernism

"Sunday Morning Apples" (1922/1924), was dedicated to William Sommer,[6] and in the opening stanza of the poem Crane immediately draws attention to the similarities between poetry and painting when he describes "those purposes/That are your rich and faithful strength of line." (*CP* 7)[7] Not only does he pun upon the meanings of poetic/painted lines, Crane is also identifying an aesthetic quality of Sommer's work that he had commented upon previously in letters. Writing to Gorham Munson, Crane reported Alfred Stieglitz had criticized Sommer's paintings for "the lack of finish evident in so much of it." However, Crane believed that Stieglitz and "other critics" were wrong to overlook "the positive and timeless qualities" in the "quality of line in Sommer's work" (*OML* 116–17). When he mentioned "other critics," Crane was thinking about a recent judgment by the art critic Paul Rosenfeld, to whom Crane had sent a number of Sommer's paintings, and who was to pointedly hear about Sommer again when Crane read "Sunday Morning Apples" at his party in 1924. Rosenfeld's assessment two years earlier, according to Crane, included comments about how Sommer "was not a notable man at all – had no personal vision – his work a mixture of halfdozen [sic] modern influences – and couldn't draw a head on man, woman or animal!" (*OML* 99).[8] Crane had sent the pictures along with the novelist Sherwood Anderson, who had offered to show them to Rosenfeld, but the latter's negative appraisal served to effect a final break in relations between Crane and Anderson. Crane's notion in his letter that certain critics "are so obsessed with the importance of current developements [sic] in art that they fail to recognize certain positive and timeless qualities" also suggests a significant aesthetic choice. When Crane "discovered" Sommer, he praised him by saying that "I prefer Sommers' [sic] work to most of [Henri Gaudier-] Brzeska and Boardman Robinson" (*OML* 61). It is certainly significant that Crane finally rejects Anderson, the man whose work he had admired beyond any other, because it demonstrates how Crane was positing an aesthetic independence, one that marked a shift away from the Midwest modernism he had identified with his own Ohio background, and towards a more European notion of art. By setting up Sommer against Gaudier-Brzeska in particular, who had been championed by Ezra Pound, Crane also advocated for an alternative strain of modernity in the visual arts. Crane's assertion of Sommer's "positive and timeless qualities" suggests again, in a similar way to the persistence of Decadence in his work, a refusal to disregard the past. In the same letter in which he discussed Rosenfeld's rejection of Sommer, he lamented this modern tendency, exclaiming "God DAMN this nostalgia for something always 'new'. This disdain for anything with a trace of the past in it!!" (*OML* 17).

As a tribute to Sommer's work, "Sunday Morning Apples" adopts those "positive and timeless qualities" very directly. In this ekphrastic poem Crane tries to develop a means by which the poet can represent the experience of seeing an artwork as well as reflecting upon the time during which the artwork was made; a fascination both with time and with the act of looking. Murray Krieger describes the traditional understanding of ekphrasis as "the attempted imitation in words of an object of the plastic arts, primarily painting or sculpture" (4), and in "Sunday Morning Apples," it seems that Crane is referring to at least three paintings by William Sommer, or at least three images derived from them. There is the "ripe nude with head/reared," the "boy [who] runs with a dog before the sun," and the "[b]eloved apples of seasonable madness." Each of these were drawn from the similar features of nudes, children, animals, and apples which commonly appear in Sommer's work.[9]

In his earlier discussions with Carl Schmitt, Crane had already investigated the possibilities of blurring aspects of the "space arts" with those of the "time arts." "Sunday Morning Apples" is not just an ekphrastic piece of work though, for it and "Interludium" explore some of the key representational concepts associated with ekphrasis. According to

Murray Krieger, a crucial point in any discussion of ekphrasis is "the semiotic status of both space and the visual in the vain representational attempt of words to capture these within their temporal sequence" (4). In both ekphrastic poems, Crane uses the present tense to give some sense of an immediate experience with an artwork. "Interludium," Crane's poem about Lachaise's sculpture *La Montagne Héroique*, opens with the lines: "Thy time is thee to wend/with languor" (*CP* 158),[10] indicating that the statue contains its own temporal condition within, suggesting a monumental and eternal quality for a sculpture that draws both on Western religious iconography and upon ancient indigenous American cultures. In "Sunday Morning Apples," Crane creates an eternal present in which to situate his representation of the paintings. The "ripe nude" is "[b]ursting on the winter of the world," the boy "runs with a dog" as they are "straddling/Spontaneities," and the apples are described as being part of a continuous process as they "feed your inquiries with aerial wine." Here Crane is attempting to recreate that experience of standing and viewing the painting and entering into a dialogue with it. Acknowledging the "vain representational attempt of words" to accurately represent the artwork, Crane uses sound patterning to simulate the sensational interaction with the art and adopts the present tense to turn the reader into the viewer. This self-conscious attempt to offer an equally powerful but different experience is also a reflection upon what it is like to create a piece of art, and as John Norton-Smith has suggested, the poem "attempts to give an account of the creative process" (41). This process is based upon insight gained from close observation, for just as a painter constantly studies his subject, so too does the poet, and this process is exemplified in the empirical, "scientific" technique that Crane describes.

As Crane wrote in "Modern Poetry," in recent times "[a]nalysis and discovery, the two basic concerns of science, became conscious objectives of both painter and poet" (*CP* 261). In the third stanza of "Sunday Morning Apples," Crane describes Sommer's painting in scientific terms, as the boy and dog are "straddling/Spontaneities that form their independent orbits." As Robert K. Martin has observed, Crane's ideas about representation in art are indebted to Clive Bell, whose work Sommer had read and subsequently passed onto Crane,[11] and in this poem Crane is directly engaging with Bell's history and analysis of Impressionism in his book *Art*. Bell wrote:

> When art is as nearly dead as it was in the middle of the nineteenth century, scientific accuracy is judged the proper end of painting. Very

well, said the French Impressionists, be accurate, be scientific. At best the Academic painter sets down his concepts; but the concept is not a scientific reality; the men of science tell us that the visible reality of the Universe is vibrations of light. Let us represent things as they are – scientifically. Let us represent light. Let us paint what we see, not the intellectual superstructure that we build over our sensations. That was the theory: and if the end of art were representation it would be sound enough. But the end of art is not representation [...] (111–12).

As Bell sees it, the end of art is to create beauty and thereby generate emotion in the viewer, even if that art is non-representational. In "Sunday Morning Apples," Crane draws upon Bell's description of Impressionism's attention to "the visible reality of the Universe" as "vibrations of light" when he describes those "[s]pontaneities that form their independent orbits,/Their own perennials of light." Rather than sharing Bell's distrust of the scientific method, he shows that he is interested in exploring the connection between the scientific observer and the object and in combining an intellectual interrogation of the object with an aesthetic appreciation of its beauty. Having watched his friend paint the apples with such intuition, he asks Sommer now to "[p]ut them again beside a pitcher with a knife,/And poise them full and ready for explosion –/The apples, Bill, the apples!" These lines suggest that Crane himself will now try to use his words as artistic materials to gain the same insights, but that the approach he adopts is not unlike that of the visual artist: the apples will be "poise[d]" in a still life arrangement with a knife and pitcher nearby, a frequent combination in Sommer's paintings.

Crane's interrogation of the apples in the poem allows him to challenge modes of representation and perception and to consider the value of representing objects within forms of art whilst engaging with a contemporary modernist literary style. The exclamation of "the apples!" suggests a moment of revelation, and whilst such emphasis upon an epiphany recalls the last lines of Crane's earlier poem "October-November," the Imagist focus upon an "intellectual and emotional complex in an instant of time" (Pound, "A Few Don'ts by an Imagiste" 84) is also similar to the artistic methods favored by William Sommer: a determined focus upon the precise presentation of one image or object. Crane wrote that he "believe[d] with Sommer that the 'Ding an Sich' method is ultimately the only satisfactory creative principle to follow" (*OML* 72), and this focus upon "the thing itself" served to challenge notions of representation. In his 1781 *Critique of Pure Reason* Kant had argued that we can only know the world with certainty, and thus know "things in themselves," through the way in which objects appear to us. As Keith Ansell Pearson and Duncan Large have explained, "[t]his means that the traditional aspirations of metaphysics cannot be met, simply because they rest on the belief that it is possible for us to transcend the sensory conditions of our nature and so arrive at a knowledge of the nature of things themselves" (5). However, even while he explores its possibilities, Crane suggests that visual and verbal art can significantly complicate the "ding an sich." In the first place, he understands he has only "seen the apples that toss you secrets," and that the knowledge derived from these "things" is subjective. The "secrets" that Sommer shares with the apples are different to those that Crane will receive – if he receives any insight at all. There can be no universal knowledge of the things in themselves.

Secondly, "Sunday Morning Apples" also suggests that art's subjective approach can lead readers and viewers to question the nature of reality and how we perceive it. In the second stanza, for instance, "there are challenges to spring/In that ripe nude with head/reared/Into a realm of swords, her purple shadow/Bursting on the winter of the world/From whiteness that cries defiance to the snow." In the first instance, this ripe nude is out of place, for such ripeness should be associated with spring or summer, and yet this figure is present in "the winter of the world." In addition, Sommer's presentation of the nude and its shadow appears on the canvas so powerfully and brightly white that the color seems to challenge the reality of the real snow outside. Rather than imitate life, art here seems to outdo it and offer possibilities for a queer aesthetic: if normative reality itself is challenged, even in doubt, then alternative possibilities of expression and reality may be equally valid.

The challenge to artistic and heteronormative reproduction

The images of fertility and sexuality in both "Sunday Morning Apples" and a second ekphrastic poem, "Interludium," echo Crane's concern with the creative process, and, in the way in which they offer a challenge to reality that it is also a challenge to normative versions of fertility, suggest the queer potential in challenging aesthetic representation possible by focusing closely upon objects like the apples. "Sunday Morning Apples" hinted at but never fulfilled the potential implied in the images of the "ripe nude" and the apples "ready for explosion"; the apples did not, after all, explode in a moment of sexual, procreative climax. Crane's queer aesthetic destabilizes the generative heteronormative process so that both ekphrastic poems present an internal conflict between the potential for reproduction and its failure.

"Interludium" was inspired by, and dedicated to, *La Montagne*, a sandstone sculpture by the French-American artist Gaston Lachaise whom Crane met in 1923, but whose work Crane would have certainly seen previously in the *Dial*. Lachaise was a prominent figure in the magazine, which published reproductions of eighteen of his works, and four major and several smaller articles about him appeared there before 1929. Lachaise's work in fact could be said to set the tone for the illustrated material in the *Dial*, since his relief *Dusk* was the frontispiece for the inaugural issue under Scofield Thayer's editorship on January 20, 1920.[12] Although *La Montagne* (originally entitled *La Montagne Héroique*) was commissioned by the artist George L. K. Morris for his estate in Lenox, Massachusetts, a reproduction of it appeared in the *Dial* in March 1921, entitled simply *La Montagne*,[13] and it seems likely that this is the version of the sculpture to which Crane is responding.

In "Interludium," Crane presents a forerunner to his symbolic Pocahontas in *The Bridge*: a divine figure who represents fertility, one who is "illimitable," and whose "open dugs" (a term that connotes both animal and human features) not only allow the speaker to "subsist" (suggesting the cultivation of land) but also seem to control the movements of the life-giving orb of the sun. Yet despite the suggestive images of fertility, the poem actually spends more time highlighting how the sculpture's self-contained nature, its density, conflicts with the possibility of reproduction. If the "ripe nude" was out of place in the winter landscape of "Sunday Morning Apples," here *La Montagne* is described as "fostering/thyself." Rather than contemplate the procreative impulse of a goddess of fertility, the word "fostering" instead suggests the raising of another person who is not a relative by blood. The final stanza describes the sculpture as "Madonna," and the intimated virginity of this figure seems confirmed in the reference to her as being "untried" in the third stanza, and in the way that the speaker is "natal to thy yielding." This is imagery that confuses birth with sexual consent under the auspices of fertility and subsistence from the land. Such imagery is linked to a more general sense of incompleteness: the repeated prefix "un-" in "unfurling," "untried" or "untenanted" suggests this, as do the ideas that the arms might spread, or hands "yield their shells," both of which are presented as actions in the future. Continuing this sense of unfulfillment, sleep is "forbidden," and in the sculpture itself "wide/partitions" are noticeable.

The phrase "challenges to spring" in "Sunday Morning Apples," just like the repeated doubting of fertility in "Interludium," questions heteronormative reproduction, and figures this queer conflict in imagery of incompleteness. Ekphrasis is the site chosen for this conflict because it also grapples with reproduction: the aesthetic challenge of transferring one form of art into another. In examining this, these poems simultaneously explore aesthetic concerns and the possibilities of sexual alterity.

The further challenge: abstraction

In order to present these possibilities, Crane also makes use of linguistic abstraction, which allows him to challenge normative representation whilst also making a connection with his reader. As Charles Altieri has asserted, American modernist poets sought to use an abstract style because "there is no other way to tease out from our empirical representations the range of states we bring under the penumbra of self, and there is no other way to make visible the sense of intersubjective connectedness that this diversity affords" (12). Both "Interludium" and "Sunday Morning Apples" provide abstract imagery, but also show that Crane was experimenting with formal techniques in order to present this abstraction. In "Interludium," an impulse towards abstraction can be seen in the frequency and repetition of the "un-" prefix, which creates fragmentation, the poet hinting at many ways in which the sculpture might be broken apart physically and linguistically, such as in the description of it "unfurling," or mention of its "wide/partitions." Such an impulse is echoed in "Sunday Morning Apples," where the final image hints at violent abstraction, "poise them full and ready for explosion." This description seems to mimic the form of many Cubist works that attempt to capture, in the words of Guillaume Apollinaire, "the immensity of space eternalizing itself in all directions at any given moment" (265). In preceding parts of the poem, Crane's abstraction can also be traced through the image of the circle or near-circle. The nude's "head" reappears in "the sun," which gives way to "independent orbits" (elliptical paths), and which appear again in the forms of the apples and even typographically in the form of the brackets "(called Brandywine)," which, if brought together, would form a perfect circle. Crane himself was well aware of Cubist form, not only through his discussions with Sommer, but also through his own experimentation with Cubist drawings.[14]

Sherman Paul is right to assert that "Sunday Morning Apples" "is cubist" (84), and the influence of Cubism behind this poem dramatizes a conflict between the whole and the fragmented where one relies upon the other to exist: we comprehend a fragmented piece only because we know what it is like as part of a whole. John Berger has suggested that

> [f]or the Impressionists the visible no longer presented itself to man in order to be seen. On the contrary, the visible, in continual flux, became fugitive. For the Cubists the visible was no longer what confronted the single eye, but the totality of possible views taken from points all round the object (or person) being depicted (18).

Such concepts in Crane's work show that he considered a process of abstraction as a possible way of solving the problem of representation. Abstraction offered Crane a means of seeing around and beyond the object; into the secrets that the apples reveal to Sommer, to view the "independent orbits" of the boy and the dog, or to view the future possibilities that are enclosed within *La Montagne Héroique*. Crane takes the sense of Cubism further than just the perspectives that can be seen, and offers his reader access to the unseen – at times spiritual – dimensions of the object. In his discussion of the relationship between another visual artist and Crane, Langdon Hammer has explained how the "representational function" in Alfred Stieglitz's photos "is de-emphasized in favor of formal pattern and symbolic statement" ("Stieglitz, Crane, and Abstract Form" 4). According to Hammer, Crane saw in Stieglitz's work

> acts of representation that point to something within it, a deep plane of relation understood as what is abstract. [...] What [Crane] was attracted to, as he describes it, is the process of abstraction, the act of the eye extracting the essential from the visible, which [Crane] sees as a passage "through" representation (4).

Crane adopts the same process in his use of ekphrasis and his treatment of Sommer's paintings and Lachaise's sculpture. Crane believed that, in his use of abstraction, Stieglitz got closer to the "ding an sich," since he was able to depict "the essences of things [... which] are suspended on the invisible dimension whose vibrance has been denied the human eye at all times save in the intuition of ecstasy" (*OML* 149).[15] Crane's attraction to techniques of abstraction like ekphrasis – literally a "speaking out" – and his connecting of abstraction with ecstasy – a state outside oneself – suggests an attempt by Crane to step outside his work and connect with his reader. Responding to Dorothy Newman's suggestion that some of Stieglitz's photographs are "erotic," Hammer comments that both Stieglitz and Crane

> use abstraction to forge an intimacy with the reader or viewer, an intimacy that transgresses the conventions of ordinary social relationships to connect people on a deep level. The abstract and the erotic merge, then, in the way that each throw us into "ultimate harmonies," as [Crane] said about [Stieglitz's] photographs. He had in mind, I think, the "defamiliarizing" of ordinary experience [...] ("Stieglitz, Hart Crane, and Abstract Form," 6).

In the opening chapter of this book I showed how Crane equated the queer with the aesthetic in "Faustus and Helen." In these later poems, he starts with concrete objects and then uses abstract techniques like ekphrasis to link himself with his reader by appealing to what Charles Altieri calls "intersubjective connectedness." Deeming language sometimes ineffective, as being too close to straightforward representation, Crane seeks instead other queer means by which he can make that connection with his reader. As Hammer indicates, this is a kind of defamiliarization, since the relationship that Crane creates with his reader is highly unusual in a way that "transgresses" what is normative, queering both the visual and the verbal, and the way in which we respond to each. As I will now go on to argue, Crane's apprenticeship to visual artists and his study of their creative processes and products, lead him to consider ways in which he might make further visual and material connections with his reader/viewer through his work.

Doubleness and the crisis of perception

Despite many attempts throughout 1921 to interest friends and experts in William Sommer's work, Crane was only partially successful in his promotion of the painter. Sommer's work appeared in the *Pagan*, he provided the cover illustration for an issue of the little magazine *Secession*, and Crane managed to sell some pieces to Gorham Munson and William Carlos Williams. But a planned exhibition in New York never materialized and Crane became gradually frustrated at Sommer's lack of enthusiasm in promoting his own work.[16] However, in a 1925 letter, Crane told Waldo Frank that he had

> finally found out why Sommer ha[d] been so remiss about joining in with me in my several efforts to expose him to fame and "fortune."

He hates to let his pictures leave him. Against that impasse, I guess, nobody's efforts will be of much avail. It's just as well, of course, if he has triumphed over certain kinds of hope. I admit that I haven't, at least not entirely. I still feel the need of some kind of audience (*OML* 205).

Crane's admission here that he needs "some kind of audience" is telling, since it goes some way to explain why the poems generally placed later in *White Buildings* and written between 1923–1925, such as "Possessions" (1923–1924/1924), "Recitative" (1923–1924/1924), "Lachrymae Christi" (1924–1925/1925), "Legend" (1924/1925), "The Wine Menagerie" (1925–1926/1926), and "Passage" (1925/1926), are so fascinated with images of sight and being seen. Implicitly, Crane acknowledges that "audience" by punctuating these poems with direct addresses to the eyes of his readers/viewers; "[w]itness," "[l]ook steadily," "[r]egard" and "[s]ee" are some of the imperatives that feature in these lyrics. As I suggest throughout the book, Crane's work is dependent upon relationality, in making a visual as well as a verbal connection with his readers, so that they might "read" him in different ways. But in offering these connections, Crane is also acknowledging two other things that result from his involvement with visual art: a general concern about the representation of reality, and the potential difficulty of "seeing" him/his meaning in the first place (both in terms of his linguistic "obscurity" and his queerness).

Reality

Crane's poems address issues of perception through Pater's concept of the "impression" as he formulates it in his "Preface" to *The Renaissance*:

> To see the object in itself as it really is, has been justly said to be the aim of all true criticism whatever; and in aesthetic criticism the first step towards seeing one's object as it really is, is to know one's own impression as it really is, to discriminate it, to realise it distinctly (1).

Pater is adapting Kant's theory of the "ding an sich" with which Crane was also familiar. But Pater's analysis is also bound up very directly with the personal interpretation of an object. As Jesse Matz has discerned, Pater suggests the necessity for a certain kind of relationality, and this is something that Crane presents in his poetry:

> [A]s Pater's impression sets it up, aesthetic judgment means turning inward and finding one's capacities for judgment incomplete; it means

discovering self-alienation, and trying to correct the problem through engagement with another kind of person. However limited this engagement might seem, its outreach puts sociality where "aesthetic ideology" sees isolated, introverted, and irresponsible selves. Its recourse to collaboration puts social intersubjectivity at the heart of the aesthetic: this, perhaps, is what made the progression from Arnold to Pater to Wilde hard for the public to take, and what gives Impressionism, even when its collaborations seem suspect, its special dissidence (55).

The "sociality" that Matz identifies in Pater is essential to the way in which Crane's poetry works. Just as Pater created a collection of figures situated in or connected with the Renaissance within his book, "a community of subjects defined through indecision and delay," as Heather Love (*Feeling Backward* 65) has described it, so too Crane had a vision of "a new order of consciousness," telling Stieglitz that he and Crane were "accomplices in many ways that we don't yet fully understand" (*OML* 155–56). If he felt that this "new order" was necessary to change America, he also felt that the connections that he made with his readers/viewers were also essential in the process of creating the artwork itself. Whereas, as Matz suggests, Pater looked inside himself and suggested an "impression" that identified "self-alienation" as the problem that required "another kind of person," Crane instead promoted a doubleness in his writing that retained the integrity of the self but affirmed a link with another person as a way of overcoming the difficulties of perception to which everyone within the world was subject. Such an affirmation is clearest in his poem "Recitative" (1923–1924/1924) in which doubleness acts as a metaphor for the essential relationship between the speaker of the poem and its reader/viewer.

It appears in the opening stanza, which seems to invite the viewer to look at what the mirror shows, as if to confirm that the image seen there will be a double of the one looking. The poem begins: "Regard the capture here, O Janus-faced/As double as the hands that twist this glass" (*CP* 25).[17] Yet rather than give confirmation, this presentation instead offers confusion. One early draft read: "As double as the hands that crash this glass," as if to suggest that obstacles have been set up to confuse the vision of the speaker (qtd. in Weber 224). In the final version the image is "capture[d]," like a prisoner, the addressee themselves is seen as "Janus-faced," which implies duplicity (*WUD* 724), and the hands are involved in the manipulation of the image itself. There is a general questioning of our perceptions, just as the mirror itself – particularly in the earlier version of the poem, is deemed inadequate. As Christopher Nealon has remarked about the poem "Legend," "our beliefs about 'the mirror,' in this case the world of presumably docile mimetic representations, are insufficient actually to render experience" (32). Crane questions how anything can be determined authentic if our perception of simple reality is constantly in doubt. If the image of ourselves is in question, so too is our environment, when Crane tells his reader in "Recitative" to "watch/ While darkness, like an ape's face, falls away,/And gradually white buildings answer day." Crane's use of the pun here, a double meaning since aping something means to "mimic" it (*WUD* 61), questions fundamental notions of place and time and the dual pleasure and danger of the multivalency of meaning. If, in "Sunday Morning Apples," Crane had previously exhibited tendencies towards scientific analysis, here he further endorses an empirical approach that calls on his reader to witness with him his (disoriented) experience. To do so, and to acknowledge the difficulty of experience, brings the reader closer to the poet's subjective world, creating once again a form of relationality. That subjectivity is figured in the "plate of vibrant mercury" that the speaker describes in the second stanza, an image that encourages the sense of disorientation: the vision in the plate of liquid mercury suggests a complexity that encompasses both a same-sex connection with another (the "brother in the half" to whom the plate of mercury is offered), and a sense in which the poet is also recognizing that his own self is unfixed, which may be a more truthful representation than the image produced in a mirror.

This conflict between inner and outer worlds occasions the crisis of perception that runs through the poem, particularly in the use of the idea of doubleness (or "duality"). In a 1924 letter to Allen Tate, Crane elaborated upon the various perspectives contained within the poem:

> Imagine the poet, say, on a platform speaking [the poem]. The audience is one half of Humanity, Man (in the sense of Blake) and the poet the other. ALSO, the poet sees himself in the audience as in a mirror. ALSO, the audience sees itself, in part, in the poet. Against this paradoxical DUALITY is posed the UNITY, or the conception of it (as you got it) in the last verse. In another sense, the poet is talking to himself all the way through the poem, and there are, as too often in my poems, other reflexes in the poem, also, which it would be silly to write here – at least for the present (*OML* 182–83).

This explanation acknowledges the role that an "audience" plays in his work. For "Recitative" therefore and in other poems, Crane writes the poem whilst envisaging an audience that hears and *sees* his work. Crane also suggests that the poem needs to be read, or seen, on several levels at once, a concept that prefigures his theory of the "logic of metaphor" as he expressed it in "General Aims and Theories" (1925), and in his discussion with Harriet Monroe in the pages of *Poetry* in 1926.

Crane's explanation to Tate is also complex because of Crane's own eagerness to justify his writing style. The addition of "(as you got it)" suggests some relief that Tate had managed to "get" his writing. In the sense that doubleness could result both in complexity and obscurity, Crane knew that it was something to be welcomed and of which he must be wary. In a letter to Gorham Munson in 1926, he explained that

> [p]oetry, as far as the metaphysics of any absolute knowledge extends, is simply the concrete <u>evidence</u> of the <u>experience</u> of a recognition (<u>knowledge</u> if you like). It can give you a <u>ratio</u> of fact and experience, and in this sense it is both perception and the thing perceived, according as it approaches a significant articulation or not. This is its reality, its fact, <u>being</u> (*OML* 232).[18]

In the sense that poetry is "both perception and the thing perceived," it mimics Crane's concern about doubleness. The danger of his theorizing in this letter is that in aspiring towards "absoluteness," the poem becomes hermetically sealed and fixed, incapable of evolution. Such total subjectivity would render any dissidence resulting from his impression, and any affirmation of Crane's sexuality, meaningless, since it would have no connection to the "outside" or the normative world. Relegated to this sealed-off space, the speaker and his subjects would have no place in that normative world. Lee Edelman observes that by using phrases such as "concrete evidence" in this letter, Crane is exhibiting "a certain epistemological unsteadiness" (*Transmemberment of Song* 34), and this "unsteadiness," again suggests Crane's desire that he be "seen" clearly in his poetry, that somehow the material might take over from the visible. Edelman continues in his analysis:

> The "fact," given contextual significance as the object of scientific investigation, denotes the world's otherness, its externality, while "experience" internalizes and interprets the world by integrating it into the self. Crane's persuasive strategy clearly assumes the hierarchical privileging of the inside over the outside even as it attempts to define poetry as the resolution of that binary opposition (34).

Certainly Crane is making a link between "fact" and "experience," but he does not seek to privilege one over the other. By holding the two in tension or conflict, Crane seeks to draw attention to the problems of perception in the modern world, opening up his poetry and refusing to restrict himself to a sealed-off existence. In doing so, Crane actually proposes a far riskier poetics: just as his abstract style sought intimacy with the unknown reader, so here he makes a deliberate attempt to relate his own subjectivity to his reader's, by fusing his own "experience" with that of his reader. In suggesting that everyone is subject to the same crisis of perception, Crane draws his own queer experience closer to that of his readers, whether queer or not. Rather than suggesting that poetry is a "resolution," Crane instead posits it as an (aesthetic) meeting point for the "social intersubjectivity" advocated by Pater.

Looking and touching

Poetry's ability to contain multitudes, especially contraries, ensures that it has its own particular dissidence, and Crane's emphasis upon the crisis of perception implies that this is a dissidence to which everyone can relate. Acknowledging, however, that each person's dissidence will be subjective, Crane seeks to overcome this by "meeting" his readers through visual and material means.

"Recitative" opens with the invitation to "[r]egard," and continues with the offering of "a plate of vibrant mercury/Borne cleft to you, and brother in the half." Crane's poem is a negotiation, for as it constantly addresses and offers moments of literal reflection to the reader, it seeks to show the similarities and connections between the author and that reader. It addresses Crane's "obscurity" by acknowledging that such obscurity is both linguistic and sexual; Crane's queerness as Otherness cannot be understood. Crane certainly does not deny his sexuality, indeed the doubleness to which he draws attention and the "twin shadowed halves" suggest the differences and similarities between the speaker and his interlocutor. However, in the course of the poem's argument he suggests that the continuing crisis of perception allows for the possibility that queerness is all around us, and that in living through such confusion, the queer individual and the heterosexual share experience. The final sections of the poem then assert a certain freedom, derived through shared language and presence.

Having made the visual connection, Crane enters into a more intimate, physical relationship with his reader. He suggests ways in which both he and they are oppressed within their shared world, through the mechanics of capitalism, and then offers a means of escape. Crane identifies a concept that is not shared, the way in which "[t]he brain's disk [is] shivered against lust." But, rather than linger on this gap in understanding, he mentions it merely as a strategy to draw attention to another, more crucial gap: "the same nameless gulf" with which *both* the queer man and the heterosexual are concerned. This is the oppression of capitalism, which appears first in the second stanza's allusion to Mercury, the Roman god of commerce, and re-emerges in the fifth stanza's description of the "atrocious sums/Built floor by floor on shafts of steel." Endorsing this shared interest, Crane repeats the word "let" in each of the last three stanzas: "Let the same nameless gulf beleaguer us," "let her ribs palisade," "let us walk through time with equal pride." This is a different kind of invitation to the visual invitations of "Regard," "Inquire," and the others, since "let," set against these oppressive, dominant structures, suggests permission, an allowance, in spite of opposition. At the same time, another of its meanings is "to suffer," in the sense of suffering someone to do something. By the end of the poem the invitation to "let" has become more and more genuine, as the speaker and his reader have "suffered" what has gone before, and Crane hopes his speaker has been persuaded of their intersubjectivity and interrelatedness, which enables them to share "equal pride."

This process of increased intimacy mimics the actual drafting of the poem, which in its substitutions of "how can you bear" for "you cannot bear"; "inquire" for "resist"; "ignore" for "decline," and even "let us walk" for "walk through Time, yourselves," suggests a gradual collective overcoming of that suffering and oppression, and endorses a kind of negative progress from the beginning to the end of the poem.[19] Such negative progress is demonstrative of the interest and difference at the heart of the relationship that Crane has set up between his speaker and his reader. The final lines confirm this negative progress, but do so by equating the text on the page with something physical. From repetition (the "alternating bells," suggesting sexual difference and the "echo") is derived unity and equality, which is rendered physical in the invitation to walk and vocalized in one of only two rhymes in the poem between "stride" and "pride." Repetition in this respect is an assertion of presence. The "things" that are being echoed make up a more human, relational rejoinder to the material things of capitalism. In addition, since a "recitative" is "a species of musical recitation in which the words are delivered in a manner resembling that of ordinary declamation" (*WUD* 1096), Crane is highlighting a performance that is delivered from memory. It is something lasting, and rather than being on the page, it exists inside – or is inscribed into – the body.

Crane's choice to foreground his poems in *White Buildings* with issues of perception is clear from the first page. Ernest Smith suggests that, in placing it at the beginning of the collection, Crane intended the poem "Legend" to be "a key, map, or guide by which to read this writer's work" ("Spending out the Self" 162). This is a poem that, like several others, questions the authenticity of what we see, opening with the assertion that: "As silent as a mirror is believed/Realities plunge in silence by…" (*CP* 3).[20] This key image of mirroring, which figured so prominently in "Recitative," is one instance of the rhetorical trope of chiasmus, which Lee Edelman describes as "a crossing [like the letter X or Greek letter chi (χ) from which the term is derived] that can be charted as a design of reversal or inward bend" (*Transmemberment of Song* 7). In "Recitative," the double image to be found in the "glass" is chiastic, and in "Legend" (1924/1925) the trope appears several times, in the mirror image at the start and twice more in the second stanza:

> I am not ready for repentance;
> Nor to match regrets. For the moth
> Bends no more than the still
> Imploring flame. And tremorous
> In the white falling flakes
> Kisses are, –
> The only worth all granting. (*CP* 3)[21]

Edelman's description of "inward bend" is apparent here, and the kisses mentioned here might be represented on the page as xxx. In these lines, just as he did in "Recitative," Crane suggests a kind of negative progress. Here that negativity is presented when Crane says that he is "not ready for repentence;/Nor to match regrets," where "match" may mean both "to furnish with its match," or "to purify, as vessels, by burning a match in them" (*WUD* 818). The use of rhetorical structure confirms this idea of progress, and Edelman describes how "chiasmus, as one of Crane's favored rhetorical structures, comes to figure a progression by means of reversal or negation" (*Transmemberment of Song* 7). But in its bending towards or crossing over, chiasmus is also demonstrative of the connection between the speaker and the reader and the intersubjectivity that Crane has been trying to foster. As the conclusion of "Recitative" suggested, Crane sought to develop the visual connection he was making with his reader into something physical, and in his use of figuration, he aspires to reach out and touch that reader. This assertion of a material poetics or physicalization of language was something he discussed in letters and in prose. Writing to Waldo Frank in 1923, Crane observed that

> [w]hat delights me almost beyond words is that my natural idiom (which I have unavoidably stuck to in spite of nearly everybody's nodding, querulous head) has reached and carried to you so completely the very blood and bone of me (*OML* 135).

Crane celebrates not only that his particular, "natural," style, portrayed here as dissident, alternative, resistant to his contemporaries, has been successful in finding an audience (and Frank was not a member of the minority, queer audience but rather a successful novelist and critic), but also that it carries something of himself with it, in order to "meet" Frank. Rather than presenting obscurity therefore, which might cause readers not to "get" Crane, the poet presents his own style as the very means by which he does in fact make a connection. In his prioritizing of chiasmus as a key element of this corporeal style, Crane's work prefigures the phenomenology of Maurice Merleau-Ponty, whose unfinished work entitled *The Visible and the Invisible* treated the body as a "chiasm," the same kind of "crossing over" that the rhetorical trope indicates. As Thomas Baldwin has explained, Merleau-Ponty's term for this conception of the body "is 'flesh' (*chair*) and he insists that it is an 'ultimate notion', a 'concrete emblem of a general manner of being', which provides access both to subjective experience and objective existence" (247). To demonstrate this new idea, Merleau-Ponty focusses upon the action of touching one hand with the other hand:

> When one hand touches the other, the world of each opens upon that of the other because the operation is reversible at will, because they both belong (as we say) to one sole space of consciousness, because one sole man touches one sole thing through both hands. But for my two hands to open upon one sole world, it does not suffice that they be given to one sole *consciousness* – or if that were the case the difficulty before us would disappear: since other bodies would be known to me in the same way as would be my own, they and I would still be dealing with the same world. No, my two hands touch the same things because they are the hands of one same body. And yet each of them has its own tactile experience (257–58).

This concept recalls Walker Evans's photograph of Hart Crane's hands discussed in the Introduction. The chiastic crossing over presented there was an invitation to a viewer to see the hands as their own, and a challenge too, for the peculiarity of the pose also encouraged them to try it out for themselves. The conceptualization of physical presence and corporeal experience that Merleau-Ponty explores here has resonance with Crane's attempts to present himself to his readers on a material level. Crane's aspiration in *White Buildings*, to retain his queer identity and yet also take part in the normative world, is also reminiscent of the hands in the bodily chiasm that are the same and yet different. The first part of "Faustus and Helen" (*CP* 27) makes use of the chiastic technique twice: in the bending of the speaker towards Helen, and in the self-referential image of the approach to the flame, which recalls the bending of the moth towards the flame in "Legend" and the inexorable progress of the moth in "The Moth That God Made Blind" towards the sun. Whilst the use of chiasmus prefigures the moment in which the speaker can "hold you endlessly," entering an embrace which, as Merleau-Ponty has it, takes place "in one sole world," so too the poem gives equal place to "[t]hat world which comes to each of us alone." In the privileging of the speaker's visual understanding of Helen as opposed to those who had "brittle, bloodshot eyes," the subjectivity developed here recalls Pater's concept of the "impression" as he expressed it in his "Conclusion" to *The Renaissance*. There he explained how "[e]xperience, already reduced to a group of impressions, is ringed round for each one of us by that thick wall of personality through which no real voice has ever pierced on its way to us, or from us to that which we can only conjecture to be without" (153). This contained space, Pater goes on to say, is limited by time, "in perpetual flight" (153), and "[i]t is with this movement, with the passage and dissolution of impressions, images, sensations, that analysis leaves off – that continual vanishing away, that strange, perpetual, weaving and unweaving of ourselves" (154). In this respect, such closed spaces are only temporary, for they seem to exist only as long as we perceive ourselves as bodies, just as the body of Helen can only be constrained for so long by material or physical means, before it enters into a world beyond the physical one, beyond the body.

Lee Edelman notes that chiasmus "moves toward the condition of a trope for the self-reflexive quality of Crane's poetics, the desire for the stability of a wholly self-enclosed literary structure" (*Transmemberment of Song* 7). Yet as I have been arguing, such an ideal or utopian structure, in which, perhaps, the queer individual might escape from societal and literary oppression, is not the ideal for Crane, for he seeks connection, not disconnection. In considering what he calls the "ideality" of experience, Merleau-Ponty observes that

> [i]t is as though the visibility that animates the sensible world were to emigrate, not outside of every body, but into another less heavy, more transparent body, as though it were to change flesh, abandoning the flesh of the body for that of language, and thereby would be emancipated but not freed from every condition (267).

These lines suggest a need for the visual and the material to work in consort with the linguistic in order to best explain and explore experience. In his poetics, Crane seeks to overcome his perceived linguistic obscurity with visual and material clarity. In the "Voyages" sequence, which formed the final part of *White Buildings*, he reasserted his concept of perception in order to set in time and place a queer relationship. To do so, he fused a sense of an eroticized body with language and vision to celebrate how he had "seen the Word made Flesh" (*OML* 186). In this way, as in "Faustus and Helen," Helen's eroticized body disappears into the "transparent," even invisible world of language, and yet it can be conjured up once more whenever the poem is read and the language is made visible.

The blurring of the material and visual recalls Crane's use of ekphrasis which, in its literal meaning of "speaking out," hints at the dialectic of inside/outside that concerns him. The need to make connections in Crane's work however, can often surpass the inner/outer boundary, which, as the following chapter reveals, can frequently mean transgressing in some way. The need to transgress also indicates that the kind of ideality represented by the corporeal chiasmus cannot always be sustained.

3
Spatiality, Movement, and the Logic of Metaphor

Hart Crane was notoriously peripatetic. He wrote much of *The Bridge* not in New York City, or even in Cleveland, but on the Isle of Pines, Cuba, where Crane's mother's family had a plantation.[1] And in 1930, the year of *The Bridge*'s publication, he lived in at least five different locations. Both *White Buildings* and *The Bridge*, as well as "Key West: An Island Sheaf," a collection of nineteen poems based on his experiences in Cuba and unpublished during Crane's lifetime, frequently make clear Crane's assertion that "poetry is an architectural art" ("Modern Poetry," *CPSL* 260). Towards the end of my first chapter, I argued that Crane's poetics are frequently cognate with Walter Pater's description of a subjective space of experience, and the queer architecture that exists within Crane's work is always conscious of the modernist landscape around it. As Andrew Thacker has argued, "[m]odernist writing [...] is about living and experiencing 'new times,' not in the abstracted location of literary history, but in specific spatial histories: rooms, cities, buildings, countries and landscapes" (13). It is important to emphasize that, despite the apparent fixity of the *places* from which Crane draws his inspiration, from the Brooklyn Bridge, various streets in New York City, the city's harbor and subway to the prairies, Cape Hatteras and Ohio, it is *spaces* that predominantly make up the architecture of Crane's work. Michel de Certeau provides a useful indication of why this might be the case in his association of space with movement and change and his suggestion that place "excludes the possibility of two things being in the same location" (117). *Space, instead of place*, therefore offers the possibility of multiplicity, a resistance to what de Certeau terms "univocity," and is thus an apt location for Crane's poetics. In his choice of vocabulary that was frequently ambiguous in meaning, sometimes through the use of words that were archaic or obsolete, and in his word play and use of puns, Crane grants words several different meanings at once, opening the way for multiple voices to be heard. One of the formal features that Crane sought to develop, "interior form," used "the possibility of two things being in the same location" to create a dense, layered effect.

Crane's understanding of space can be understood in Kantian terms. As Roger Scruton has said, "Kant argued that space and time, far from being concepts applicable to intuitions, are basic *forms* of intuition, meaning that every sensation must bear the imprint of temporal, and sometimes of spatial, organization" (41). In Crane's case the description of sensations is affected by space, just as the spaces he describes are affected by sensations. What is more, to negotiate the spaces in his work is to negotiate his queerness. According to Dianne Chisholm, "queer space demarcates a practice, production, and performance of space beyond just the mere habitation of built and fixed structures" (10). Crane's work involves these three dynamics of queer space, but this chapter focuses particularly on the queer production of space and queer practices within it. Early gay and lesbian literary theory focused upon the "homotextual space" as being one of escape. Jacob Stockinger suggested that "the most frequent type of homotextual space is the closed and withdrawn place that is transformed from stigmatizing into redeeming space" (143). He also noted how

> [o]ne can also deliberately free oppressive space by seeking out the marginal space of the open countryside, which is privileged space for the homosexual because it marks both his ostracism and the chance to recuperate his "unnatural" love in nature (143).

It is hardly surprising that Stockinger's 1973 proposal speaks so much of "stigma" and "oppressive space," for he was writing very much as an anti-homophobic critic, rather than as a queer one.[2] However, recent queer theory helps to demonstrate that Crane's own approach to his depiction of queer modernist spaces was affirmative, even insistent, rather than limited or cautious. Crane presents queer spaces not as stigmatized, but as spaces that represent active resistance to heteronormativity. His work creates subcultural spaces within modernity and gives individuals within those spaces legitimate voice. In his creation of alternative spaces Crane adopts a stance of queer negativity, an idea I have already briefly explored, one that is always aware of the heteronormative. As much an affirmation of queerness as it is a negation of normativity, this queer negativity turns heteronormative society's sense of the queer individual as sterile and limited back on itself in order to advocate possibilities for the queer individual and queer poetics.

Crane's spatial practices are also his textual practices, as his description of movement figures his transgressive aesthetic both as a queer practice and as one that seems to be contrary to the technological thrill of modernity. As becomes apparent, the kind of spatial practice that might be associated with a queer writer, cruising, is a divisive one for Crane, and he finds it compromised by the capitalist structures of a modern urban environment. Analyzing Crane's spatiality can also throw light upon the early reading, or misreading, of Crane's work, and suggests both why readers like Harriet Monroe and Yvor Winters were not able to comprehend Crane's poetry, and also why a key concept, the "logic of metaphor," is best understood as a queer, spatial practice.

Enclosed spaces

In *The Production of Space*, Henri Lefebvre identifies "dominant space" as that which is "a space transformed – and mediated – by technology, by practice. [...] Dominated space is usually closed, sterilized, emptied out" (164, 165). By contrast, there is "appropriated space," signifying space that, it might be said, is taken back to "serve the needs and possibilities of a group" (165). Crane's poetry creates spaces that seek to take back or appropriate space from heterosexual domination. Lefebvre notes that "[a]ny revolutionary 'project' today, whether utopian or realistic, must, if it is to avoid hopeless banality, make the re-appropriation of the body, in association with the re-appropriation of space, into a non-negotiable part of its agenda" (166–67). In his poem "The Wine Menagerie" (1925–1926/1926), Crane seeks to re-appropriate both the body and space from being dominated by heterosexual normativity by means of self-conscious and self-critical expression.[3] In doing so, he also gestures towards his own "revolutionary project" that has utopian aspirations.

Crane fills "The Wine Menagerie" with spaces in which the queer speaker finds himself trapped; such as "glozening decanters," which are said to "[w]ear him" and to which he feels "conscripted" (*CP* 23).[4] The speaker draws attention to the deceptive nature of these decanters: they are dominant spaces that seem to control and oppress him. Their "glozening" suggests their abilities to flatter or misinterpret, whilst the bottles reflect only part of the speaker ("in crescents") "on their bellies"; images that would normally both suggest something limited about the speaker and also infantilize him, placing him as if inside a womb. The references here to "[s]low applause," "cynosures" (which can mean "any thing to which attention is strongly turned" [*WUD* 329]), and the acknowledgement of conscription, which implies he is being compulsorily forced into a certain mode of behavior, suggest the ways in which the speaker is self-consciously aware of the ways in which he is part of a dominated space, but that within that space he is also performing a role.

The following stanza, however, directly challenges that dominated space by questioning its authenticity, describing the "imitation onyx wainscoting." Whereas Crane often uses gender ambiguity when referring to sexual contact, here he makes it clear that the speaker is observing a male–female couple. Sexual intercourse itself is set against the false background, and is degrading. That background is made up of base materials; either elemental like the snow or coal, or sordid like the manure. This animalistic production mimics the violent behavior of the human couple, for as the man "takes her" with "the forceps of a smile," so the woman's eyes are "[m]allets." The images of performance continue to be employed here, but the speaker is presented as being on the outside, able to "regard" the scene played out below him and comment upon it. In this way he presents the heterosexual couple as Other, their coupling the production of a suitably sullied space. Later in the poem, the speaker draws attention to the ways in which this sexual practice is bound up with the space itself:

> Each chamber, transept, coins some squint,
> Remorseless line, minting their separate wills –
> Poor streaked bodies wreathing up and out,
> Unwitting the stigma that each turn repeals:
> Between black tusks the roses shine!

Gazing around this structure, the speaker is in a Dantean Inferno where sex is portrayed as a kind of torture. It is horribly claustrophobic, as the mirroring of sound in "[e]ach chamber" suggests the impossibility of escape. And yet this kind of sexual intercourse is given a religious backdrop: a transept is "[a]ny part of a church that projects at right angles to the body" (*WUD* 1403). Crane uses the image with heavy irony, linking heterosexuality with the Church as if to challenge the validity of the only socially acceptable form of sex. But with that comes the "stigma that each turn repeals," a stigma that shows on these bodies the mark of the Fall, for in that moment of knowledge, Adam and Eve acknowledged their sexualities. The speaker presents this stigma as inevitable, just as the sexual intercourse that he describes ("[e]ach chamber [...] coins some squint,/Remorseless line") is inevitable and obvious. No matter whether the first parents tried to hide their nakedness and eroticized bodies, Crane suggests that sexuality itself will always overwhelm any attempt to dismiss it: the "black tusks" will penetrate the "roses', which will "shine." As Gordon Tapper has argued, these may be inescapable because they are both representative of the human body and of the unconscious, "chambers of the mind, images of the unconscious echoed by the other peripheral spaces and architectural dividers that fill the poem" (64).

The way in which the heterosexual couples are enclosed within spaces where the queer speaker can view them suggests a reversal of the panoptic gaze that Michel Foucault has described as one of heteronormative society's weapons against queerness and criminality:

> The panoptic mechanism arranges spatial unities that make it possible to see constantly and to recognize immediately. In short, it reverses the principle of the dungeon; or rather of its three functions – to enclose, to deprive of light and to hide – it preserves only the first and eliminates the other two. Full lighting and the eye of a supervisor capture better than darkness, which ultimately protected. Visibility is a trap (*Discipline and Punish* 200).[5]

Vision in "The Wine Menagerie" is not just alcohol-induced, but queer, appropriating through the act of looking the dominated or oppressed space in which the queer individual is normally trapped. Instead of the queer subject being studied and judged, the situation is reversed. The queer speaker "see[s] constantly" and the heterosexual couple are trapped in their visible space, their sexual activity "shin[ing] " out. This reversal suggests not only Crane's resistance to normativity but also a socially, even socio-politically-engaged, strategy that was concerned with the ways in which his own sexual identity might be represented as an authentic alternative to the norm.

Utopian spaces?

In "The Wine Menagerie," Crane had explored the place of such subjectivity by emphasizing the contrast between the heterosexual spaces where "[e]ach chamber, transept, coins some squint,/Remorseless line, minting their separate wills," and the *revelation* of a queer sexuality which promises "[n]ew thresholds, new anatomies!" (*CP* 24).[6] As opposed to the "separate wills" of the heterosexual couples, here the queer speaker creates an ideal, enclosed space, a "tear" in which he retains a certain degree of selfhood whilst also being "within another's will." In contrast again to the heterosexual, the "new anatomies" suggest that the queer individual is a different species, free of the kind of lapsarian "stigma" that is associated with the couples described in the previous stanza. The "[n]ew thresholds" can have both corporeal and metaphorical meanings. Thomas Yingling contends that the phrase means "the naming of the body as a threshold, as an entry – be it through sexual pleasure or through drunkenness – into an intersubjectivity that is as far removed from Otherness as one can imagine" (136). In fact, it is heterosexuality which is "Othered" here, converted into an alien and sordid concept in which the participants may be physically joined, but emotionally and spiritually distanced from each other.

Crane continues this theme by contrasting the spaces of the brothel, where sexual relationships are set against false backgrounds or described in terms of the financial transactions that they really are ("coins," "minting"), with the world of the "tear." That space is the result of "competence," a word that can mean "property or means of subsistence sufficient to furnish the necessaries and conveniences of life, without superfluity; sufficiency; such a quantity as is sufficient" (*WUD* 261). Far from the financial associations of the relationships in the brothel, the queer relationship is presented as having value only in its human union. However, Crane notes that this enclosed, utopian space cannot last because the speaker acknowledges that the attraction of lust is too much. He sees a "receptive smile" in the face of another man, and the purity and ideality that the "tear" of the previous stanza represented is negated. As John Norton-Smith has observed, in his use of "[r]uddy, the tooth implicit of the world," Crane plays upon the phrase "nature red in tooth and claw," highly appropriate for this poem full of "menagerie" imagery and suggestive of the way in which the queer relationship is suddenly perceived by Crane to be little different to the heterosexual animalistic lusts that he described in previous stanzas (110).[7] The attraction between the two is figured in sound ("chimes"), and the speaker illustrates his self-conscious disappointment in his succumbing to his sexual desires when he describes this "flame" (where "flame" means a lover) as nothing more than a "shell," presenting a relationship that is no more than surface. However, the break that the speaker proposed with "[n]ew thresholds, new anatomies!" can still be traced despite these disappointments. The speaker draws a contrast between the lustful bodies he has observed and his own, for whereas they were "[u]nwitting" about the "stigma" that marks them, a seemingly endless damnation, the queer speaker of the poem gives voice to the "wit that cries out of me," implying both self-consciousness and self-knowledge. This self-awareness is presented through paradox: the flame is one of "gaunt repose," and the "shell" is "[t]olled once, perhaps by every tongue in hell." These are linguistic contradictions. A flame in repose is an impossible state, and a shell being "tolled once" is opposed to the definition of the action, since "tolling" suggests a repeated ringing. However, in presenting these gaps in sense, Crane is offering spaces into which optimism might enter. Rather than the unadulterated and unrealistic optimism of travelling in "a tear/Sparkling alone, within another's will," the speaker's sense of newness is to be found in the "new dominoes of love and bile." This is an acknowledgement that, in this game of dominoes, an ideal match cannot be made perfectly; and an unrestricted utopian state is not worth striving for. Instead, the queer subject must create and inhabit spaces that balance the ideal with the real and certain oppression that he must suffer in the world. Despite all the difficulties, by the end of the poem that balance is rendered possible, as the queer subject reincorporates the lover – figured as an "exile" from the normative world – into his body in the doubling action of folding. The exile is compared to the puppet Petrushka in Igor Stravinsky's 1911 ballet, who is killed by the Moor when he pursues the ballerina, yet reappears as a ghost in the final scene. This pivoting, one of a number of processes of conscious incompletion that Crane uses, intimates that a queer utopia might be found in constant movement. But in Crane's use of the Stravinsky ballet, Crane draws attention to the poem itself as an active aesthetic object, since it can reach out beyond its own space to pull in and then synthesize different forms of aesthetic expression.

Commenting upon the notion of queerness as an ideality, José Esteban Muñoz declares that "[q]ueerness is that thing that lets us feel that this world is not enough, that indeed something is missing" (1). Muñoz is contending that queerness is itself utopian, but not as something hermetic. Instead, Muñoz considers the possibilities of queerness speaking from a position of subcultural strength:

> Turning to the aesthetic in the case of queerness is nothing like an escape from the social realm, insofar as queer aesthetics map future social relations. Queerness is also a performative because it is not simply a being but a doing for and toward the future. Queerness is essentially about the rejection of a here and now and an insistence on potentiality or concrete possibility for another world (1).

Muñoz's allusion to the performativity of queerness recalls the emphasis upon spaces of spectacle in "The Wine Menagerie." Whereas the heterosexual couples practice unconscious disunity, the queer speaker's self-consciousness and awareness of the performed and limited nature of his behavior allow him to identify possibilities for newness and change rather than continued stigmatization. Muñoz affirms that "queerness exists for us as an ideality that can be distilled from the past and used to imagine a future" (1). In this focus upon issues of futurity as regards the creating of new worlds and times, Muñoz enters into (and for the most part resists) certain assertions derived from the recent debate within queer theory over the anti-social or anti-relational thesis. This provocative discussion began in 1995 with the publication by Leo Bersani of his book *Homos*, in which he contended that "self-shattering," which Bersani says "disrupts the ego's coherence and dissolves its boundaries," is a form of jouissance that "is intrinsic to the homo-ness in homosexuality. Homo-ness is an anti-identitarian identity" (101). This "anti-identitarian" theory was developed more recently by Lee Edelman. In *No Future: Queer Theory and the Death Drive*, Edelman attempts what he calls "a truly hopeless wager": that "turning the forces of queerness against all subjects, however queer, can afford an access to the *jouissance* that at once defines and negates [queer individuals]" (5). Edelman argues that by embracing negativity, and in particular rejecting the cult of the child within society, queerness is essentially antisocial, for by denying a future, queerness denies reproductive futurity and a continuation of humanity. By drawing both on the kinds of utopian ideas that Muñoz promotes and also the anti-relational thesis of Edelman, it is possible to find valuable ways to investigate Crane's use of space.

As is evident from the foregoing discussion of "The Wine Menagerie," Crane does aspire to a form of alternative spatiality. To create it he affirms negativity, not in a way that suggests resignation, but in the process, as he said, of "affirming certain things" and asserting his sexuality (*OML* 118). In this respect I draw upon Edelman who argues that, by "accepting and even embracing" the common "ascription of negativity to the queer," the queer subject can turn negativity back on itself,

> [n]ot in the hope of forging thereby some more perfect social order – such a hope, after all, would only reproduce the constraining mandate of futurism, just as any such order would equally occasion the negativity of the queer – but rather to refuse the insistence of the hope itself as affirmation, which is always affirmation of an order whose refusal will register as unthinkable, irresponsible, inhumane (*No Future* 4).

Edelman's assertion matches the way in which, in "The Wine Menagerie," Crane recognizes the unsustainability of a utopian structure, a "more perfect social order." It cannot last. Instead – and here my argument departs from Edelman's polemic and moves closer to Muñoz's stress on potentiality – Crane does find hope in the creation of alternative spaces. His creation of these frequently occurs through actions of queer negativity, by being engulfed or relinquishing agency. The adoption and consequences of those actions can be seen in the drafts and final versions of the six-part sequence of poems entitled "Voyages" (1921–1926/ 1923–1926),[8] which brings *White Buildings* to a close.

Atopias

The "Voyages" sequence demonstrates most clearly that the spaces that Crane creates through the language of his poems are spaces of resistance. In their queerness, these spaces figure alternative desires and push back against the pressures of normativity. Since Crane does not seek to create "some more perfect social order" in such spaces they cannot be called utopias, so I propose to describe such spaces as atopias, adopting a term and its sense from Roland Barthes. At various points in his work, Barthes returns to this idea, suggesting in *A Lover's Discourse* that *atopos* refers to a situation in which

> [t]he loved being is recognized by the amorous subject as "atopos" (a qualification given to Socrates by his interlocutors), i.e. unclassifiable, of a ceaselessly unforeseen originality (34).

Elsewhere he concludes that "the pleasure of the text is scandalous: not because it is immoral but because it is *atopic*" (*The Pleasure of the Text* 23). Although Barthes uses "atopic" to refer to a state and not as a spatial term, later in his definition of "atopos" he describes how stereotypes of emotion have "no more room in this relation without a site, without *topos*" (*A Lover's Discourse* 36). I adopt atopia therefore to refer to the way in which Crane creates spaces that are unclassifiable. His resistance is in acknowledging the normative but at the same time asserting queerness. Such spaces are frequently in flux, their only contingency being linguistic, and even here the multivalency of Crane's diction means that this contingency can frequently be in doubt.

In "Voyages" (1921–1924), the sea is just such a shifting, alternative space, and evidence of this can be seen by examining the early drafts of the "Voyages" sequence. To do so is to uncover how some of the multivalency of Crane's important images is created. In the published version of "Voyages II," for instance, the female-gendered sea seems to look favorably upon "the pieties of lovers' hands," but this sense is even clearer in an earlier draft of the poem, in which the sea is seen as complicit in the relationship:

> And though
> in terror of her sessions she enlist us
> to her body endlessly, subscribe. She
> is our bed.[9]

Whereas before it was the lover's body that was compared with the sea, here the speaker urges the other to "subscribe," as "she enlist[s] us/to her body endlessly." The female sea acts as an atopic space in which the sexual relationship can be continued without fear of reprisal. The fact that it appears "endless" means that it cannot be defined, that there is no temporal certainty about it. Throughout the revisions of "Voyages" there is also a sense that the speaker wishes to give up his and his lover's agencies to the sea; that he desires – to use another Barthesian term – "engulfment." Being engulfed represents the position of queer negativity which Crane adopts, for "on those occasions when I am engulfed," Barthes explains, "there is no longer any place for me anywhere, not even in death." (*A Lover's Discourse* 11). For Crane being engulfed is a positive thing: "not even in death" means an escape from death. Engulfment thus allows the queer subject to inhabit a space outside normative boundaries, but without accepting the extreme negativity that will deny hope and futurity. In the earliest draft of "Voyages II," A32, the speaker observes how: "the steeping measureless years/enclose me in this accident," and as early as A33, he requests: "[t]ake us in time, O seasons clear." In A36, he sees how "[a]dagios of passing isles that snare/brief labial tides, enlist us termlessly," whilst in A37 he describes how "[f]rondage of dark islands, breathing/the crocus lustres of the stars –/repeated ease, repeated awe/enclose me, aching with the night." In A39, he urges: "suspend us, — aching with the night/that trails its rites from isle to isle." This negation of agency, which resurfaces in the final version of the poem in the line "[b]ind us in time, O Seasons clear, and awe," places a certain amount of strength and faith in the image of the sea. This decision might seem foolish, considering the warnings of "Voyages I," that "[t]he bottom of the sea is cruel," but in giving up control the speaker sounds a note of desperation. In his repeated urgings to "hasten" and emphasis upon "while they are true," the speaker draws attention to the fact that the atopia is fragile, recalling the fleeting nature of the Paterian "impression."

The queer flâneur

Whilst such fragility acknowledges that normativity is constantly exerting pressure on queer spaces, these areas in Crane's work can also take the form of normative spaces with queer potential. In depicting queer experience, Crane also describes how queer individuals move through these spaces. Jan Ulrick-Désert has suggested that "[a] queer space is an activated zone made proprietary by the occupant or *flâneur*, the wanderer" (21), but although the figure of the flâneur/flâneuse has been assumed to be one of the key characters of modernity, introduced by Baudelaire and then theorized by Walter Benjamin, Crane's queer subjects do not practice the same kind of flânerie.[10] Their roles in his poetry are far more complicated, not least because the flâneur is an urban creature – "[t]he crowd is his domain," says Baudelaire (*Selected Writings* 399) – and many of those moving through Crane's landscapes are to be found in non-urban environments such as the figures in "The River" (1926–1929/1928) or "The Dance" (1926–1929/1927). They are also to be found traversing abstract locations, including, as has been described, atopic spaces. In addition, Crane's queer subjects are not subject to chance in the same way as the Baudelairean flâneur who, although it is claimed he is seeking "that indefinable something we may be allowed to call 'modernity'" (402), which Baudelaire defines as "the transient, the fleeting, the contingent" (403), he nonetheless does so by idling. Crane's subjects travel with a purpose in mind and in a certain direction.

Like the descriptions of the flâneur as a person "for ever in search" (*Selected Writings* 402), it is certainly true to say that Crane's textual spaces are full of motion: the layered spaces of "Black Tambourine," which have potential for alternative *meanings*, are actually kinetic in their presence. Crane himself indicated that he saw this poem as containing space in a 1922 letter to Sherwood Anderson. Here, Crane illustrated his own method by quoting sections of two poems by John Donne, the first of which featured such spatial metaphors as "lattices of eyes,/[...] labyrinths of ears," and the second a number of puns: "break off this last lamenting kiss,/Which sucks too [punning on 'two'] souls and vapours both away/[...] And let ourselves benight our happiest day [suggesting both 'benighted' as ignorance and as a literal process of becoming night]."[11] Following these Crane declared,

> [w]hat I want to get is just what is so beautifully done in this poem, an "interior" form, a form so thorough and intense as to dye the

words themselves with a peculiarity of meaning, slightly different maybe from the ordinary definition of them separate from the poem. If you remember my "Black Tambourine" you will perhaps aggree [sic] with me that I have at least accomplished this idea once (*OML* 79).

As is clear from my earlier discussion, Crane's sense of visuality transferred itself to his poetics, and his use of ekphrasis suggests that he understood words to be material things. Where Murray Krieger notes that "words are not [...] pictures, and do not, in any literal way, have 'capacity'" (3), Crane counters with the idea of "an 'interior' form," in which space can actually be *produced* within language. "Black Tambourine" offers a number of puns that challenge normative meaning: "interests" can mean both those of the black man himself, but also – in respect to "the negro question," which early readers of this poem thought Crane was addressing, and the history of African-American slavery – his financial value to a "cellar"/"seller."[12] So too the "mid-kingdom" is placed by "lying," but is also deemed deceptive in its capacity to "lie." The carcass may be "quick" to attract flies because of the heat and its decomposition, but can also seem "quick" or alive because of the movement of the feasting insects.

By drawing attention to "Black Tambourine," Crane celebrated the way in which he had married content to form, and his use of space is vital to that success. The black man in the cellar has been frequently read as a marginal figure within society representative of Crane's own sexual Otherness, but it is in the introduction of a form that is "thorough and intense," and the creation of spaces through the linguistic dimensionality of words, that queer Otherness emerges.[13]

But the production of space in this poem is also connected with spatial practices. When the "[g]nats toss in the shadow of a bottle," and the "roach spans a crevice in the floor," the actions of these animals are continuous, giving the spaces a sense of constant motion or flux. Whereas, for Michel de Certeau, a place "implies an indication of stability," space can be considered unstable since it is "composed of intersections of mobile elements" (117). This instability can be seen in Crane's spaces, since it is through their very instability, in terms of the description of movement within them and the poet's use of diction and syntax, that they assert themselves against the normative.

Elsewhere in *White Buildings*, Crane also addresses another element of Baudelaire's flâneur: his fascination with the modernity derived from the high capitalist moment. Baudelaire says that "[t]he aim for [the flâneur] is to extract from fashion the poetry that resides in its historical envelope, to distil the eternal from the transitory" (*Selected Writings* 402). According to Benjamin,

> [t]he flâneur is the observer of the marketplace. His knowledge is akin to the occult science of industrial fluctuations. He is a spy for the capitalists, on assignment in the realm of consumers (427).

This is the man in Baudelaire's essay who observes the latest fashions and makes a note if "bonnets have widened and chignons have come down a little on the nape of the neck" (401). In his poem "Possessions," Crane interrogates the modern capitalist city through the queer spatial practice of cruising; a practice, Mark W. Turner has affirmed, "that exploits the ambivalence of the modern city, and in so doing, 'queers' the totalizing narratives of modernity, in particular *flânerie*" (46). According to Dianne Chisholm "the cruising flâneur is piqued with desire – desire that the city itself has induced with its intoxicating promenade of commodities" (46). Chisholm explains that "the cruising flâneur is on the outlook for love, where the gay gaze is misrecognized for the look of the commodity" (46).[14] Cruising is of course the stereotypical spatial practice of the queer subject and since it is based, as Chisholm suggests, upon seeing and gazing, it can also be considered as an aesthetic practice (46). Turner describes cruising as "the moment of visual exchange that occurs on the streets and in other places in the city, which constitutes an act of mutual recognition amid the otherwise alienating effects of the anonymous crowd" (9). This is a mutual recognition of sexual attraction, which may then lead to one man "picking up" the other, and may or may not then lead to sex. "Possessions" (1923–1924/1924) dramatizes a queer experience of modernity: two linked conflicts that are prefigured by the notion of the queer flâneur, between movement and inertia, and between the attraction and repulsion towards capitalism.

The conflicts of cruising

In the first stanza of the poem (*CP* 18),[15] Crane adopts his reader into the mechanics of cruising. Indeed with the opening line's invitation to "[w]itness," suggestive of eye contact, the poem may be said to cruise the reader. Punning on the opening line, Michael D. Snediker observes that "the poem picks up the reader faster than 'this trust' becomes a tryst" (64). Implicit in the cruise is the knowledge that there is a risk involved: as George Chauncey has detailed, undercover agents frequently sought out and arrested "degenerates."[16] But Crane's concern with "trust" goes beyond a simple need for confidence in the authenticity of the other man or, in fact, beyond "trusting" that there will be some kind of sexual liaison at the end of the cruise. He infers a more general issue of "trust"; that the cruise will not result in emotional damage. Writing to Jean Toomer, to whom he shortly afterwards sent the first draft of "Possessions," Crane admitted:

> For a while I want to keep immune from beckonings and all that draws you into doorways, subways, sympathies, rapports and the City's complicated devastations (*OML* 161).

In its trepidation about and realization of these "complicated devastations," the poem bears witness to Crane's real concerns about the dangers of cruising. The first line of "Possessions" is an admission, a confession, and a boast, as if to expose to his reader the kind of risk he is taking. But "trust" can also imply credit, as in the giving and taking of financial credit and, with the addition of "the key, ready to hand" and the description of how "the flesh/Assaults outright for bolts that linger/Hidden," Crane begins to equate the notion of a cruise with the imagery of a financial transaction, suggesting that some corporeal gesture can give way, unlock the bolts, to a sexual liaison. This "fixed stone of lust" therefore suggests a gemstone, a focus of material wealth and desire that also represents an object of sexual desire, but the speaker's "linger[ing]," his "undirected" movements, and the stone's "fixed" nature, all suggest that this first part of the poem is registering Crane's desire to "keep immune from beckonings." In claiming that "Crane has written what is probably the first poem of the modern urban homosexual in search of sex," Robert K. Martin suggests that Crane's "hesitations [are] the result of fear and self-oppression. He desires and yet he fears; he will go and yet he hesitates" (*The Homosexual Tradition in American Poetry* 128).

The second stanza offers more reasons for that hesitation, as Crane continues to link the prospect of cruising to what Mark Turner has described as the "economy of sexual exchange," with its invocations to "[a]ccumulate" and "account the total" (51). The speaker challenges not just himself but also his reader: with all that he already *knows*, should he enter into this transaction? Should he head out into the street? His reluctance to enter into this "economy" is represented by the way in which he presents himself as a performer. After the initial desire for a "witness," the second stanza contains images of the performing arts; "the screen" and the dance imagery, and the sense of being "prepared" to act or deliver lines. The first part of the third stanza confirms this act. As if entering from off-stage, the speaker suggests both his acting out of the role and the way in which he feels compelled to take part in the practice of cruising; "[a]s quiet as you can *make* a man" (emphasis added). The speaker takes up the stone in a way that mimics the way in which, as Chisholm has suggested, "the gay gaze is misrecognized for the look of the commodity" (46), and as if he were on the lookout for something to purchase. The material wealth of the "stone" is representative of the whole city, part of "the City's complicated devastations," which Crane spoke about in his letter to Toomer. Fully into the cruise, the speaker holds the stone to the light as if to check its value and authenticity. The parallel that Crane draws here between the first person "I" within the cruise and the "I" who is "turning, turning on smoked forking spires" equates this striving for value and authenticity with the phallic imagery of the "spires" and the helpless state of the speaker in intercourse.

The penultimate stanza acknowledged that the cruise left the speaker "[w]ounded by apprehensions out of speech," and in the final stanza Crane seeks to retrieve language from its usurpation by materialism. The notion that Crane associated these "apprehensions" with American society is confirmed by a letter he wrote to Gorham Munson around this time where he lamented, "O God that I should have to live with these American restrictions forever, where one cannot whisper a word, not least exchange a few words! In such cases they almost suffice, you know" (*OML* 127).[17] An earlier draft of this last stanza (qtd. in *OML* 164) shows Crane addressing these restrictions as he grapples with the adequacy of language in respect to the needs of the body. Crane draws attention to "the page" being read, but whereas in the final draft of the poem "the page [...] finally burns," perhaps with the intention of suggesting a more aggressive form of deletion prefiguring the "ras[ing]" that takes place in the last two lines, here there is intimation that the page has been "turn[ed]," suggesting an underlying optimism. Reference to the "blind sum" also suggests a retort to the activity of cruising which, as has been described, is so dependent upon the look and the gaze. The commodity is still there in the "sum," but the fact that it is "blind" removes some of its threat. Whereas before the page could not be written because the words could not be spoken, now there is a sense that the page can be turned and changed. In this way speech, and by extension writing, is given back its own authenticity.

The final three lines of the draft version of the poem are virtually the same in the final version, with one exception detailed below. The "pure possession," which will come and "rase/All but bright stones wherein our smiling plays" is frequently seen as a purifying gesture occurring at a point where, as Gordon Tapper suggests, "purity and impurity are reconciled by an 'inclusive' poetic language, a language embracing both the ordering effect of closed form (the stately iambic pentameter, the rhymed couplet), and the disruptiveness of 'rase,' a word over which the reader hesitates as if confronted with a misprint" (34). Tapper is right here to show the ways in which the final lines address the issue of purity and impurity, and to draw attention also to the "disruptiveness" of those final lines. However, the source and reason for that purification needs to be interrogated further. The last lines of the poem merely return the speaker to his initial concerns about "the fixed stone of lust" and his earlier embrace of materialism, but Tapper is quite right to suggest that instead of disrupting the reader positively, the word "rase" can disturb. Although it can mean "[t]o scratch or rub out [...] to erase," and also suggest the effect of "the heart [which] is fire" in "[t]o level with the ground [...] to destroy," Crane's decision to spell the word with an "s" also indicates the legal meaning: "[a] measure in which the commodity measured was made even with the top of the measuring vessel, by scraping or striking off all that was above it" (*WUD* 1087). Rather than seek to purify, therefore, "the inclusive cloud" and "the white wind" seek to homogenize, even normalize, and this impulse must be particularly concerning for the queer speaker. In addition, this normalizing influence destroys everything except for the "bright stones wherein our smiling plays." In another letter to Jean Toomer around the time of the composition of "Possessions," Crane noted the subsiding of a "strange tempest" that he had been feeling:

> It has left one conscious thing (at least this and perhaps more) that evil accumulates, if not in us, at least in pockets and domains of the world without. And that the mark + gauge of our progress is quite obviously to be told in the successively more intense attacks of the dark force upon us – as we continue to defy it always more persistently (*OML* 163).

At the conclusion of "Possessions" what remains is "accumulat[ion] " of "that evil," just as much of the poem dramatizes the ways in which

Crane struggles with and tries to "defy it." Whatever this "evil" may be, its general nature and the way in which Crane assumes that Toomer is also affected, suggests something of the struggle of the artist in a society that has little place for him. In presenting the "bright stones" as the conclusion, Crane provides an aesthetic reminder of an experience that would otherwise pass into nothingness. Mark Turner has explored how cruising leaves nothing more than "urban traces" that are made even less sure by the ambiguous situations in which cruising often occurs; urban spaces where the uses of those spaces are often overlapping (49–56). In his treatment of cruising, Crane splices together the two halves of Baudelaire's definition of modernity: "the transient, the fleeting, the contingent; it is one half of art, the other being the eternal and the immovable" (403). The speaker seeks to document "[u]pon the page" what in the final version is a "[r]ecord of rage and partial appetites"; to present the experience truthfully in a way that will prove "eternal and immovable," and be something to "possess." Crane wrote of such aspirations when he told Alfred Stieglitz, in words that recall Baudelaire's flâneur inhabiting the crowds, that "[w]e must somehow touch the clearest veins of eternity flowing through the crowds around us – or risk being the kind of glorious cripples that have missed some vital part of their inheritance" (*OML* 162). Crane questions the value of a spatial practice like cruising since, being bound up with notions of commodification, it rejects language, leaving the speaker "out of speech."

A poetics of transgression

Despite his uncertainty about cruising, Crane nevertheless makes a connection in "Possessions" between spatial practices and the expression of his sexuality, and between language and movement. In both *White Buildings* and *The Bridge* Crane makes repeated reference to walking as a spatial practice that is also a form of resistance to the normative forms of movement and normative forms of speech. Michel de Certeau has proposed that "[w]alking affirms, suspects, tries out, transgresses, respects, etc., the trajectories it 'speaks'" (99), and the "trajectories" of Crane's "walks" frequently move along these lines. In *White Buildings* in particular, walks figure the ways in which Crane's aesthetic transgresses normative boundaries. The structural form of *The Bridge* transforms walking into what might be considered a "deregulating" or liberalizing practice, whereby the Bridge itself is made corporeal. The impetus of deregulation is also one of enunciation, and in the following sections I argue that the "speaking" of spatial experience that characterizes

Crane's poetics is also related to the ways in which his work was misread by early readers.

Crane adopts walking as a spatial and poetic practice as early as his poem "My Grandmother's Love Letters" (1919/1920) (*CP* 6).[18] The poem offers two powerful moments of transgression. The speaker, first of all equating the memories found in love letters to space, does not draw back from entering and inhabiting that space, walking it as if on a tightrope, giving the sense that the grandson's reading of the letters or considering of his grandmother's desire are illicit activities. Yet it becomes clear that the exploration of this space is in the interest of the speaker and not his grandmother, for the poem suggests that she may no longer fully comprehend the nature of the desire contained within the space of those letters. More significantly, when the speaker leads her "by the hand" he creates new spaces that are representative of his own alternative form of desire, something that, he knows, she will not be able to understand, and it is in this incomprehension that the emotional core of the poem is to be found. The rhyme of "hand" and "-stand" represents both the matching of steps as the grandson leads the grandmother, but also another kind of equality. Despite the secret knowledge that the speaker has about his sexuality, which might make him seem utterly Other, he knows simultaneously that his grandmother too has desired in a way that he can never fully comprehend, just as she will not be able to grasp the characteristics of his desire. The speaker's remark, "[a]nd so I stumble," suggests a physical manifestation of that impasse.

The use of walking to denote differences between queer and heterosexual desire appears in other poems in *White Buildings*. In "Stark Major" (1923/1923), the male subject is described as leaving an apartment whilst his lover, pregnant with "[h]er mound of undelivered life" (*CP* 10),[19] laughs and calls out her lover's name as he descends the stairs. In detailing the various moments of his departure, and his walking away from the building, the speaker provides a critique of heterosexual relations that is in itself transgressive. Now the lover's role has been fulfilled, providing the means by which the female has become pregnant, he is diminished. His walking away is symbolic of the end to desire, the "lover's death," and suggests too a rejection of that manifestation of heterosexuality: the pregnant female. The poem also suggests a preoccupation with the "sterility" of the queer person. The lyric voice, unlike many of the other poems in the collection, is not first person; it is detached, suggesting a speaker in a position to offer comment from the outside.

A poem that rejects the limited aspects of heterosexuality, "The Wine Menagerie" (*CP* 23–24) also uses walking to denote an approach that contravenes normal social behavior, as the speaker walks away from scenes of heterosexual desire and the conflict that results from it. Holofernes, over whose shins the speaker steps, was slain by Judith, who had seduced him with her beauty whilst Salomé, in Oscar Wilde's 1891 play, causes John the Baptist to be executed after he fails to return her lustful advances. The walking that the speaker encourages traverses the body of the dead Holofernes (a kind of violation) and goes "[b]eyond the wall," a movement away from the normative and towards a queer space in which the "exile" can be reincorporated. The word "exile" suggests someone banished from walking on their native soil, with a root meaning in the word "sole," as part of the foot. To re-embrace the "exile" is to reassert someone or something that is transgressive, an impulse that is encapsulated by the need to travel by walking – an idea to which I will return shortly.

Crane's poem "Legend" offers, as argued previously, a chiastic trope as a way of making a physical connection with the reader. If that trope is exemplary of a form that contravenes the rules of the page, the conclusion to the poem suggests a subtle transgressive shift in its meaning (*CP* 3). Christopher Nealon has described this poem as "an opening gesture of defiance by a young gay man who has assimilated a certain rhetoric of homosexuality as self-indulgence or failure of will, or personal excess, and who then claims exactly that 'failure' as the source of his poetic powers" (33). The conflict that Nealon identifies here is represented by the hybrid movement of walking ("step") and dancing ("caper"), for it is precisely in his splicing together of two actions that Crane presents his "gesture of defiance." Offering a state caught between the quotidian and the celebratory, Crane suggests an optimistic moment of queer negativity in which he partially asserts a queer selfhood in his opening poem. Like "My Grandmother's Love Letters," "Legend" formally complements its themes with its stylistic traits: just as the rhymes in "My Grandmother's Love Letters" formed an equality of misunderstanding, so the assertion of the self here is deemed to happen in a contradictory fashion. It will occur "drop by caustic drop," yet the "perfect cry" will form "some constant harmony," in spite of any societal pressure that would force the queer subject to conform. With the transgression of movement comes the transgression of time, as Crane breaks temporal rules through his fusing of three temporal moments or periods: "legend," "youth," and "noon." Just as it stands at the beginning of the book to show that Crane intends to question notions of perception, so too "Legend" asserts that *White Buildings* will be a collection that will actively seek to cross the boundaries of the known and the unknown.

Crane brought a sense of transgression into *The Bridge* that was centered on the Bridge itself as a structure. As part of a description of his new relationship with Emil Opffer, Crane described how

> I have been able to give freedom and life which was acknowledged in the ecstasy of walking hand in hand across the most beautiful bridge of the world, the cables enclosing us and pulling us upward in such a dance as I have never walked and never can walk with another (*OML* 187).

As in "Legend," which Crane wrote a few months after this letter, Crane blurs dancing and walking and, just as in the poem and its "opening gesture," Crane's use of movement suggests the production of a space that exists somewhere between public and private worlds. Crane and his lover walk through a very public space ("the most beautiful bridge of the world"), yet dance across it "hand in hand" in an intimacy that could hardly be more indiscreet and challenging to normative society.

The Bridge is prefaced by an epigraph from the Book of Job, which introduces the association between this movement of walking and transgressive identity:

> From going to and fro in the earth,
> and from walking up and down in it (*CP* 41).[20]

Crane uses the words of the ultimate transgressor, Satan, in answering God's question "Whence comest thou?"[21] to suggest that the linked poems contained within *The Bridge* are derived from restless experience. This is a thorough form of experience, since the speaker's identity is fashioned from his coverage of the three dimensions of the earth: breadth, length, and height. Yet in its parallel with Crane's description of actually walking across the Bridge, the epigraph also suggests a further dimension to that experience that passes *through* or "in the earth." This is the unmeasurable dimension of the queer "ecstasy of walking hand in hand," something "thorough and intense" as Crane said of his concept of "interior form," and which exemplifies Crane's ideal that a poet should have "a sufficiently universal basis of experience" ("General Aims and Theories," *CPSL* 218).

Space deregulated

A bridge itself is the perfect structure to contain queer experience. De Certeau's description of the bridge as a symbol illuminates some of the ways in which Crane uses it in his work:

> As a transgression of the limit, a disobedience of the law of the place, [the bridge] represents a departure, an attack on a state, the ambition of a conquering power, or the flight of an exile; in any case, the "betrayal" of an order. [...] [I]n recrossing the bridge and coming back within the enclosure the traveler henceforth finds there the exteriority that he had first sought by going outside and then fled by returning. Within the frontiers, the alien is already there, an exoticism or sabbath of the memory, a disquieting familiarity. It is as though delimitation itself were the bridge that opens the inside to its other (128–29).

The bridge is the natural space of the exile, one of transgression, and a space that creates the means for movement to bring about "a disquieting familiarity" or queerness. The process by which laws are broken and boundaries are broken down might be termed deregulation, exemplified by the bridge and prominent throughout Crane's work. It is a form of resistance, for it addresses the ways in which heteronormativity considers queerness to be a limitation, and then seeks to negate it. As De Certeau suggests, this kind of process is a form of movement, and that movement is frequently a pedestrian one. Before *The Bridge*, deregulation took place in "For the Marriage of Faustus and Helen," which Crane referred to as "a kind of bridge" (*OML* 120). The lines that close the poem (*CP* 32) suggest the value of walking as an aesthetic practice. In representing the "imagination," the image of walking meets and goes beyond "despair," and also rejects language that has become corrupted or useless: whether through materialism (the "bargain"), because it is meaningless ("vocable" is "a word considered as composed of certain sounds or letters, without regard to its meaning" (*WUD* 1481)), or whether it is language which passively supplicates ("prayer").

Deregulation is figured in *The Bridge* as a compulsion to move. Thomas Yingling has suggested that "[t]he problem of the modern, as it is figured at the outset of *The Bridge* is the problem of motion, the problem for the homosexual who understands himself as displaced, the fact that nothing 'stays' him" (191). Certainly the speaker and the queer subjects in the poem are always on the move, but because they seek to break out of the demarcated spaces in which they are placed by heteronormative society. In this respect, walking is deviant because in its adoption of a purely human form of movement it rejects the modern, technological modes that limit human potential, an issue I discuss in the final chapter of this book. The speaker in "The Dance," which posits a connection between the land and the Native American, says that "I could not stop" as he goes on foot to his dance (*CP* 63), whilst the speaker in "Cutty Sark" (1926–1929/1927), a section that celebrates the technology of the old clipper ships, tells of how "I started walking home across the Bridge..." (*CP* 73).[22] The addition here of an ellipsis followed by five further dots across the page, ostensibly to denote a section break, also suggests a continuous movement that never ends. In "To Brooklyn Bridge," the Bridge is "silver-paced/As though the sun took step of thee, yet left/Some motion ever unspent in thy stride" (*CP* 43), suggesting that deregulation and the containing of potential is a crucial part of the Bridge's design.[23] At the conclusion of "Cape Hatteras" (1926–1929/1930), the part of the poem most cognizant of modern technology, the speaker urges Walt Whitman to be "[a]foot again, and onward without halt" (*CP* 84).[24] In doing so, he assures Whitman that "[r]ecorders ages hence, yes, they shall hear/In their own veins uncancelled thy sure tread," thereby endorsing the elder poet's work entitled "Recorders Ages Hence" and its own description of a speaker who "saunter'd the streets curv'd with his arm the/shoulder of his friend, while the arm of his friend rested/upon him also" (qtd. in Whitman 276).[25] In suggesting the presence of "thy sure tread" in "their own veins uncancelled," the "Cape Hatteras" speaker seeks to deregulate space. Here, I suggest, Crane is using a particular definition of "cancelled," which means a space enclosed as if with a lattice (*WUD* 189–90), and in its uncancelling the image thus suggests an opening up of that space through which Whitman can now make a corporeal connection with his "recorders." In this respect, the bridging takes place between Whitman's time and Crane's own, and the process of deregulation, as de Certeau says, "opens the inside to its other," where the "other" is the speaker's twin in the "eternal brotherhood" Crane seeks to celebrate.

Yet Crane also saw deregulation as a means of resistance to the negation of his poetic practice. When Harriet Monroe wrote to him in 1926 asking him to clarify the metaphors that he used in "At Melville's Tomb" (1925/1926), the poem he had sent for publication in *Poetry*, Crane responded with a description of his "dynamics" or "logic of metaphor." Rather than Monroe's actual criticisms, significant here is Crane's interpretation of those criticisms, for he understands them to be a direct attack on both his style and sexual/authorial legitimacy. He tells Monroe that

> [t]he nuances of feeling and observation in a poem may well call for certain liberties which you claim the poet has no right to take. I am simply making the claim that the poet does have that authority, and that to deny it is to limit the scope of the medium so considerably as to outlaw some of the richest genius of the past ("A Discussion with Hart Crane," 36).

When Crane speaks here of "authority', he is defending not just his authority as a poet, but also his authority to be a queer individual *and* a poet, and for the work he produces to be legitimate. He aligns himself with geniuses of the past by suggesting not that he is like them, but that *they* are like *him*, and that to "outlaw" them – literally to remove them like the queer individual from protection under the law and thus societal legitimacy – would be to outlaw his work and his person too. In his "logic of metaphor" Yingling finds Crane using "a simultaneous multiplication of signs and obfuscation of meanings," and "refusing 'natural' language and employing in its stead a language full to the very limit of meaning" (41). Yet in his reply to Monroe, Crane actually seeks to deregulate or de-limit meanings and logic, suggesting that

> as a poet I may very possibly be more interested in the so-called illogical impingements of the connotations of words on the consciousness (and their combinations and interplay in metaphor on this basis) than I am in the preservation of their logically rigid significations at the cost of limiting my subject matter and perceptions involved in the poem (*CP* 234).

Crane parallels freedom of style with freedom of expression, and in response to Monroe's claim that "[t]he packed line should pack its phrases in orderly relation" ("A Discussion with Hart Crane," 35), he offers instead a poetics that deregulates semantic space, breaking out of the linear, logical form that Monroe advocates towards something that might move "to and fro [...] up and down." In such a situation, words can harbor entirely different, *dis*orderly relationalities to each other.

The logic of metaphor, space, and the phatic aspect

It is notable that when Crane tried to explain his poetics to Monroe, he used metaphors of movement; the motion of a boat through islands, or an airplane at speed. In his earlier essay, "General Aims and Theories," upon which Crane drew when replying to Monroe, Crane spoke of his aspirations for his particular style in a similar way:

> It is my hope to go *through* the combined materials of the poem, using our "real" world somewhat as a spring-board, and to give the poem *as a whole* an orbit or predetermined direction of its own. [...] It is as though a poem gave the reader as he left it, a single new *word*, never before spoken and impossible to actually enunciate, but self-evident as an active principle in the reader's consciousness henceforward. [...] [T]he entire construction of the poem is raised on the organic principle of a "logic of metaphor," which antedates our so-called pure logic, and which is the genetic basis of all speech, hence consciousness and thought-extension (*CPSL* 220–21).

The "logic of metaphor" is a spatial construction that offers an alternative space produced through movement. Crane's adoption of this logic when faced with criticism also shows how it is a resistant practice, and that Crane is resisting a normative construction of poetics. His desire to "to give the poem *as a whole* an orbit or predetermined direction of its own" may owe something to Eliot's emphasis upon impersonality, but it is also a decisively independent assertion of an aesthetic separate from the normative, and one dependent for its existence upon space and movement. In this respect, when Harriet Monroe admitted that she could not understand Crane's use of language she was also admitting to an inability to understand this spatial aesthetic. Without access to, or rather, without the willingness to access, the kinds of queer spaces Crane was describing in his work, she would and could not have access to the linguistic spaces created by the logic of metaphor, and for her it would always remain illogical and incomprehensible. In her criticism, Monroe drew attention to the "succession of champion mixed metaphors, of which you must be conscious" ("A Discussion with Hart Crane," 35). Lee Edelman has identified one of the key tropes of Crane's poetry to be catachresis, "the means by which Crane claims new ground for his poetics. It allows him to extend meaning through the radical mixing of metaphors and through the improper naming of objects or actions that lack proper names of their own" (*Transmemberment of Song* 7–8). Monroe's criticisms therefore describe precisely one of Crane's queer modernist strategies. Her inability to understand Crane's work is representative of a broader "conscious" or unconscious misunderstanding of his sexuality and how his sexuality affects his work. Edelman suggests that "Crane's catachrestic ideology was deeply informed by his sexuality, and that one of the things it aspired to do was to find a language whereby Crane might articulate a desire for which no 'proper' language existed" (43).

Crane's efforts to find that language were grounded in spatial terms: "to go *through* the combined materials of the poem, using our 'real' world somewhat as a spring-board." Crane suggests that the poet must seek an alternative space to the "real" world for his poetics. De Certeau's writing once again serves as an apt description of Crane's sense of place when the critic observes that "space is like the word when it is spoken, that is, when it is caught in the ambiguity of an actualization [...]. In contradistinction to the place, it has thus none of the univocity or stability of a 'proper'" (117). These ideas describe what I am terming the deregulating urge of Crane's aesthetic, which suggests the possibility of multiple voices within the text, not just the normative, single one. Crane's queer textual space also rejects the kind of "stability" to which Monroe alludes when she idealizes poetry that "pack[s] its phrases *in orderly relation*" ("A Discussion with Hart Crane," 35, emphasis added). As Edelman suggests, Crane aspired to create a language for his "improper" desire, and he found the means to do so by fusing language and space. By going "through" the materials of the poem, Crane seeks to emerge into an atopic space (and time) that is to be found thereby beyond the normative, "caught in the ambiguity of an actualization." It is the location where the impossible and possible meet; where a word is present but cannot be enunciated and where space is realized in action, caught midway between different states. In this respect it is a space where the poem, as has been common throughout Crane's work, is always on the move. As a result of this aesthetic, the final section of *The Bridge*, which on the surface seems to be the part which attempts to unify the rest, proves to be anything but a synthesis. "Atlantis" (1923–1929/1930) frequently draws attention to the thesis and antithesis of its argument but cannot, and is not intended to, provide the synthesis, a fact that Crane's critics have frequently misunderstood. One of the earliest critics of *The Bridge*, Yvor Winters, described "Atlantis" as "an attempt to embody another non-existent 'destiny' in miscellaneous concrete details" (29), with the understanding that Crane was "headed precisely for nowhere, in spite of all the shouting" (25). Yet essentially this is the point. Crane's own queer logic is procedural, emphasizing the need to continue to go "through," but without a certain destination. When Crane used a section from Seneca's *Medea* as the epigraph to "Ave Maria" (1926–1929/1927) (*CP* 45), the first section of the poem (after the dedication to the Bridge), he was quite conscious of the implications of the Latin phrase "ultima Thule," and the lines: "Tethys will disclose new worlds/Nor shall Thule be the ultimate bound of earth."[26] This is a place that may be approached but never reached. As José Muñoz puts it, "[q]ueerness is not yet here" (1). Since synthesis is not what it seeks, "Atlantis" constantly moves through conflicting spaces (*CP* 105).[27]

For instance, although the second stanza offers "[o]ne arc synoptic," such unity is challenged by the "labyrinthine mouths of history" that remain to be negotiated. In the description of the ships as "[c]omplighted," Crane's neologism suggests a catachrestic opposition of "comply," "light," and "completed," with a negative sense of yielding in "comply" asserted within a breath that might be positively "completed." When the voices say that they "ply" a song of love, the implication is an energy that both *folds* the woven fabric of those voices (suggesting a matching of materials), but also energy that bends or yields, which would seem to compromise the impulse to "[m]ake thy love sure." In acknowledging the need to resist a synthesis that might satisfy the narrative arc of normative structures, Crane identifies the necessity to retain the Other, for to synthesize is to become only one thing and to deny the sense of possibility and relationality that the call and answer represented here affords.

Crane claims that "the organic principle of a 'logic of metaphor,' [...] antedates our so-called pure logic, and [...] is the genetic basis of all speech, hence consciousness and thought-extension" ("General Aims and Theories," *CPSL* 221). At the same time as these ideas suggest the real possibility of progress and growth in the assertion of the "organic," they also suggest a queer strategy that seeks to return to a linguistic starting point. It is from such contrasts that the essential energy that moves *The Bridge* forward is derived, for Crane relies upon a structure that itself depends upon contrasting points in space; either side of the Bridge tension is created by contrasts within the steel cables that support it. This movement, and the logic of metaphor itself, recall what de Certeau has called the "phatic aspect,"

> the function [...] of terms that initiate, maintain, or interrupt contact, such as "hello," "well, well," etc. Walking, which alternately follows a path and has followers, creates a mobile organicity in the environment, a sequence of phatic *topoi*. [...] [It is] like a series of "hellos" in an echoing labyrinth, anterior or parallel to informative speech (99).

The phatic aspect suggests a production of space through movement that moves forward and backward simultaneously, a sense of space that is presented in the final stanza of "Atlantis" and thus the final lines of *The Bridge*. These lines offer ambiguities and doubts: whilst suggesting the possibility of unity and conclusion, the stanza also offers infinity, an endlessness. Crane directly questions the possibility of fusing time (represented by the serpent) and space (the eagle), and his concluding line is certainly inconclusive. "Whispers" may go unheard or be misheard, whilst an "antiphony" is a form of "alternate singing" in which the song is "sung alternately by a choir or congregation divided into two parts" (*WUD* 60), which connotes a sense of division rather than synthesis. The final "swing" is an incomplete motion which, depending on the viewer's perspective, might be from side to side or from backwards to forwards. By considering De Certeau's comments alongside Crane's final lines, the conclusion can be seen as a phatic aspect, and the continuous motion with which *The Bridge* leaves the reader as an invitation to answer the "series of 'hellos' in an echoing labyrinth." The phatic aspect's position of being "anterior or parallel to informative speech" suggests an equivalent impulse to the logic of metaphor, which "antedates our so-called pure logic and is the genetic basis of all speech," and exists through connotation. Just as the "hellos" may or may not overlap and answer each other in space of the labyrinth, so the logic of metaphor relies on the reader, who "responds by identifying this inflection of experience with some event in his own history or perceptions – or rejects it altogether" (*CPSL* 235). The overriding impulse at the conclusion of "Atlantis," and throughout *The Bridge* in the repeated imagery of the circle that Crane employs, is the desire to return to a beginning, and the final section goes back to the structure of the Bridge itself where it began in the dedication.

In its conscious presentation of oppositions, doubts and the aspiration to return, "Atlantis" goes beyond just the structure that acts as its inspiration and seeks to occupy a space which, as the several references in this part to the color white suggests, is blank and thus full of possibility, not just for the Bridge, but for the queer identity of the speaker. Commenting upon Foucault's analysis of the life of the hermaphrodite, Herculine Barbin, Judith Butler proposes that Foucault

> implies a critique of the metaphysics of substance as it informs the identitarian categories of sex. Foucault imagines Herculine's experience as "a world of pleasures in which grins hang about without the cat." Smiles, happinesses, pleasures, and desires are figured here

as qualities without an abiding substance to which they are said to adhere. As free-floating attributes, they suggest the possibility of a gendered experience that cannot be grasped through the substantializing and hierarchizing grammar of nouns [...] and adjectives [...]. Through his cursory reading of Herculine, Foucault proposes an ontology of accidental attributes that exposes the postulation of identity as a culturally restricted principle of order and hierarchy, a regulatory fiction (*Gender Trouble* 32–33).

Butler's conclusions illuminate the situation of "Atlantis" in their observations about gender, resistance, and language. The space to which Crane aspires at the end of *The Bridge* (one in constant motion, incomplete, full of doubts) is a space where the expectations of gendered desire are erased. The result is an atopia, which might also be said to be asocial in the respect that it challenges the dominant, heteronormative substance and hierarchy. As Butler intimates when she describes the "free-floating attributes" of language that serve to define, identity is to be found in connotation, and just as she sees Foucault as offering an "ontology of accidental attributes," so Crane's logic of metaphor prioritizes connotation (a linguistic and sexual freedom) over denotation (social norms and "proper" language). Incorporated into *The Bridge* therefore is Crane's resistance to heteronormativity, a resistance that is simultaneously fashioned through language and through the production of space. Crane does offer queerness in space as a form of freedom, both for the speakers who inhabit his poems and in terms of the language they use and the forms through which that language is presented. That kind of freedom can also be seen in Crane's temporality, which will be examined in the following chapter. As I shall explain, the poetry's continuing commitment to the queer negation of the heteronormative and its attention to a queer temporality, which assembles strategies and processes to produce moments "out of time," serve to make Crane's work difficult to place temporally as well as spatially.

4
Temporality, Futurity, and the Body

Critics who have chosen to deal with Crane's use of time have, generally speaking, felt compelled to examine *The Bridge*, and many of these critics have explored Crane's use of history, rather than his experience of temporality. In the previous chapter, I showed how recent developments in queer criticism have redefined queer space, and approaches such as these can provide a different frame for the study of Crane's poetics from both a queer and a modernist perspective. This helps to shift analyses away from the familiar ground of history and the development of technology that brings about the "conquest of space and time" in *The Bridge*. In offering a queer reading of Crane's temporality, I juxtapose the "Voyages" sequence alongside parts of *The Bridge* as one way of breaking that ground, and of suggesting the wider possibilities for looking at Crane's use of time. In doing so I use selections of the "Voyages" manuscripts to further disrupt a conventional, normative reading of the sequence, but also to show how a genetic reading of the drafts and versions can illuminate Crane's choices in the final form of the poem. This process of reading through the versions also demonstrates how Crane's writing and revision processes – frequently seen as chaotic – were often considered and precise.[1] This methodology is akin to Dirk Van Hulle's definition of a genetic critic as one who focusses "on the temporal dimension of writing and regard[s] a work of literature as a process rather than a product. The end result remains inextricably bound up with its textual memory, that is, the numerous textual transformations that preceded its publications" (2).

Out of time and out of history

Many previous critics have considered Crane's writing of "history" to be inadequate. Such criticisms are frequently a result of the mislabeling of

The Bridge as an "epic" poem, and the misunderstanding of Crane's use of time in *The Bridge*, viewing it as the result of either a longing for the past or a conflict with historical narrative. Homophobic criticism or an assumption that Crane did not possess "an excess of brains," as Joseph Riddel remarked (98), have also played a role in this misreading of the temporal in Crane's poetry. It is only latterly that Crane's non-normative temporal strategies have been recognized as consciously achieved, but the analysis of such strategies – consciously queer, consciously modernist – have hitherto been applied almost exclusively to *The Bridge*. In one of the more recent and successful treatments of Crane's histories, Christopher Nealon sums up critics' difficulties with Crane's work by noting that he appears to them "not a modernist or a metaphysical or a romantic poet but somehow all of these, ransacking 'the history of styles' and floating lost beyond it" (13). If critics have considered Crane difficult to place, they have also considered his attempts to "write history" as a failure, especially if compared to the contemporary historical epics of T.S. Eliot or Ezra Pound. Suzanne Clark Doeren sees Crane as a victim of the critical theory that Eliot promoted and which was taken up by disciples such as Allen Tate and Yvor Winters, two men who also happened to be friends of Crane and early influences upon subsequent critical opinion of him. Eliotic (and then New Critical) theory, Doeren says,

> could not allow for a poem to function rhetorically as part of the historymaking business – a theory that demanded of history the very rational continuity Crane was bringing into question, a theory that thought modern culture essentially disconnected from the past. These early critics assumed that, to be successful, Crane's poem must involve the creation of a unity, an (impossible) joining of the traditional and the modern. Furthermore, since the tradition was bankrupt, the only possible unity would appear as a modern belatedness, the regret for a lost and more unified past (20).

Thus Tate and Winters both accused Crane of writing backwards: Tate suggested that *The Bridge* could be placed at the end of Romanticism, and Winters heavily criticized Crane for including and praising Walt Whitman.

The form of *The Bridge* has also affected critics' understanding of Crane's use of time and history. Just after Yvor Winters had reviewed *The Bridge*, Crane wrote in response:

> Your primary presumption that *The Bridge* was proffered as an epic has no substantial foundation. You know quite well that I doubt that

our present stage of cultural developement [sic] is so ordered yet as to provide the means or method for such an organic manifestation as that (*OML* 428).

Nevertheless, critics have persisted in labelling *The Bridge* an epic, and part of the reason why so many critics are unable to see further than this poem and issues of history, is precisely because it has been consistently described as an epic poem. In some respects, this has been a teleological reading of the poem, since it automatically compares *The Bridge* to other modernist epics such as Ezra Pound's *Cantos*, which he famously described as "a poem including history" ("Date Line" 86). Donald Pease, for instance, sees Crane nostalgically reaching back in time to his twin influences, Whitman and Blake, to splice together epic form and prophecy. According to Pease, he "then correlates a series of central moments in the epic history of America as common efforts to sing that song until – as Blake did for England – Crane conflates all of American history into that single moment when the total form of America's epic turns into the prophetic act of Atlantis rising from the sea" (273). Writing more generally about Crane's work, Joseph Riddel contends that "it was virtually certain, given his obsession with temporality, Crane would aspire to write an epic – or more accurately, to turn history into myth, to collapse the epic and the lyrical forms, by way of presenting not only the ideal that must *in*-form history but the very act of transformation by which the ideal is purified of history" (96). Both Pease and Riddel suggest the strain that Crane seems to place upon history, and the strain he places upon his own poetics as a result. Both of them, like Tate and Winters, are also working from certain normative expectations of what the poem should look like and be, an approach which seems to run deliberately against the grain of Crane's stated project. Daniel Gabriel, in a much more nuanced reading of *The Bridge* as a modernist epic to set alongside *The Waste Land*, *The Cantos*, and William Carlos Williams's *Paterson*, argues that "it is unprofitable to read it merely as a lyrical sequence, or as a long lyrical poem. Such a reading can only reduce its important historical/cultural status – for it is a 'cultural text,' a poetic 'document' of a transitional culture." Instead, Gabriel suggests that the poem is "a hybrid of lyric and epic modes, a mixture of two distinct but related discourses. These two modes assume a dialectical relationship, and yet form an unconventional synthesis (a disunified unity) through a complex and elusive structure" (2). Of the criticism about the epic mode of *The Bridge*, Gabriel's analysis seems to me the most satisfying, since it offers a way to read the poem that is both in agreement with

Crane's own vision for the work, and also engaged with the elements of the poem that attempt to incorporate national identity, an approach that might ordinarily be called "epic." In addition, it is more in accord with my own queer reading of the poem, particularly Gabriel's sense of *The Bridge* as being "a disunified unity," which suggests the resistance to normative time and space encapsulated in a poem that can still be a complete artistic work, even if it deliberately concludes, as I will show, in an open-ended way.

Gabriel himself acknowledges that his study is not concerned with the social history depicted in *The Bridge*, but instead is interested in exploring a more abstract version of history in which "history as chronology or knowledge became disrupted by another precept: radical disjuncture" which served to re-define history "as lyric discourse" (8). Rather than see the representation of history in terms of this kind of cultural-formal shift, I argue in this chapter that such "disjuncture" is the result of Crane's attempt to find the right structures with which to present queer experience in the present and in the past. However, critics' attempts to understand Crane's supposed "failure" to deal with history through form or content has led them to think that Crane must have been at war with it. Commenting upon the irony of previous critics' perception of *The Bridge* as being not historical enough, John Carlos Rowe claims that this is because it "is an extended attack on the very idea of American history, whose obsession with the past or future has exhausted the synergy of the present" (607). In this conflict, Joseph Riddel explains, the "poet-quester" of *The Bridge* must "be sacrificed in his role, for he is to be destroyed with his vision. The enemy is history. And yet, to go one step further, he restores the vision, purifying it of history, in his act of sacrificing himself to it, in the suffering that attends the rejection of the Word by the world" (94). Riddel's commentary may be from the mid-1960s, yet it is frequently cited in criticism of Crane's work, and has remained influential. Nevertheless, Riddel's assertions for the need for the poet-quester to combat an historical narrative, to suffer, and to sacrifice himself as an act of purification, all suggest homophobic critical tropes that were common in discussion of Crane's work until the 1990s, criticism that pities Crane one moment whilst it damns him the next. Even after Thomas Yingling's book was published in 1990, fellow critics still equated Crane's writing in *The Bridge* with these kinds of tropes. Gert Buelens, for instance, writing in 1992, considered Crane to be a Romantic poet, striving to return to the past "to a place beyond the here and now, in his search for the experience of wholeness that he himself saw in the mythic bridge" (251). Buelens emphasizes what he sees as Crane's desire to harmonize with the past in order to accept and transcend the present. These emphases, upon a striving for wholeness and an inability to be comfortable in the present gesture once again towards the difficulty of placing Crane in a normative society. Christopher Nealon, commenting upon this difficulty, observes that "[t]his subliming of Crane out of literary history is always linked, I suggest, to a notion that he fails to write history; this notion is linked, in turn, to his homosexuality" (13). Instead of reading Crane as a queer writer, critics of the past have most often read him as someone who was out of time and place.

Critics more comprehending of Crane's queer aesthetic have explored how labels for his work, which imply a certain kind of temporality, are problematic. Although he chooses to adopt the term "epic," Thomas Yingling also describes how "[t]he homosexual poet – particularly when his intentions are toward as culturally authoritative a text as epic has traditionally been expected to be – has no ground on which to stand" (197). Certainly I would argue that this is one of the reasons that Crane decides to adopt a mythical, rather than straightforward, linear, or normative history in his work. Jared Gardner suggests that Crane applied the "new vocabulary for his sexuality" that he had developed in *White Buildings* to create "a version of America's history and traditions. In doing so, he attempts to inscribe his sexuality as the correct reading of the myths that define American culture, myths whose supposed misinterpretations have led to the degradation of modern society" (33–34). As I will go on to discuss later in this chapter, Crane's adaptation of particularly American stories, legends, and myths (and myths which have been re-read as having New World significance, such as the Eden narrative) enables him to critique the heteronormative world.

Yet whether they adopt a queer reading or not, several critics have observed that Crane's poetic techniques frequently challenge normative temporality. In his analysis of *The Bridge*, Riddel argues that "[t]he compressed images, the ellipses, the forcefully collapsed syntax and metaphors – all reveal a poem which tries to deny the temporality of language, to distill the pure logos from the dross of the world's words. At the same time, this style calls attention to its own processes, and the stresses of its effort" (99). Where Riddel sees these as strains and failures in Crane's depiction of time I argue that, in *The Bridge* and in "Voyages," these kinds of techniques and the self-consciousness of the writing are used by Crane to assert a queer view of the world. It is no surprise, therefore, that Riddel views these strategies as false ones, since they fit within a non-normative framework that is alien to him. Other critics though have noted the same kind of techniques used by Crane: Clark Doeren draws attention to "a necessary shattering of cohesiveness" in Crane's writing (21), whilst Rowe observes that "Crane's very poetic style relies in ironic allusions, doubled images, and prolepses to suggest the 'temporality' of the poem as bridge in the very rhythms of writing" (608). Allen Grossman identifies something like the blurring of temporal periods when he asserts that "Crane invests the present not with intelligibility, but with the unreachability, of the past, and the past with the urgency of the present, thus burdening his hope (the enrichment of present time) with the unobtainability of memory and the unexchangeability of particular experience" ("Hart Crane and Poetry" 232).

It is worth reiterating that most of these critics see Crane's concern with temporality exhibited only in *The Bridge*, and then only in Crane's response to history. This chapter seeks to go beyond this limited viewpoint by examining "Voyages" alongside *The Bridge*. In doing so, I will examine how a key element of Crane's aesthetic is his response to and description of time, and that through his embrace of ideas and techniques concurrent with modernism, Crane offers a challenge to heteronormative conceptualizations of time. If, as the previous chapters have argued, Crane's work is animated by the search for and development of a suitable language for queer experience, the relating of that experience, whether in a personal environment ("Voyages") or a grander, national one (*The Bridge*) is dependent upon discovering a relevant and coherent concept of time. Examining Crane's queer temporality against a backdrop of modernist philosophy, using the work of Friedrich Nietzsche and Martin Heidegger, serves to draw out from an exemplary strain of modernist thought about time certain complexities that Crane exploited. This, in turn, exemplifies the way in which Crane's queer approach allowed him to enter into these processes of thought and yet also stand apart from them.

Furthermore, Crane's adopting and maintaining of a "poetry of negation" both subscribed to what he saw as Eliot's style, and departed from it in asserting a queer position, challenging reproductive futurity and normative temporality. Such a challenge is often centered on Crane's use of the body in his texts, and the body that intervenes in the temporality of the poetry needs to also be considered as a body that desires, for such desire is figured in various stylistic strategies that appear in "Voyages" and in *The Bridge*. These strategies, such as the creation of gaps, flux, the difficulties of closure, and the use of repetition, are typical both of modernist poetics and also temporal tropes.

As with Crane's use of space, process and movement are crucial aspects of his engagement with temporality: Nealon perceptively remarks that Crane "is a genius at describing processes that live inside other processes" (*Foundlings* 30). Often, Crane's use of time is a process, that is to say it is continuous, rather than halting; progressive, rather than protracted. Such a process is rarely linear. As I argued earlier, the poems embrace movement, and even as "Voyages" and *The Bridge* are replete with verbs and moments of advance, they are equally full of the kind of movement that can be seen in temporal terms, since it works backwards as well as forwards. Such motion, even in the form of repetition, is an assertion of a queer identity, a process of independent and continual creation in spite of the forces of normative temporality.

The "Moment"

In the course of the Third Part of Friedrich Nietzsche's *Thus Spoke Zarathustra* (1883–1885), Zarathustra challenges his listeners with "the riddle that I *saw*, the vision of the loneliest. – " (Kaufmann 268). He describes how he set out along a path, only to be confronted by a creature, "half dwarf, half mole," the "spirit of gravity," who dragged him down continually until they reached a gateway. Here, Zarathustra addressed the dwarf:

> "Behold this gateway, dwarf!" I continued. "It has two faces. Two paths meet here; no one has yet followed either to its end. This long lane stretches back for an eternity. And the long lane out there, that is another eternity. They contradict each other, these paths; they offend each other face to face; and it is here at this gateway that they come together. The name of the gateway is inscribed above: 'Moment.' But whoever would follow one of them, on and on, farther and farther – do you believe, dwarf, that these paths contradict each other eternally?"
>
> "All that is straight lies," the dwarf murmured contemptuously. "All truth is crooked; time itself is a circle" (Kaufmann 270).

Zarathustra then draws the dwarf's attention to the gateway, "Moment," asking him:

> "Must not whatever *can* walk have walked on this lane before? Must not whatever *can* happen have happened, have been done, have

passed by before? And if everything has been there before – what do you think, dwarf, of this moment? Must not this gateway too have been there before? And are not all things knotted together so firmly that this moment draws after it *all* that is to come? Therefore – itself too? For whatever *can* walk – in this long lane out *there* too, it *must* walk once more. [...]

[M]ust not all of us have been there before? And return and walk in that other lane, out there, before us, in this long dreadful lane – must we not eternally return?" (Kaufmann 270).

According to Martin Heidegger, the collision between past and future to which Nietzsche's tale seems to aspire but does not describe is possible for someone "who *is himself* the Moment, performing actions directed toward the future and at the same time accepting and affirming the past, by no means letting it drop" (*Nietzsche, Volumes One and Two* 56). As Ronald Schleifer notes, this means that the dwarf is a mere spectator, and "situates himself [...] precisely 'nowhere' in relation to time" (111). Schleifer asserts that "[t]he 'Moment' of the advent of the second Industrial Revolution, the moment of twentieth-century Modernism, is precisely when, in history, narrative, and science, the possibility of a view from nowhere, the possibility of forgetting time and temporality by reducing it to spatial figures – of reducing time simply to an accident that can *always* be disregarded – is lost" (111). According to Schleifer, this happens because the "collision" that Heidegger describes is inevitable during this moment of Modernism; a result of "the abundances of material, intellectual, and quotidian life" (111–12).

In one important respect, Crane represents that someone "who *is himself* the Moment," a writer who was fascinated by modern technologies and prospects of progress, whilst at the same time cursing his contemporaries for "this constant nostalgia for something always 'new'. This disdain for anything with a trace of the past in it!!" (*OML* 117). But in another respect Crane also takes up the position of the dwarf, *deliberately* situating himself in no space and "nowhere," since, as I have already indicated, to adhere to the Modernist Moment entirely would be to subscribe to normative principles. Instead, in his appropriation of a number of the stylistic strategies used by his avant-garde contemporaries, Crane reserves the right to speak a "truth [that] is crooked," and to challenge, distort, and queer the Modernist Moment. In doing so, Crane's work continues to present conflicts to the reader. In his use of time, however, it is possible to consider the conflicts in Crane's work as comprehensible within modernist writing, as occupying that space of "collision" legitimized by Heidegger's interpretation of Nietzsche. As Langdon Hammer accurately describes it, adopting a phrase from Crane's poem "Recitative," modernism can be described as

> "Janus-faced" because it is ambiguous, not only ethically and politically, but historically so, being both old and new, peering both backward and forward in time. It is forward-looking in its manifold forms because it attacks the genteel monopoly on culture [...] But modernism looks backward too, because it institutes and enforces its own monopolies of cultural prestige, reasserts hierarchies of sexual and racial difference, and reconstructs traditional authority in restrictive ways (*Hart Crane and Allen Tate* 9).

In particular then, rather than *sabotaging* modernism from within, Crane uses modernism's own tools to fashion an alternative strand of modernist poetics, one that is sometimes resistant to the dominant strand (especially to any assertion of a sexual hierarchy), and sometimes complementary to it.

Negation and futurity

As I observed in the previous chapter, Lee Edelman has argued that queerness is essentially antisocial. It proposes no future for itself, and by existing on its own "negative" terms, also stands in the way of any human future. Queerness represents, says Edelman, reversing an advertising slogan from a 1990s U.S. public service campaign, "the side of those *not* 'fighting for the children', the side outside the consensus by which all politics confirms the absolute value of reproductive futurism" (*No Future* 3).[2] Edelman's controversial polemic – controversial because it might be seen as sanctioning the prejudices of homophobic America – is useful in thinking through the frequent presentation in Crane's work of a negative strain of thinking and expression. In addition to his exploration of space, this strain can be discerned in the concern with futurity, which in Crane's poetry is exemplified in the treatment of the figures of children and the family structure. This is linked to issues of sterility (or reproductive futurity) and, by extension, the treatment of time itself, which, as I have already indicated, is frequently subject to debate about whether it should be considered as linear or circular. Crane's queering of time involves an impulse towards "no future," or at least an alternative future, and in favor of the negativity that can bring about these situations. This was something he himself identified as early as 1922 in a letter to Allen Tate about T.S. Eliot:

> The poetry of negation is beautiful – alas, too dangerously so for one of my mind. But I am trying to break away from it. Perhaps this is useless, perhaps it is silly – but one <u>does</u> have joys. (*OML* 86)

In response to some comments from Tate about Eliot, Crane goes on to discuss him in more detail in a subsequent letter to Tate, dated June 12.[3] Crane suggests that "[h]aving absorbed [Eliot] enough we can trust ourselves as never before, in the air or on the sea. I, for instance, would like to leave a few of his 'negations' behind me, risk the realm of the obvious more, in quest of new sensations, <u>humeurs</u>" (*OML* 89–90). Writing to Selden Rodman about *The Bridge* in 1930, Crane described the poem "as a whole [to be], I think, an affirmation of experience, and to that extent is 'positive' rather than 'negative' in the sense that *The Waste Land* is negative" (qtd. in Edelman, *Transmemberment of Song* 266). In each of these examples, Crane occupies an ambiguous position. He understands Eliot's negativity to be a kind of "cultural pessimism," to which Crane would like his poetry to act as antithesis, even antidote. David Bromwich notes that *The Waste Land* may bring to light "a sort of knowledge, but it is knowledge at the cost of experience, and what it confirms is a negation of freedom" (43). For the sake of freedom – and specifically here, freedom from temporal heteronormativity – Crane affirms negativity in order to reach a more positive, optimistic outcome.

In the first section of "Voyages" (1921–1926/1923–1926), "Voyages I," the speaker offers a warning to a group of children on a beach that he first names as "[b]right striped urchins" in the opening stanza. By comparing an early version of the poem, "The Bottom of the Sea is Cruel,"[4] to the final version, it is possible to see that the warning is concerned with non-reproductive futurity (*CP* 34).[5]

Crane described the initial draft "as a kind of poster," even suggesting that it might be titled "Poster," and the reworked stanza suggests Crane's original intention of a "stop, look and listen" warning, as Crane tells of the "line/You must not cross." The kids are described in terms of brightness in a way that implies a visual aesthetic has guided Crane's writing. The children are "brilliant," which suggests they have unsullied selves, and an innocence that is moral, sexual, and behavioral; the kids "frisk" and "[f]ondle" without, it seems, any concern over future repercussions. Crane's alteration to the next lines, changing "bleached/ with the time and the elements" to "bleached/By time and the elements," further develops this concern with futurity. The "shells and sticks" suggest genitalia, and whilst it is possible to read them both as phallic symbols, the partnering of shells and sticks, and the ungendered description of the "kids," also suggest both feminine and masculine associations. The first version of the lines ("*the* time and *the* elements") suggests a specific time and place for this bleaching to have occurred, situating these sexualized children in one particular moment. But the revision indicates that in being "bleached/By time and the elements," the speaker is referring to a non-specific, generic time. In doing so, he also suggests that previous generations inform the sexual behavior of these children, whether they know it or not, and that death – or "no future" – is an inevitability.

Such an assertion, that the adopting of negativity will bring about a positive outcome, is in keeping with the references in the sequence to the stories of the Book of Genesis: the casting out of Adam and Eve from Eden is implied here and the entrance of Death into the world, as well as the attempt by God to subsequently purify that world, as if Crane is drawing attention to the very mythical constructs of a normative society that excludes him, appropriating them and demonstrating their flaws. The great flood of the Bible and the renewal of God's relationship with mankind through a covenant given form through a rainbow, are continual reference points in the sequence. Such imagery of salvation appears in "Voyages II" when the speaker asks that he and his lover should be bequeathed "to no earthly shore until/Is answered in the vortex of our grave/The seal's wide spindrift gaze toward paradise," and it is made explicit in "Voyages VI," where the island of "Belle Isle" is described as a "fervid covenant," where "rainbows twine continual hair." The speaker in "Voyages II," acknowledging the lack of futurity, asserts the negativity that counters heteronormative understandings of what queerness actually *is*. In this way, queer temporality counters the way in which it is commonly perceived by heterosexuals: as being only comprehensible in terms of the past, a perception derived, as Guy Hocquenghem observed, from the fact that a normative society would have it that

> every homosexual must […] see himself as the end of a species, the termination of a process for which he is not responsible and which must stop at himself. […] The homosexual can only be a degenerate, for he does not generate – he is only the artistic end to a species.

> The only acceptable form of homosexual temporality is that which is directed towards the past, to the Greeks or Sodom; as long as homosexuality serves no purpose, it may at least be allowed to contribute that little non-utilitarian "something" towards the upkeep of the artistic spirit (107–8).

The final lines of "Voyages I" affirm negativity, and imply that these children will be destroyed by the sea. In this way, Crane prepares the reader for the ensuing concerns over mortality and immortality that feature as key ideas throughout the remainder of the sequence and in *The Bridge*. Crane forces the reader to begin his sequence with an ending, one that seems to challenge heteronormative understandings of generative, linear progress. In his embrace of this impulse towards death and negativity and thus a non-normative way of living a life, Crane challenges not only reproductive futurity, but also temporal understanding more generally, suggesting that a linear conception of time is not the only way of comprehending progress.

In *The Bridge*, particularly in the second part entitled "Powhatan's Daughter," Crane maintains that challenge to reproductive futurity, revealing the male-female relationships to be unstable, even asexual, and presenting a challenge to patriarchal society itself. In "The Dance," he describes Pocahontas, a symbol of the continent, the land, and of fertility, to be "virgin to the last of men…" (*CP* 65).[6] Her body bursts "into bloom," but her fertility seems assured by the union of the two male figures: her husband, the Native brave Maquokeeta, and the speaker of the poem himself. In "Quaker Hill" (1927-29/1930), Crane laments the decline of a grand hotel, and sees the advancement of corrupt material wealth replacing the spiritual values of the past. In this environment, where the speaker must "[s]houlder the curse of sundered parentage," acknowledging the failure of the heteronormative family structure, the speaker cries out "[w]here are my kinsmen and the patriarch race?" suggesting thereby a confusion about futurity and the possibility that a lineage might end.

In "Van Winkle" (1923–1929/1927), the speaker's memory provides him with clear images of attempts to oppose and extinguish the failing family structure. First he describes a cinder pile from his youth "[w]here we stoned the family of young/Garter snakes" (*CP* 55),[7] snakes that are set up in opposition to the speaker and his "monoplanes/We launched – with paper wings and twisted/Rubber bands." The "mono" here figures singularity or sameness rather than a male-female couple of difference, and "twisted" suggests the opposite of the heterosexual figures in "Faustus and Helen"; "those untwisted by the love of things/irreconcilable" (*CP* 26). The struggle continues to be represented temporally, as the "rapid tongues [...]/flittered from under the ash heap day/After day," suggesting the continuing presence and recurrence of this particular family, rising again and again, it seems, from the ashes. And yet with the intervention of Rip Van Winkle who, Jared Gardner observes, in his own myth "left his wife to join a community of men in the woods" (36), the speaker is able to challenge the stability of reproductive futurity. Van Winkle introduces a sense of temporal instability, "[h]e woke and swore he'd seen Broadway/a Catskill daisy chain in May –," and the speaker endorses such instability through his own use of memory, drawing upon it to recall the emotional failings of parents. He remembers, and reflects on why it is that his memories consist of: "the whip stripped from the lilac tree/One day in spring my father took to me" and then "the Sabbatical, unconscious smile/My mother almost brought me once from church/And once only, as I recall – ?" Each time, failure is figured through linearity. The earlier, complex images of the snakes and their tongues, which are both circular as "garter" snakes and linear in their morphology, give way to the confusion of the daisy chain, which may be both linear and circular. But those images associated finally with the family, the whip and the smile that disappears, are representative of the linear process of reproductive futurity, and they, finally, are seen to fail. The mother's smile, after all, "[d]id not return with the kiss in the hall." Interpreting the stoning of the garter snakes as indicative of a "childhood suppression of desire," Gardner proposes that "[t]hrough the guidance of Rip, the poet imagines the biological family at the root of this repression, so the renouncement of the family which begins here becomes an act of recovery of sexual identity" (37). Given that Van Winkle himself represents a character out of his own time who has also – albeit accidentally – renounced his own family in Washington Irving's tale, he is an early representative of the new "brotherhood" that replaces the biological family in *The Bridge*, and will find its truest example in Walt Whitman.

If the "recovery of sexual identity" is brought about here through the failure of linearity, elsewhere in his poetry Crane creates spaces in or of time that serve to challenge a normative understanding of time that looks backwards and forwards. On the one hand, Crane's work produces gaps that serve to challenge linear time and reinforce the text's erotic content through linguistic structure, whilst elsewhere, he blurs temporal periods in a way that suggests an understanding of time as being in continuous flux.

The body and temporal gaps

The earliest draft for "Voyages II," dated September 27, 1924 by Crane, and entitled "Notes for Voyages," contains three stanzas and a single line:

> That night off San Salvador
>   the stars there slipped a step, it was
> a guide, a perfect measure to me, say
>   The water brought you clear into a day, –
>   a clasp and diaspon you danced...
>
> There -- the steeping measureless years
> enclose me in this accident, I ask
> wreak hell or worse into this step;
> Serene, I know your flesh shall rest
> as kissing all that deck, the stars [prostrate]
> call back your words...and with some other there
>
> Chants there an octave   and it brims
> more than confession...in which your tongue
> slips mine
>
>   governs...whose moving shoulder distracts (A32)[8]

This draft of the poem is noticeable for the way in which time shifts from one period to another. Whilst the opening stanza is set in the past, the second brings the action into the present. "[T]he steeping measureless years/enclose me" of the second stanza is linked to the first by an ellipsis, suggesting a temporal gap, a moment where futurity is in doubt.[9] The word "[t]here," followed by two dashes, seems to act both as a marker to a time in the past (an indication of nostalgia, acknowledging that the moment has been lost), and also as an assertion, as if to prove the truth of what has just gone before. And in the final version of the poem, San Salvador occupies the present tense: "as bells off San Salvador/Salute the crocus lustres of the stars" (*CP* 35). This experimentation with shifting tenses through the drafting process, which eventually comes to prioritize the present, suggests that moment's relative importance for the speaker and the poet. The later urgency of the published version of the poem – stanza three urges "onward," whilst the fourth stanza encourages the listener twice to "hasten" – accentuates that desire to keep things in the present time. But the mark of queer temporality is that it tries to break out of a fixed temporal reality. As

Edelman notes, "the efficacy of queerness, its real strategic value, lies in its resistance to a Symbolic reality that only ever invests [queer individuals] as subjects insofar as [they] invest [themselves] in it, clinging to its governing fiction, its persistent sublimations, as reality itself" (*No Future* 17–18). Crane frequently finds ways of realigning temporal reality, and in his drafting of "Voyages II," he indicates an alternative space and time that he has found through a material and temporal slippage.

Nealon has said that gaps – what he calls "interstices" – are integral to Crane's poems, arguing that

> the overall effect of the lyrics in *White Buildings* is to suggest that the interstices between moments or sensations or perceptions constitute the realm of experience most worth poetic attention, because those interstices are both mimetic and creative: both difficult to render and, because of that difficulty, the possible source of new and shared knowledge about desire and change (*Foundlings* 31).

Nealon proposes a different kind of difficulty to that normally associated with Crane and other modernists, one not rooted in the words themselves, but *between* them. Such gaps can be regarded as queer spaces, not in which to hide (like Wilde in *De Profundis*), but to exploit. In addition, it is worth considering how such gaps may themselves figure erotic desire. In *The Pleasure of the Text*, Barthes asks,

> [i]s not the most erotic portion of a body *where the garment gapes?* In perversion (which is the realm of textual pleasure) there are no "erogenous zones" [...]; it is intermittence, as psychoanalysis has so rightly stated, which is erotic: the intermittence of skin flashing between two articles of clothing (trousers and sweater), between two edges (the open-necked shirt, the glove and the sleeve); it is this flash itself which seduces, or rather: the staging of an appearance-as-disappearance (9–10).

"Notes for Voyages" emphasizes the same kind of erotic moment and represents it as an "accident," creating the same kind of seemingly illicit excitement that Barthes describes, as if the speaker has discovered a secret. The body of the speaker enters into an erotic moment as time (represented in this maritime situation by the stars which normally enable time to be told) slips; a slippage later given further erotic implications by being associated in the poem with the "tongue" of the lover, which is both corporeal and a confirmation of the eroticism of language to which Barthes draws attention. As Shannon Winnubst has observed, recent queer criticism such as Edelman's has made it clear that

> various other kinds of dominant social norms [...] [have] emerged through these analyses as energized by and grounded in a temporality that orients us always and only towards the future. We are rendered docile, most often at a wholly unconscious bodily level, through our unwitting obedience to the future. Particularly, as we do not conceive temporality as a constructed aspect of living existence, we do not interrogate its power over our lives and the norms that we unconsciously enact (138–39).

In "Voyages" and elsewhere, Crane makes us aware of the way in which we interpret time on an "unconscious bodily level," and one way he does so is by making the body a prominent feature. Elizabeth Freeman has suggested that a "sensation of asynchrony can be viewed as a queer phenomenon – something felt on, with, or as a body, something experienced as a mode of erotic difference or even as a means to express or enact ways of being and connecting that have not yet arrived or never will" ("Introduction" 159). By asserting the body, and the eroticized body in particular, queer temporality maintains its own unavoidable existence in the present. In "Voyages," particularly through the drafting of "Voyages II," Crane pushes this boundary still further, identifying the space of queer temporality to exist, as Freeman suggests, somewhere between the present and eternity, an indefinite (if positively existing) future and an alternative reality. To assert the body is to place oneself within the Nietzschean/Heideggerean "Moment," occupying that space of collision where past, present, and future meet.

In this initial draft for "Voyages II," A32, the speaker implies that the slippage he identifies is also a gap in social oppression that the speaker can exploit. Just as Edelman suggests the value in queer people embracing their perceived negativity, the speaker here seems to demonstrate his new resistance to such oppression by inviting it; "I ask/wreak hell or worse into this step" (A32). Together with the later diction of "confession" and "governs" in this poem, we might perceive the relationship in the terms described by Guy Hocquenghem, in which "[a]ll relationships between the homosexual and his circle are trapped in the problematics of confession, in a guilty situation where desire is criminal and is experienced as such" (90).[10] It is certainly important not to underestimate the extent to which Crane shows awareness of his difference, for it exemplifies the tremendous pressures upon him personally. Nevertheless, this draft also shows an assertion of sexuality that is greater than simply guilt. Crane writes, "it brims/more than confession... in which your tongue slips mine," suggesting not that the speaker feels some kind of guilt at taking note and learning from this "accident," but that on the contrary the value gained from that moment of slippage is of far greater significance. That confession, which might ordinarily be seen as leading to spiritual fulfilment or forgiveness, is rejected in favor of bodily fulfilment; "your tongue/slips mine." In a way it also recalls the lines which appear in "Legend," the poem which opens *White Buildings*: "I am not ready for repentence;/Nor to match regrets" (*CP* 3).[11]

In "Voyages III," it seems that Crane wants to commemorate his relationship by encapsulating it in the phrase the "tendered theme," and in A32 he asserts that what is enclosed within "the steeping measureless years" as a result of the accident needs to be a form of permanent record: the body is not simply a site of pleasure, but also a site of memory. In a later draft of "Voyages II," Crane presents a similar position when he demands: "Take us in time, O seasons clear" (A33). Despite the human body's evanescence, and despite the disapproval of society, the speaker remains "[s]erene," for "I know your flesh shall rest/ as kissing all that deck, the stars/call back your words." This exemplifies what Carolyn Dinshaw has called "a queer desire for history" (qtd. in Freeman and others 178), for if, as Hocquenghem suggests, normative sexuality demands that queer people have no future, in the face of such oppression it is important that the speaker asserts how not only the text but also the body is a repository for history. Despite this "accident," a seemingly one-off, unforeseen event, the body, eroticized and described in elemental terms as "flesh" here, retains the experience. The constant references to hands in the "Voyages" sequence, and elsewhere in Crane's writing (for example in the poems "Episode of Hands" (1920/unpublished), "Possessions," "Recitative," and "The River" and "The Harbor Dawn" sections of *The Bridge*), emphasize that necessity to make connections and make history through body-to-body contact, and its enduring possibilities for sexual intimacy. In the final version of "Voyages II," the sea "rends/As her demeanours motion well or ill,/All but the pieties of lovers' hands" (*CP* 35). Such moments recall Evans's photograph of Crane's hands that was discussed in the introduction to this book, and draw attention once again to Crane's concern with making connections with others in the world. Just as Merleau-Ponty described how the touching of hands could summon up a world beyond, here the "pieties" of hands may be able to placate the world of the sea.

In this presentation of the body therefore there is something greater at work than just personal histories. In A32, the way in which "the stars there slipped a step" is echoed by "in which your tongue/slips mine," and by linking the two ideas, points to the universal or cosmic implications of this temporal slippage. Just as "Voyages I" offers a general warning that goes beyond the kids on the beach, the impulse behind the words of instruction that punctuate the final version of "Voyages II" are intended to engage the reader. Phrases such as "[t]ake this Sea" and "[m]ark how" (*CP* 35), imply that the experience should have relevance outwards, beyond the queer individual.

Temporal gaps in "Voyages" are issues of presence and absence, but in *The Bridge*, gaps act as lacunae into which queer characters in the poems fall, since time in the poem is frequently unpredictable and unreliable. In "Indiana" (1927–1930/1930), the pioneer mother acknowledges the failure of her husband to strike gold during the Rush (*CP* 66).[12] The family was caught in a temporal gap, "too late, too early," and rather than blaming the land, the mother describes the years themselves as if they were enigmas. This makes Crane's poem suggest something broader, that the famed Colorado Gold Rush of 1859, rather than granting instant access to a fortune, was to many a myth, associated merely with sterility and pain. In its depiction of a momentary relationship set up between the pioneer mother and Native American mother as they see each other across the trail, "Indiana" shows Crane's concern for those forgotten, even abused by history. As well as challenging received ideas about Gold Rush success, "Indiana" also continues *The Bridge*'s challenge to futurity: the patriarch of the family is dead, and the first-born son is leaving not just the state but the country to seek the family fortune which his father failed to find in Colorado. Despite her pleading, the mother's final words suggest great doubt about whether her son will return:

> Come back to Indiana – not too late!
>   (Or will you be a ranger to the end?)
> Good-bye…Good-bye…oh, I shall always wait
> You, Larry, traveller –
>   stranger,
>   son,
> – my friend –

In this last part of "Indiana," Crane employs typographical devices to give a sense of the temporal concerns of the mother: her fears are enclosed in brackets, as if to show that we are entering her consciousness; the ellipses suggest an agonized parting, as the mother seems to call her son back even though bidding him farewell; and the poem seems to acknowledge, with her, that she is unlikely to see him again. Just as the lineation denotes his physical movement away from her so too the language suggests his loss, moving from his name, Larry, through "traveller," "stranger," "son" to "my friend." This represents a gradual confusion of his identity and an emotional distancing of him from her, which ends with a final dash that connects her sense of him with nothing but empty space on the page and on the land.

The section that follows "Indiana," "Cutty Sark," also features a character who has lost all sense of time and identity (*CP* 71). The epigraph to this section is from Melville's poem "Temeraire" (from his 1866 volume *Battle-Pieces*), "O, the navies old and oaken,/O, the Temeraire no more!" (*CP* 69), which chronicles the retirement of the celebrated warship Temeraire, and thus also the rise of the ironclad ships that featured in the Civil War and began to replace the oak-hulled vessels. In the same way, the human subject of this part has reached the end of his useful life as a sailor, and finds himself a victim of time. His obsession with notions of temporality allows Crane to develop his discussion of futurity, which emerges from the beginning of his speech in the phrase "now remember kid," a concentrated blending of present, past, and future. Just as in "Indiana," where time and loss is associated with the body, so here the sailor's failings, "weakeyed watches," which suggests a fundamental dereliction of duty and a breakdown of identity, are associated with corporeal features. The sailor seems a perfect illustration of Winnubst's claim that "[w]e are rendered docile, most often at a wholly unconscious bodily level, through our unwitting obedience to the future," for when the mariner's "bony hands/got to beating time," this action seems to be entirely unconscious, the impetus coming from the hands themselves rather than the sailor. As in "Voyages," where the eroticized body is associated with a crucial moment in time, so here time is interpreted through a body charged with sexuality. Samuel R. Delany is correct in suggesting that "Cutty Sark" is linked to "Cape Hatteras" through that section's epigraph: "The seas all cross'd, weather'd the capes, the voyage done...," which is drawn from Whitman's "Passage to India."[13] The remainder of Whitman's stanza describes how "fill'd with friendship, love complete, the Elder Brother found,/The Younger melts in fondness in his arms" (538). And as Delany convincingly suggests, the old sailor from "Cutty Sark' is representative of "the Elder Brother," as the poem looks both backwards to another old sailor, Columbus, in "Ave Maria" and forwards to Whitman's role in "Cape Hatteras." In this way, "the elided homosexual (and incestuous) resolution of the epigraphic passage confirms the homosexual subtext of the previous section, 'Cutty Sark', as it makes a bridge between 'Cutty Sark' and 'Cape Hatteras'" (Delany 221). This link is developed further by the sailor's avowal that "I'm a/Democrat" (*CP* 71), a reference that recalls both Whitman's *Democratic Vistas* (1870) and his project of reaching out to all Americans and including them. As Stephen John Mack has observed,

> [a]ffirming the "democratic process" has become a rhetorical cliché in the United States. Whitman, however, understood the radical implications of the emphasis on process. For one thing, rather than privileging stability, order, the known, it renders them targets of habitual suspicion. As a social value, process elevates inventiveness, experimentation, *becoming* – and the likely chaos associated with both – over stasis and tradition. It also elevates the unknowable future over secure past: "Thus," he writes in *Democratic Vistas*, "we presume to write, as it were, upon things that exist not, and travel by maps yet unmade and a blank" (141).

The sailor in "Cutty Sark" represents an aspect of time that Crane seeks to reject. There is significant irony that the character who needs "stability, order, the known," is encapsulated within perhaps the most stylistically chaotic of all the passages in *The Bridge*. The fact that the speaker fails to pick up the sailor, and that he is nearly hit by a wharf truck, demonstrating his inability to exist on land, shows Crane drawing the contrast between the sailor, a Democrat of the past, and the speaker himself, who is a figure gesturing towards the future, and the future queer embrace of the true Democrat, Walt Whitman. As the sailor remains stuck in the "secure past," so the speaker "started walking home across the Bridge...," associating himself instead with "process," "becoming," and "the unknowable future." In this case, Crane confirms the disorientation of "Cutty Sark" (named, after all, partly after Crane's favorite whisky), since the meeting with the old sailor was something of a diversion: the "Elder Brother" was not in fact found here, but the speaker, and the reader too, are instead required to journey on to discover him in the following section.

Temporal blur

In "Van Winkle," the character of Rip too is caught in a liminal temporal space between periods; "he, Van Winkle, was not here/nor there" (*CP* 56), with the punctuation and the lineation accentuating the slow realization of his dislocation. But "Van Winkle" also demonstrates another temporal strategy that Crane uses in *The Bridge* to remove readers from the normative temporal framework; the blurring of one time period or history into another. The title of the section itself hints at the possible connection to be drawn between old New Amsterdam and New York. And many of the characters who appear in "Van Winkle," like the characters throughout this section of the poem, "Powhatan's Daughter," are constantly on the move, and can be regarded as immigrants to America: the conquistadors Francisco Pizarro and Hernán Cortes, and the English captain John Smith. And just as the historical lines are blurred, so too are the real and fictional ones. Crane draws upon not only Washington Irving's tale of Rip Van Winkle and "The Legend of Sleepy Hollow," but also Henry Wadsworth Longfellow's "The Courtship of Miles Standish" for the character of Priscilla and by extension, the Pilgrim Fathers.[14] In addition, the hurdy-gurdy, an instrument played by Italian immigrants on New York streets, is a link back, as Lawrence Kramer notes, to Columbus's arrival in the New World as detailed by Crane in the earlier section "Ave Maria" (27), whilst the tenement that Van Winkle sweeps is located on "Avenue A," an area of Manhattan where many immigrants lived during the 1920s (28). And Van Winkle is also an immigrant, both in space – as a Dutch colonist – and in time, trespassing here upon the 1920s.

In the marginal notes to "Van Winkle," "Memory" is described as "time's truant," and Crane, like other modernists, used memory as a technique to suggest temporal unreliability and further challenge normative conceptions of time. In the opening of "The River," he offers a fragmentary version of reality that is both a temporal and spatial collage (*CP* 57).[15] Here, each dash represents a shift in time and perspective: glancing at the posters on the board is like looking through recent history, where an advert for a past minstrel show (Bert Williams had died in 1922) is still visible through other advertisements. The invitation to "[s]tick your patent name on a signboard" becomes fragmented, combining it with an earlier call (attributed to Horace Greeley in an 1865 edition of the *New York Tribune*) to conquer the West (Kramer, ed., 33). The rhythm of the following line, "Tintex – Japalac – Certain-teed Overalls ads" mimics the staccato, fragmented nature of the description. Yet at the same time, the river itself is "[t]ortured with history, its one will – flow!" Crane's use of time here, as both full of stopping points and yet also in continuous movement, is a governing feature of several sections of *The Bridge*.

In "Quaker Hill," Crane describes "that docile edict of the Spring/That blends March with August Antarctic skies" (*CP* 92),[16] and the beginning of this part of the poem is seen through the eyes of cattle, whose idea of time is detached from human pressures, alien to the normative and seeing only "the seasons fleeting." It is an appropriately disorienting gesture for a section of the poem that describes the abandoned, grand hotel that once commanded time and space in the formerly "Promised Land."

In "The Tunnel" (1926–1929/1927), the speaker emerges from the struggle through the infernal subway, to proclaim that he has successfully negotiated the river, albeit underground (*CP* 101).[17] The speaker marks his progress by the structures in the city, which are themselves subject to typical clock time, but he has been "[t]ossed" from this space into one where time is rendered meaningless, described as if it were at the edge of civilization. As it was in "Voyages," futurity is in doubt, with "Tomorrow/And to be" surrounded by ellipses, indistinct markers of time. In addition, "hands," which might represent the hands of a clock, no longer have meaning, for they are both "unaccounting" and, exploiting the double meaning possible, they "lie."

Recurrence and sameness

As part of his project to destabilize normative time, Crane inscribes "Voyages" and *The Bridge* with certain tropes of temporality that can be grouped under the title of recurrence – forms of replacement, returning, reproducing, and rehearing. Although different in use to the creation of gaps and temporal blurring, I consider these ideas as temporal because they nonetheless distort the linearity of normative time. They designate different ways in which same-sex desire and sexuality are figured, and this frequently includes issues of temporal and reproductive futurity.

The first stanza of the published version of "Voyages II" describes an intimate relationship between the lovers and the sea (*CP* 35). Crane uses "wrapt" to describe the lovers' bond, a word which, as Ernest Smith observes, suggests both "wrapped" and "rapt." It appeared early on in the drafting process, testifying to one of the original intentions of the poem, to capture different ways of representing the doubleness of the lovers, and describes both a visual fascination and a physical embrace, as if the couple is wrapped in each other's arms (*The Imaged Word* 114–15). The description of the love as containing "inflections" suggests a love with an accent, as being non-normative.[18] But the embrace will not continue indefinitely. By thrusting a belly that seems so full and fertile towards the moon, emblematic of female, and therefore heterosexuality and a certain type of futurity, the sea seems to be mocking this inflected, sterile love. The sea represents, after all, a space of "eternity." Despite this, the "wrapt" quality of the love is also an early example of the way in which queerness is figured in "Voyages II." Linguistically it is one word wrapped into another, but it also suggests the way in the poem by which one thing overlaps, even envelops another as one moment flows into the next. The intensity and contained nature of "wrapt" contrasts with the perceived hostility of the "great wink of eternity." In its neologistic quality, "wrapt" fits Roland Barthes's definition of an erotic word:

> the word can be erotic on two opposing conditions, both excessive: if it is extravagantly repeated, or on the contrary, if it is unexpected, succulent in its newness (in certain texts, words *glisten*, they are distracting, incongruous apparitions – it matters little if they are pedantic [...]). In both cases, the same physics of bliss, the groove, the inscription, the syncope: what is hollowed out, tamped down, or what explodes, detonates (*The Pleasure of the Text* 42).

In "Voyages," Crane uses words that "glisten," whether by adopting words from unexpected registers (such as "diapason," which he carries over from musical terminology), by bending the rules of grammar (to transform "particle" into a verb, as he does below), or by refashioning a word so that it carries a different meaning in a certain context (as with the word "superscription," also below). Crane presents a distinctly queer eroticism, one that provides an alternative understanding of language. He extends the metaphors of recurrence, and thus the possibilities for Barthesian eroticism, by filtering them through the body of the sea, and here the sea, which shifts its personality as frequently as its currents, acts as a discreet correspondent, one who knows of the queer relationship between the lovers, and is a confidante. An early draft reads:

> The emulating tides that ~~stroke~~ **stride**
> our sides and clothe by pawing coves
> ~~the~~ the superscription of ~~a~~ **our** perfect lust, - -
> timeless as your towering, ~~falling~~ ~~covered~~ **floating** hair
> processioned of me in the gamut deep
> and ~~sleepless~~ **termless** ~~teeming~~ orbit lair, **particle**
> **the teeming** (A33, recto)

In "emulating," the speaker implies the copying of one action by another individual; in "clothe," he suggests how one image – a naked body? – can be replaced by one covered; and in "superscription" (one definition of "superscribe" is: "[t]o write or engrave on the top, outside, or surface" (*WUD* 1328)), the speaker suggests the way in which the sea legitimizes the queer relationship, by clothing it. That relationship is figured through a fusion of body and text, the "superscription" being the way in which one body meets another in sex or "perfect lust." The initial line "superscription of a perfect lust" draws attention to the way in which, in corporeal terms, anal intercourse might be described as one body "writing over" another in its identical (or "perfect") shaping. In the final version of the poem, Crane makes this imagery even clearer by adding a figure that seems to mimic bodies in a sexual act: "superscription of bent foam and wave" (*CP* 35).

In other drafts, and in the final version, Crane uses further words and phrases of recurrence. "Repeated ease, repeated awe" signifies both the quality of the sea through our reactions to it when becalmed or stormy, and also suggests through sound ("ease [...] awe"), something of the movement of its tides.[19] In a phrase that echoes the early drafts of "Voyages III," Crane also mentions how "the stars/call back your words," suggesting once more the importance of words and speech, even to the point of having them repeated. The figure which symbolizes recurrence or return, the "prodigal," who appears in the final version as "my Prodigal," in earlier drafts was even more explicitly identified as a physical lover:

> Bells ringing off San Salvador
> on scrolls of silver, ivory sentences
> brimming confession, O prodigal,
> in which your tongue slips mine, -- (A37)

By repeating himself, Crane suggests a desire for sameness that gives textual form to his queer desire. The repetitive motion of the "emulating tides" of A33 interact sensually with the body as they "stroke" and "clothe," and when the description of how the stars "slipped a step" is echoed by "your tongue/slips mine" in the A32 draft, the effect is to give the moment, and the relationship, a sense of the eternal, taking it out of time. Just as in Heidegger's reading of Nietzsche's "Moment," the body crucially enters into the stream of time and can behold both past, present, and future together. The "accident" of the A32 draft is seen by the speaker to be fortuitous, it works, perversely, as a "guide," for this slippage in time and space seems to create an alternative space to reality in which the speaker can exist with his lover. For after the slippage, "[t]he water brought you clear into a day," and there is some degree of contentment in the speaker finding himself "enclose[d]." In this early draft for "Voyages," there is a sense that such a space, out of normative time, allows the speaker to disregard any attacks on his sexuality. Indeed, he says "I ask/wreak hell or worse into this step" (A32). The speaker acknowledges that his object-choice of another man as subject of this sequence, will provoke both social and religious ostracism. But this relationship is essential to him, and he feels compelled to take advantage of this "accident." He understands that the implications of this choice are great, for it will affect both present and future. Although the word "accident" does not appear in the final version of the poem, its presence is felt in the fourth stanza, where the speaker urges the listener to "hasten," as if the slippage of time from previous drafts will not last for long, and so the lovers should take advantage of the situation whilst they can.

Self-consciousness

In their figuring of queer desire through recurrence, Crane's texts also suggest a degree of self-consciousness and performativity that Robert K. Martin has identified as characteristic of a queer text. For Martin such a text "presents itself as both subject and object of desire, a text in the act of beholding itself, often through the mirror of the other, and loving itself" ("Roland Barthes" 293). Martin's commentary suggests a text in process, one in which a negotiation of what the self means is ongoing. In *The Bridge*, this self-consciousness is most obvious in "Cape Hatteras." Here the speaker enters into a mediated relationship with the temporal against the background of new technologies that conquer that time and space:

> time clears
> Our lenses, lifts a focus, resurrects
> A periscope to glimpse what joys or pain
> Our eyes can share or answer – then deflects
> Us, shunting to a labyrinth submersed
> Where each sees only his dim past reversed…(*CP* 77)[20]

On the one hand it seems as if time allows the speaker to experience a certain amount of objectivity, empathy, and clarity. Yet time's unpredictability leads the speaker into a self-conscious phase that sees that speaker enter into a zone that is entirely subjective. This same self-consciousness is evident in later sections of "Cape Hatteras," when "Adam and Adam's answer in the forest/Left Hesperus mirrored in the lucid pool," or when "[d]ream cancels dream in this new realm of fact/ From which we wake into the dream of act;/Seeing himself an atom in a shroud –/Man hears himself an engine in a cloud!" Each example – in the case of Hesperus quite literally – offers the chance for the speaker to view or experience themselves in the moment. Yet there is also the self-conscious acknowledgment, as was evident in "Voyages," that such an instant can only last for a short period of time. This concern with the temporary can also be traced to contemporary discussions of the "queer moment." In their book *Regarding Sedgwick*, Stephen M. Barber and David L. Clark identify an apparent conflict in Eve Kosofsky Sedgwick's thinking between different modes of temporality. On the one hand, she has been concerned with the idea that "[i]n the short-shelf-life American marketplace of images, maybe the queer moment, if it's here today, will for that very reason be gone tomorrow" (*Tendencies* xii). But at the same time, Sedgwick also asserts that "something about *queer* is inextinguishable" (viii). This conflict, which the unpredictable nature of time in *The Bridge* reflects, suggests an impulse that needs to keep making itself known – often through the assertion of the body – rather than risk being extinguished. As Barber and Clark say, "[i]f 'queer' exists at all, it can only be in the mode of an ongoing performativity: in a present created and sustained by the effortful acts – productions and interventions – that embody it" (2). The notion of time "ongoing," as "a present [...] sustained," is related to Sedgwick's own discussion in *Tendencies*:

> Queer is a continuing moment, movement, motive – recurrent, eddying, *troublant*. [...] The immemorial current that queer represents is as antiseparatist as it is antiassimilationist. Keenly, it is relational, and strange (xii).

Sedgwick's claims for queerness suggest the force of Crane's writing: the desire for transhistorical continuity; the assertion of the writing's kinetics: the description of constant movement, whether in the sound or lineation or in the content; as a recurrent force that continues to assert itself; and as something immemorial, with a conscious concern for past, present, and future. In Crane's work, and in "Voyages" in particular, that display of performativity is conspicuous in an attentiveness to the capacity of language, and in the knowledge that each "performance," whether it is repeated or not, can only last for a limited time. In the early draft of "Voyages III" entitled "Sonnet" (D102), this urgency is exemplified in repetition:

> Now, in the encrusting edge of years, –
> the definition of eternity – call
> One work back now, that is your name,
> That I may be, as it is, one half to blame! (D102)

The repetition of "now" suggests that the poem creates a time and space in which the love can be celebrated, and in that repetition, the "now" of the moment is matched with the "now" of the "work." The weight placed upon language itself can be seen in an earlier draft from April 1924, where "word" was used instead of "work," thereby representing both the poem and the lover himself (qtd. in Weber 395). The use of "work" here suggests that the lover can temporarily step in to fill the gap before "the [...] edge of years" becomes entirely encrusted and the chance to make the memory eternal, is lost. Although the phrase does not appear in the final version of the poem, such an urgent request is still present in the temporal references "whereto this hour" and "from dawn to dawn," and in the final line of the published poem; "Permit me voyage, love, into your hands...." It also resurfaces in "Voyages II" where, in the final version, there is an emphasis placed upon speed: "Hasten, while they are true, – sleep, death, desire,/Close round one instant in one floating flower" (*CP* 35).

The final line in D102: "That I may still be, as it is, one half to blame!" is temporally complex, and marks both the emphasis upon the importance of time, and the unpredictability of it. It encompasses future, present and past tenses; "I may," "it is," "to blame," implying an action or event in the past for which the speaker seeks to be forgiven. The line builds on "the encrusting edge of years, --/the definition of eternity --" – this moment and space that draws together past, present, and future in an attempt to preserve the relationship in words. In the final draft of the poem, the sense of these lines is incorporated into the second stanza (*CP* 36). Here, senses of death and life are fused into "transmemberment," a word that is deliberately not destruction, and not even reconstruction, but instead a conveying – in the sense of movement – of meaning. "Transmemberment," as descriptive of a process of moving across, has clear links with the way in which Crane described to Waldo Frank how he felt about his relationship with Opffer, describing himself as "changed and transubstantiated as anyone is who has asked a question and been answered" (*OML* 187). In both instances, the emphasis is upon the movement of the physical, possibly corporeal form, through the spiritual: via song in the poem and via religious ritual in the letter.[21]

Completion

So in "Voyages III," Crane maintains his queering of time, distorting the normative linear understanding of temporality. Not to do so would mean that a faithful representation of the queer relationship could not be possible. What results is an emphasis upon completion, which is presented in temporal and material terms, and which can be charted through a number of different drafts of "Voyages II." This completion is figured by images of enclosure, but these clash with images of open space and an impulse towards "engulfment," to employ Roland Barthes's term, which is both comforting and alarming. The sea represents this contrast by being once more both a friend and an enemy, and the poet explores how a non-normative space can be created as a safe haven for his love.

The images of A32 begin by suggesting completion:

>   That night off San Salvador
>   the stars there slipped a step, it was
>   a guide, a perfect measure to me, say
>   The water brought you clear into a day, -
>   a clasp and diaspon you danced...

The rhyming couplet of lines three and four suggests completion, setting up the imagery of the "clasp" and "diaspon," a misspelling of "diapason" that Crane corrects in later drafts. The bodily reference implied in "clasp," as in the holding of a partner in a dance or embrace, is obvious, but by tracking the "chain of events," as genetic critics Daniel Ferrer and Michael Groden put it (2), by which the word "diapason" evolves through the drafting process, as well as how such changes affect other words around it, we can see how Crane develops the concept of completion.

Webster's defines "diapason" as: "[t]he octave, or interval which includes all the tones of the diatonic scale," but also "[c]oncord, as of notes an octave apart," and "[t]he entire compass of tones" (*WUD* 369). Such definitions highlight the difficulty of this word, for its meaning implies both completeness ("all the tones," "concord," or "entire compass," which also implies a measurement of direction) and remoteness ("notes an octave apart"). Crane was perhaps conscious of this difficulty, because in A37 he attempted to clarify it by calling it a "perfect diapason," suggesting that he was trying to get across its sense of something homogenous, rather than heterogeneous. Nevertheless, the tension between completion and suspension persists in the revisions: in A32, "this great wink of eternity" captures the contrast between the temporal spaces of an instant and of indefinable distance; "the gamut deep/and ~~sleepless~~ **termless**" in A33 suggests the vast spaces both spatial and temporal; whilst the use of the word "subscribe" in A35 gives a sense of something being completed, of a transaction into which an individual has entered. The contrast appears too in the way in which Crane urges "until/The seal's ~~mildnrimy~~ **findrinny** sniff of paradise/Is answered in the polar [axis] of grave,/her penniless rich supscriptions" (A35). In the final version, this need for an answer, an idea to which the following section of the poem returns, becomes more ambivalent: "Bequeath us to no earthly shore until/Is answered in the vortex of our grave/The seal's wide spindrift gaze toward paradise" (*CP* 35). A sense of opposites is implied in the use of "paradise" and "polar," but the final version is notable for its shift from vertical to horizontal imagery, from "polar [axis]" to "wide spindrift gaze." This is suggestive of one of the reasons for the changes. Crane described the poems as love poems and sea poems, and whilst in A32 the emphasis was very definitely upon the lover ("a clasp and diapason you danced"), by the time Crane reaches his fourth revision, A35, the sea has taken over ("Take this Sea: whose diapason knells/on scrolls of silver snowy sentences, --"). Thus, the landscape of the poem shifts from the vertical presence of the figure of the lover to the horizontal presence of the wide open sea. The vastness of the sea and its uniqueness (indicated by the capitalization of "Sea") is once again associated with God, just as the lover is associated with something divine. Crane's use of the word "diapason" also represents how he understood experience: the "effort to describe God," an effort which, as he described later, was "limitless and yet forever incomplete," just as the diapason suggests unity and disunity at once (*OML* 192).

And yet by the final version of the poem, the two elements (horizontal and vertical/sea and lover) are brought together, with the suggestion that it is only with the addition of the body of the lover that "the dark confessions" of the sea can be completed; "Adagios of islands, O my Prodigal,/Complete the dark confessions her veins spell" (*CP* 35). The theme that surfaces here, worked through from the early drafts, is similar to that of "Voyages III": the acknowledgement that death and desire are closely linked. This is a result of the process that Roland Barthes describes using the verb as "s'abîmer / to be engulfed." Barthes's comment is useful in analyzing Crane's use of time, and it is worth noting that he defines "engulfment" as an "[o]utburst of annihilation which affects the amorous subject in despair or fulfilment" (*A Lover's Discourse* 10).[22] For the lover, Barthes explains, being engulfed by despair

> is a moment of hypnosis. A suggestion functions, which commands me to swoon without killing myself. Whence, perhaps, the gentleness of the abyss: I have no responsibility here, the act (of dying) is not up to me: I entrust myself, I transmit myself (to whom? to God, to Nature, to everything except to the other) (11).

The lover is caught in a moment out of normative time, "a moment of hypnosis," and between physical states, "to swoon without killing myself." Barthes goes on to say that "on those occasions when I am engulfed, it is because there is no longer any place for me anywhere, not even in death" (11), and these two sentiments strongly echo "Voyages II" and "III." In the final version of "III," "death [...]/Presumes no carnage, but [...]/The silken skilled transmemberment of song" (*CP* 36), and in "II," the speaker requests: "Bind us in time," and "Bequeath us to no earthly shore until/Is answered in the vortex of our grave/The seal's wide spindrift gaze toward paradise" (*CP* 35). In the ambivalence of the concluding lines of the published poem, the speaker is left in something like a temporal utopia, but whereas this feeling comes to Barthes in a moment of despair, when Crane speaks of it he is considering the union of himself and his lover. To rephrase Barthes: the speaker transmits himself (to whom? to God, to Nature, to everything *especially* to the Other).

Death and ecstasy

The concern with death can also be perceived as a concern with the death drive, which, as Lee Edelman has described it, "names what the queer, in the order of the social, is called forth to figure: the negativity opposed to every form of social viability" (*No Future* 9). Just as earlier sections of this chapter showed how an embrace of that kind of negativity actually leads to an increased sense of the future set against an heteronormative understanding of time, so an anticipation of death itself and thus an apparent end to normative time allows Crane to occupy a space that is beyond or outside normative temporality. In its constant consideration and anticipation of death as a key element in his poetic thought, Crane echoes the work of his historical contemporary, Martin Heidegger, whose work *Being and Time* (1927) offers an illuminating parallel interpretation of the relationship between the self and death. In essence, Heidegger argues that it is only in the anticipation of death that the human being's understanding of its place in the world (*Dasein*) can truly – Heidegger says "resolutely" – be comprehended. Heidegger's concept of being is one that experiences temporality in a non-normative way. As Michael Inwood notes, "[r]esolute *Dasein* runs ahead to its death, and reaches back into the past before deciding what to do in the present, the authentic present or *Augenblick*, the moment of vision" (88). This process of temporal movement is described by Heidegger as *ecstatic* temporality:

> The phenomena of toward..., to..., together with...reveal temporality as the ἐκστατικόυ *par excellence*. *Temporality is the primordial, "outside-of-itself" in and for itself.* Thus we call the phenomena of future, having-been, and present the *ecstasies* of temporality (*Being and Time* division II, chapter III, 314).

The term "ecstatic" is useful to employ when dealing with Crane, but in the past it has been a problematic one for reading his work, since Crane's own use of it (he described an out-of-body, ether-inspired experience at the dentist's as "[a] happiness, ecstatic such as I have known only twice in inspirations" (*OML* 92)) has led critics to use it as shorthand for a poetics that seems to encapsulate many moments of exclamation, especially when describing desire. Yingling argues that

> the utopian in Crane signifies a desire to escape history and becomes a site on which homosexuality – as a historical, material condition of modernity – is annihilated. [...] This sexual utopian fantasy is often figured in Crane either as death or as ecstatic dismemberment (43).

Yingling's focus here is very much upon the relationship between history and the ecstatic and, just as my previous chapter offered ways in which Crane's notion of utopia needs to be complicated, so Yingling's use of the idea "ecstatic" here requires re-assessment. Nealon is right to resist the very term ecstatic as it has been used by Yingling and others, arguing that "Crane is a writer whose sexuality is a major factor in motivating him to be neither elegiac (post-historical) nor 'ecstatic' (extra-historical) but deeply engaged with the question of what history is, how it comes about" (*Foundlings* 29). However, what Nealon and Yingling do not acknowledge here through their focus on Crane's undoubted interest in forms of history, is his equal, if not more important, focus upon futurity. In this respect, Crane's adoption of a queer temporality that does not proceed along a linear path makes time in his work far more complex than has been generally assumed. I would retrieve the term "ecstatic," considering it from a Heideggerean perspective, and suggesting its utility for describing Crane's attempts – particularly when embracing negativity and anticipating death – to occupy a temporal space and understanding outside normative time. Just as Edelman offers a resistance to heterosexual futurity and progress, so Heidegger's identification of an authentic self that is able to acknowledge its own place in the world is in itself a resistance:

> Primordial and authentic temporality temporalizes itself out of the authentic future, and indeed in such a way that, futurally having-been, it first arouses the present. *The primary phenomenon of primordial and authentic temporality is the future* (*Being and Time*, division II, chapter III, 314).

In asserting its authentic self – which it does in the *Augenblick*, or "moment of vision" – Dasein rejects the *"they-self,"* that is to say the everyday self, affected by mundane time, things, and words of the people around it (*Being and Time*, division I, chapter IV, 125). Its place, and the place that Crane aspires to inhabit, is the ecstatic one, which allows him to look backwards, forwards and around him in the present and assert this experience in his writing. Such an aspiration or moment of vision is an assertion of the same kind of self-consciousness to which I have drawn attention. Crane's own "they" is the normative world he rejects. And with it, the narratives of that world that are inevitably bound up in its histories, are rejected too. Both in his drafts and in the final versions of the sequence, "Voyages" frequently finds holes and explores images of recurrence and problematic visions of completion, whilst *The Bridge*, in its rewriting of history as myth, challenges expectations. In "Atlantis," the speaker asks "[t]hy pardon for this history, whitest Flower,/O Answerer of all, – Anemone" (*CP* 107), suggesting the inadequacy of any kind of history, and the need instead to assert something temporary, such as a flower's lifespan, or even something unwritten, since this white flower can suggest a blank page.

Crane's description of completion is frequently anything but complete, and one of the key governing features of *The Bridge*, as it is in "Voyages," is kinesis; something which is clear from the concluding sections of each poem. In "Voyages," the final imagery of "VI" suggests a continuity. The verbs are often in the form of present participles, and there is no end to "[s]till fervid covenant"; and "rainbows twine continual hair." The final stanza also presents a paradox: just as a reader is left to wonder whether "[t]he imaged Word" will ever release the "[h]ushed willows anchored in its glow," so too the very final lines seem twisted in deliberate complication. These two lines seem destined to oppose each other for ever, a textual realization of Crane's ideal for the lovers, for the "unbetrayable reply" that might be offered has an "accent no farewell can know." In the first place, it is an unusual reversal, with the reply mentioned before the farewell, but there is also no sense of completion here. The "farewell" may be spoken, but the reply cannot be understood, leaving the initial speaker waiting, incomplete.

Several sections of *The Bridge* also resist completion. "Cape Hatteras," the last section to be completed, concludes with the movement onwards of the speaker, hand-in-hand with Walt Whitman, whilst "Atlantis," the concluding section of *The Bridge* as published, has different markers denoting incomplete time; "the prophecy," "this history," "beyond time." And finally, when time seems to be drawn towards a union with space, the union is left open; "Is it Cathay,/Now pity steeps the grass and rainbows ring/The serpent with the eagle in the leaves...?" (*CP* 108). By contrast, regardless of its foregoing dislocation, *The Waste Land*, the poem to which *The Bridge* responds, ends with a shoring of fragments intended to bring about a semblance of peace, and its "Shantih shantih shantih" does act as a legitimate reply to the preceding imperatives "Datta. Dayadhvam. Damyata" (Eliot, *Collected Poems*, 79). There is a conclusion here, however unconvincing or temporary it may be, whereas *The Bridge* entertains no such closure. Instead, it ends with more movement: "[w]hispers antiphonal in azure swing" (*CP* 108).

Beyond time

Rather than suggest that the lack of a union between time and space at the end of *The Bridge* was a result of a creative failure on Crane's part, as some critics have done, I want to suggest instead that this disunion points towards a concern with materiality within Crane's work and within modernism. Like other modernist writers who emphasized the value of placing their faith in things rather than abstractions, Crane's poetry seeks to find in his words the reliability of material objects. This is the Crane who celebrated "the incarnate word" in "Voyages," and the wonder of having seen "the Word made Flesh" in the relationship that was the inspiration for much of the sequence. Yet it is also the Crane who acknowledges the difficulty of creating material language, who investigates the possibilities of spiritual or mystical means by which to create and speak this "Word," and who explores the ways in which the eroticized body may take part in that process of creation. It is this conflict between the material and immaterial that leads Crane to confront a problem of epistemology that is reliant upon experience and experiment rather than the acquisition of the knowledge of the academy.

5
Empiricism, Mysticism, and a Queer Form of Knowledge

One evening in 1926, Crane's friend and fellow writer Jean Toomer was standing on the platform of the 66th Street "L" station in New York City, waiting for a train. All at once, he began to have a mystical, out-of-body experience:

> I was changing. Throughout my entire presence I was changing. It seemed I was being taken apart, unmeshed and remeshed. I seemed to become malleable and flowing. My very substance was in motion ("The Experience" 34).[1]

After a while, Toomer felt himself gaining new insight, a kind of clairvoyance, and the sense that he was being enveloped by another body – "a new form with new faculties" (37) – which afforded him "a dimensionally higher consciousness" (37). Eventually, Toomer boarded the L train, still in the midst of this mystical experience, and was able to look around him with pity at the way in which his fellow passengers were so downtrodden and deprived of the insight he now enjoyed. He was also intrigued to know whether his new state was obvious to the other people on the train.

> One man, happening to glance my way, seemed curious. He kept looking as though trying to size me up. Evidently he was scrutinizing my body only, assuming that he was thereby taking my measure. No doubt of it, he was equating my body with myself. What a queer sensation it gave me to be taken for my body when I was so starkly aware that I was a being.
>
> Suppose you were carrying an umbrella and saw someone looking at it, taking it to be your body. Or suppose a man looked at your chest but believed he was seeing your face. Not only would you have queer

sensations; you would know that should that person have dealings with you he would behave at variance with your reality and with his own better intelligence. Whether he meant to or not, he would mistreat you, and himself (49).

Toomer, like Crane, was a marginalized figure, and his "out-of-body" experience and the articulation of that experience has real resonance with Crane's concerns about the material and immaterial and the conflict between experience and knowledge – the dichotomies with which this chapter is engaged.

The fact that Toomer perceived his body to be scrutinized by the other man speaks not merely to the difference that Toomer considered might be obvious as a result of his higher consciousness. Unspoken here is Toomer's own African-American identity. Since he did not immediately appear to be of "Negro" descent, the man's close attention to Toomer's body is all the more disconcerting, as if *he* is the one who has been given insight, rather than Toomer, and the emphasis is upon the body being a site of difficulty and challenge.[2] Toomer uses the adjective "queer" in his repeated reference to the "queer sensations" that someone might feel if their body was inaccurately perceived. This might not have been intended by him to have sexual connotations (although the way in which this unknown man continues to "size [Toomer] up" could be perceived as the beginning of a cruise), but it certainly does suggest that Toomer thinks the man perceives something different or "alternative" about his appearance.[3] Finally, in the way that Toomer describes how the man misapprehends the body in front of him, suggesting that the man might look at his chest but think he is looking at his face, Toomer presents the man as looking at him only obliquely or askance while Toomer is still in his state of elevated consciousness. This kind of perspective is a characteristic feature of the writings and discussions of alternative dimensions, challenging the normative relational perception of bodies within space, and offering thereby a revised version of knowledge about the world.

Crane also experienced moments of "a dimensionally higher consciousness," and these occasions, together with his reading of P.D. Ouspensky's work about the fourth dimension and his correspondence with Toomer led him to consider ways in which a mystical experience of the world and the writing about it might be aligned with queer experience and writing. Unlike previous chapters, which focused upon the ways in which Crane's poetry reflected his experience of the world, the examination of materiality in this chapter also considers how his work appeared to others. In fact, his frequent privileging of intense but immaterial experiences over the materiality of knowledge resulted in critical charges of artistic and personal failure from others. However, Crane's epistemology, inflected by his reading of Ouspensky, was significantly different to his critics' normative understandings of what knowledge was and how it should be accumulated. Crane's own conception of knowledge and representation of the material body was challenged by the serious concern he came to have about language's capacity to represent something with authenticity. At the same time, Crane's concern with describing the material and the immaterial in his poetry must be read against the ongoing discussion in modernist culture regarding what Ian F.A. Bell has called "the new materiality," in which Crane and his community had become engaged in the 1920s. Analysis of Crane's attempts to go beyond the material through a dimensional aesthetic can lead to a new reading of the way in which Crane uses his "materials" in *The Bridge*, particularly technological ones, and suggest reasons to re-engage with those critics who deemed this "mystical synthesis of 'America'" (*OML* 131) and its author a failure.

The difficulties of experience and knowledge

In a letter to Jean Toomer in 1924, Crane explained that he tried "to make my poems experiences" (*OML* 192). In doing so, Crane attempted both to describe powerful experiences within the poems, and to make the poems experiences for his readers. As I argued previously, Crane attempted to do this by making a material connection with those readers, particularly in his use of chiastic tropes. But Crane's language can be seen to be material in other ways too, and the juxtaposition of the material with the immaterial is designed to provide a linguistic and sensory jolt to a reader – a certain kind of "experience" – and gestures towards the deregulating process identified in my third chapter, a bending of the rules of language. A few examples might include: "the nights opening/Chant pyramids" (*CP* 19), from "Lachrymae Christi" (1924–1925/1925), "had I walked/The dozen particular decimals of time?" *(CP* 21), from "Passage" (1925/1926), "The portent wound in corridors of shells" (*CP* 33), from "At Melville's Tomb" (1925/1926), "Already snow submerges an iron year" (*CP* 44), from "To Brooklyn Bridge," and "'Make thy love sure – to weave whose song we ply!'" (*CP* 105), from "Atlantis."

Crane was aware that his frequent combination of the material and immaterial could provide a challenge to readers. This technique was part of the reason Harriet Monroe requested an exegesis of "At Melville's Tomb," and when Crane wrote an explanation of his work for Eugene O'Neill, in the hope that the dramatist would write an introduction to *White Buildings*, he identified this strategy as a major element in his poetics. He hoped, he said, "to go *through* the combined materials of the poem," and so proposed a passage through both space and through material objects ("General Aims and Theories," *CPSL* 220). Whilst Crane understood language to have the potential to be material (challenging an epistemological understanding of matter), he also understood poetry to be a form of knowledge. Writing to Gorham Munson in 1926, he stated that "[p]oetry, in so far as the metaphysics of any absolute knowledge extends, is simply the concrete <u>evidence</u> of the <u>experience</u> of a recognition (<u>knowledge</u> if you like)" (*OML* 232). Such a collision of the "concrete" or material (identified as knowledge) with the intangible or immaterial (the "experience") would bring Crane into conflict with friends and critics, who sought to understand him – and thus position him – on their own terms. They asserted that Crane's empirical strategy was an insufficient grounding for a poet. Repeatedly, and over a long period of time that extended beyond Crane's death, critics such as Gorham Munson, Malcolm Cowley, and William Carlos Williams faulted what they saw as Crane's lack of knowledge, which failed to support his experience as it was detailed in his work. As I suggest, they each had particular reasons for picking on this aspect of Crane's "education."

Crane thought that a poet required "a sufficiently universal basis of experience" ("General Aims and Theories," *CP* 218), and that "[t]he poet's concern must be, as always, self-discipline toward a formal integration of experience" ("Modern Poetry," *CP* 260). His difference from his fellow poets was that for him, issues of experience were not separate from issues of knowledge. His letter of June 16, 1924 to Toomer is characteristic of the way in which he juxtaposed knowledge and experience. On the one hand, Crane explains that his current definition of experience is "the effort to describe God. Only the effort, – limitless and yet forever incomplete" (*OML* 192). A few lines later, describing his love affair with Emil Opffer, Crane wrote that he had come to "know that such a love would forever be impossible again – that it would never be met with again, if only because one knew that one would never have the intensity to respond to a repitition [sic] of such even though it seemed worthy enough!" (*OML* 193). Crane goes on to provide a first draft of "Voyages IV" (then entitled only "Voyages"). The first stanza of that draft reads:

> Whose counted smile of hours and days, suppose
> I know as spectrum the sea and greet
> now vastly entering the reach and swarm of wings
> unknown to me; –
> from palms the severe
> chilled albatross's high immutability
> advances still no stream of greater love
> than, singing, this mortality in singleness
> aflow through clay immortally to you... (qtd. in *OML* 193)

Crane told Toomer that this poem represented "the initial exaltation" (*OML* 193) of his experience with Opffer, and so if we take him at his word – and records of Crane's drafts suggest this is indeed the earliest extant draft – this poem represents an unfiltered version of Crane's experience, or as unfiltered as a poem can be. The draft is concordant with his stated desire in this same letter "to make [his] poems experiences." The poem shows how Crane persisted in bringing together ideas of experience and knowledge, and hints at the non-normative concept of knowledge that sets Crane apart from many of his readers.

This draft of the first stanza does offer moments that hint at epistemological certainty: the "counted smile," regulation measurements of "hours and days," the "immutability" of the albatross, and the knowledge of "mortality." These might be considered unchangeable things, even facts. However, Crane complicates the stanza by compromising the basis of knowledge when he writes "suppose/I know" and admits to experiencing "the reach and swarm of wings/unknown to me." He also blurs the boundaries between the material and immaterial when he describes how mortality can "aflow through clay immortally to you..." Crane challenges the idea of knowledge by suggesting firstly that the knowledge gained from experience can be more valuable than any other kind, allowing the learner access to something important from something so immediate, and secondly that knowledge can fail – whatever they read or learn cannot prepare people for certain things.

Yet for writers like Munson, Williams, Cowley, and Allen Tate, Crane's main problem was knowledge. Munson argued that "he [did] not know enough" ("Hart Crane" 49), Cowley explained that "although he read intensely, rather than widely, there were immense gaps in his knowledge of things we took for granted" (*A Second Flowering* 192), and Tate was later to say that "[w]ith the instinct of genius [Crane] read the great poets, but he never acquired an objective mastery of any literature, or even of the history of his country" ("Hart Crane" 311). Williams meanwhile claimed that Crane

> didn't write as low as he knew, or should have known, his life to be. Instead he continually reached "up," out of what he *knew* to that which he didn't know. [...] He grew vague instead of setting himself to describe in detail – Achilles [sic] greave and shield. His eyes seem to me often to have been blurred by "vision" when they should have been held hard, as hard as he could hold them, on the object –
> [...] Crane appears to me often to have neglected the equal objectivity of words in making up his compositions. Edges, facets often escape him – to his undoing ("Hart Crane [1899–1932]" 34).

Crane's interior form, explored in my third chapter, ran contrary to Williams's notion that words should have "equal objectivity." Williams is concerned with how words should be equally "objective," but Crane's strategy was to destabilize that objectivity, granting words subjective rather than objective status by making them accrue different meanings according to the context in which they were placed in the poem. Williams's comments link Crane's knowledge with material concerns, and he equates knowledge not just with objectivity, but also with "[e]dges" and "facets." The kind of knowledge that Williams, Cowley, Tate, and Munson claim that Crane should have is one that contains "edges," which means knowledge that can be grasped, an academic knowledge that might be found in a book, for instance. It is certain: once the edge or limit to it can be found, then work can be done to extend the knowledge that exists. Since Crane does not subscribe to this kind of hard-edged knowledge, what he knows is much more difficult to discern. Williams and the others therefore were concerned that the edges of Crane's knowledge should be found, and if they were not obvious, then they should be imposed. Crane knew very well what they were proposing:

> If this "knowledge," as you call it, were so sufficiently organized as to dominate the limitations of my personal experience (consciousness) then I would probably find myself automatically writing under its "classic" power of dictation, and under that circumstance might be incidentally as philosophically "contained" as you might wish me to be. That would mean "serenity" to you because the abstract basis of

my work would have been familiarized to you before you read a word of my poetry (*OML* 233).

From his skepticism at Munson's use of the term "knowledge" as if it were a euphemism, "as you call it," to the assertion of the "limitations" to which Munson has clearly alluded, to the sense that Munson wishes Crane to be "contained" and "familiarized," there is a clear sense of Crane's outrage, and it is significant that this letter occasioned a break in correspondence that was never really renewed. Munson's comments about Crane's lack of knowledge were thinly veiled in code, but spoke of homophobic intent. He criticized Crane's "highly specialized subjectivity" (48), and wrote that Crane's

> intuitions, while valuable, are allied to *guessing*. We know that intuitions may be mistaken or even *diseased*. We know that something must be added to them – and that is certitude – to make them knowledge (50, emphases added).

It is noticeable that Munson's comments are vague. In making these comments he provides no textual substance to support them. Merrill Cole provides a convincing reason for this when he argues that Munson's refusal to identify with Crane's style "is a sanctioned ignorance, for to add specificity to Crane's 'ecstasies' would mean to implicate himself in a homoerotic form of knowing" (124). Given that Munson had been one of his first heterosexual friends to be trusted with the knowledge of Crane's queerness,[4] Munson's comments must have seemed to Crane like a particularly wounding betrayal, and it is certain that he resented Munson's choice to pass judgment on Crane the man, rather than Crane the writer.[5] As Sedgwick has argued in her discussions about the role of the closet, "the *special* centrality of homophobic oppression in the twentieth century […] has resulted from its inextricability from the question of knowledge and processes of knowing in modern Western culture at large" (*Epistemology of the Closet* 33–34). In Crane's case, homophobia was expressed through another kind of knowledge itself, combating the "epistemology of the closet" (or Crane's being out of it), with the knowledge of the academy or a group of like-minded intellectuals. That strategy, expressed in Williams's critique, ensured that Crane's work was surrounded by "edges" and that he was "contained," putting him back into the closet so that the knowledge of his sexuality, which Crane made no effort to conceal, could be hidden away.[6] As Crane understood, when he considered Munson's suggestion as proposing "automatic [...] writing under its 'classic' power of dictation," the underlying motivation of Munson and the others was to remove Crane's own voice from his work, effectively silencing him.[7]

Radical empiricism

The process by which Crane negotiated experience can be profitably compared to the "radical empiricism" (or pragmatism) promoted by William James. Even though James wrote some of his key essays outlining his philosophy in the early 1900s, Crane would have come into contact with his work in a number of places, not least in P.D. Ouspensky's *Tertium Organum* (first translated into English in 1920), in which James is quoted at length. In addition, Susan Currell has noted how "the 1920s marked the popularisation of the ideas of pragmatism more widely than ever before" (9), whilst David Bromwich has observed that "[b]ecause of its use by the pragmatists [William] James and [John] Dewey, 'experience,' in the 1920s, was a word charged with specifically American associations. It was apt to serve a common argument that the individual – most of all the individual in a democracy – possessed among his inward resources a field of experiment sufficient to define an idea of freedom" (43). The appeal of a native philosophy would have been particularly attractive to Crane, as would the emphasis within it upon self-sufficiency because of his use of a poetic logic that ran contrary to the normative and was intended to give language a sense of freedom. Radical empiricism is also valuable in describing Crane's antithetical resistance to the kind of knowledge formation that Munson and the others understood as the only legitimate one. Whereas Williams highlighted the need for hard edges, James's radical empiricism describes a blurring of those edges. James drew a contrast between his concept of radical empiricism and mosaics, observing that mosaics have a bedding of cement in order to hold their constituent pieces together.

> In radical empiricism there is no bedding; it is as if the pieces clung together by their edges, the transitions experienced between them forming their cement. [...] [T]he metaphor serves to symbolize the fact that Experience itself, taken at large, can grow by its edges. That one moment of it proliferates into the next by transitions which, whether conjunctive or disjunctive, continue the experiential tissue, can not, I contend, be denied. Life is in the transitions as much as in the terms connected; often, indeed, it seems to be there more emphatically [...] (1180–81).[8]

Crane's work particularly attends to the transitions between experiences, and the overlap here from one experience to another can be regarded as exemplary of what Crane himself called "the real connective experience" (*OML* 232), representing a queer strategy that challenges the normative and material linking of one experience to another, and instead offers something much more fluid and immaterial, a sense of experience that recalls Jean Toomer's out-of-body episode that left him "malleable and flowing." It is worth recalling here Nealon's assertion that in Crane's poetry "interstices between moments or sensations or perceptions constitute the realm of experience most worth poetic attention, because [they can be] the possible source of new and shared knowledge about desire and change" (*Foundlings* 31). Just as Crane's presentation of temporal gaps distorted temporal linearity and offered a reconceptualization of time, so knowledge, or ideas about knowledge, could be derived from the conjunctions between experiences.

"Passage" (1925/1926) exemplifies Crane's exploration of these transitional moments, and offers a commentary upon and challenge to the criticisms of Crane's "lack" of knowledge.[9] It is a poem that describes a personal rite of passage and also an aesthetic one. In her letter rejecting the poem for publication in the *Dial*, Marianne Moore suggested that "[i]ts multiform content accounts, I suppose, for what seems to us a lack of simplicity and cumulative force" (*OML* 205). Moore's description of the poem as "multiform" suggests something of the mosaic-like quality of "Passage." There are various unattributed speeches in the poem and a concerted effort to provide imagistic divisions: "the cedar leaf divides the sky"…"The evening was a spear in the ravine"…"had I walked/The dozen particular decimals of time?" (*CP* 21).[10] But there is a pattern, as the poem moves in time from dawn, through the afternoon, and into the evening. The poem also contains points of confluence between the material and immaterial, such as "Memory, committed to the page, had broke," which have their correspondence in the form of James's mosaic, as one piece of the mosaic meets a transitional space where no cement exists.[11]

With the prominence given in the poem to images of division and reduction ("My memory I left in a ravine"), the speaker seeks to challenge pre-existing knowledge and forms of knowledge acquisition, and reduce the self ("I was promised an improved infancy"). Thomas Yingling has argued that the poem represents "a secure return to the origin of knowledge and self-authorization that has before been unavailable to the speaker" (127). That Crane is also addressing his critics' assumptions about his knowledge is clear from the final three stanzas (*CP* 21–22).

The need to return to "the origin of knowledge" is figured by the Edenic image of the serpent. The poem also attempts to provide the kind of "self-authorization" that Crane would shortly afterwards propose in his letter to Munson, rejecting his idea of "knowledge." The "stolen book" represents on the one hand the kind of knowledge that Munson and others proposed for Crane yet also considered him never able to acquire. It is the knowledge acclaimed by Eliot and his disciples, and then New Criticism. This is academic knowledge represented by the laurel, a plant which *Webster's* defines as being "found about the Mediterranean, and [...] early used to crown the victor in the games of Apollo. At a later period, academic honors were indicated by a crown of laurel, with the fruit" (*WUD* 756). Crane proposes to "argue" with it, offering "transience" instead of the hard reality of the book. In addition, there is a biographical slant here, since the "stolen book" was a real one, Crane's smuggled copy of *Ulysses*, the French publication of which he had subscribed to in 1922, and which was brought over to him from Paris by Gorham Munson. In 1923, Crane wrote a flurry of letters to his family and friends outraged that someone had stolen his copy of Joyce's book whilst he was in staying in Cleveland. Langdon Hammer sees in this alleged theft the culmination of "the sexual subtexts entailed in the shifting alliances of American modernism in the mid-1920s" (*Hart Crane and Allen Tate* 137). In this reading, Crane perceived the embrace of *Ulysses* by Tate and Eliot, both of whom he considered part of a literary (and perhaps sexual) community to which he also belonged, as a betrayal. Hammer argues that Tate came to read *The Waste Land* as a poem that rejected the epic and visionary.

> For Tate, this reading of the poem provides a foundation for a community of authors dedicated to an aesthetic of impersonality, authors bound together by the classical wisdom that promotes an accommodation to limits over romantic excess. For Crane, this is the foundation for a heterosexual community that excludes him and his desires, not incidentally but necessarily and expressly, even programmatically. This community is "treasonous," moreover, because it cancels the promises Crane once believed it had made to him. Modernism, when it calls for a "renunciation" that *even Joyce demands*, crosses over to the side of the social order that required the suppression of *Ulysses* itself (137–38).

Crane was well aware of the need to find a way to acknowledge but go through Eliot's "aesthetic of impersonality," and in "Passage" the book is both the real thieved copy of *Ulysses* and a metonym for this academic community that "excludes him and his desires." Crane therefore rejects the fixity of such knowledge and instead maintains an aesthetic of "transience," the immaterial points of transition between the mosaic tiles that are reproduced in the collage style of this poem. The speaker's/Crane's decision to "argue" therefore marks the "self-authorization" that Yingling identifies. Crane explains how the misreading of his work means he is "fleeing/Under the constant wonder of your eyes," as the readers of the academic community fail to understand him. He contrasts the serpent that "swam a vertex" (where a vertex means "[t]he point in any figure opposite to, and further from, the base" (*WUD* 1471), and thus diametrically opposed to normative knowledge), with "the Ptolemies," which represent both the astronomer Ptolemy, whose geocentric model of the world was proven to be inaccurate "knowledge," and the 3rd century BCE dynasties of Egypt who created the library of Alexandria for scholars; and the scholarly knowledge Crane rejects. In his use of the serpent and its associations with the forbidden fruit of knowledge, Crane is instead arguing for the place of experience, and experience that *includes* knowledge gained from desires, just as the academic community *excludes* it. That experience is described by the "transience" in which the speaker says he is justified. Tim Dean has noted that "whereas the ellipses of Eliot's nonmimetic realist aesthetic may be brought into proper perspective by research or erudition, no form or degree of knowledge ameliorates Crane's difficulty, since his aesthetic concerns ontology at the expense of epistemology" (92). Whilst my frequent use of *Webster's Unabridged Dictionary* and historical documents throughout this book show that I implicitly dispute Dean's idea that Crane's "difficulty" cannot be elucidated through research, his assertion that Crane privileges ontology over epistemology does approach the argument I am making here that Crane places epistemology secondary to the sense of being in the world; though I regard it therefore as a privileging of phenomenology over epistemology. In this sense, the basis for Crane's knowledge is sensuous experience, and this means that Crane is consciously placing himself quite outside the modernist community to which he normally felt that he belonged. Setting Crane against William Carlos Williams, Roy Harvey Pearce claims that Crane "strove to be the great epistemological realist of the American epic," whereas Williams wanted to be "the great nominalist" (111). Certainly, as I argued in my second chapter, Crane frequently embraced abstraction rather than the "things" to which Williams held fast, and as this chapter will demonstrate, the conflict over knowledge was evident in these two poets' differing attitudes to materiality.

Yingling is right to note how Crane is "justified only 'in transience,' in the materiality of history, the materiality of the signifier, the materiality of the body" (129), since none of these things are sure in the poem, with memory being lost, the semiotic confusion of Crane's multivalent diction, and the body becoming immaterial ("I had joined the entrainments of the wind"). However, whereas Yingling determines that "[o]ne cannot overstate how far short of its desire for self-authorization "Passage" falls" (130), the foregoing discussion shows how in fact this poem marks a turning point (another definition of "vertex" (*WUD 1471*)) in Crane's relationship with his critics. The final line of the poem, in which "Memory, committed to the page, had broke," shows Crane once again demonstrating that it is the transitions or immaterial parts of experience that are most reliable, for as soon as that immaterial knowledge – in the form of memory – becomes material or enters the academic community that sought to marginalize Crane, it is broken.

The new materiality

The leader of this community, or as Crane called him, "our divine object of 'envy'" (*OML* 90), T.S. Eliot, was never far from Crane's thoughts during the 1920s. David Bromwich has also observed a number of textual echoes of *The Waste Land* in "Passage" (48–49). Given Eliot's profound influence upon Crane, such parallels are not surprising, even as late in Crane's development as 1925–1926, but this section of the chapter will address Eliot's influence by arguing that in his continued attempts to address and go beyond the elder poet, Crane adopted the teachings of mysticism and writings about the fourth dimension. By 1922, when he read *The Waste Land*, Crane was prepared to use a strategy that emphasized the immaterial world over the material to respond to and challenge Eliot's work, and he put it to use in "Faustus and Helen."

Crane's engagement with ideas of the fourth dimension and higher consciousness was stimulated by an experience very similar to that of Jean Toomer's, which opened this chapter. Like Toomer, Crane's experience began in an everyday situation – when he visited the dentist.

> [U]nder the influence of aether and amnesia my mind spiraled to a kind of seventh heaven of consciousness and egoistic dance among the seven spheres – and something like an objective voice kept saying to me – "You have the higher consciousness – you have the higher consciousness. This is something that very few have. This is what is called genius." [...] A happiness, ecstatic such as I have known only

twice in "inspirations" came over me. I felt the two worlds. And at once. As the bore went into my tooth I was able to follow its long revolution as detached as a spectator at a funeral. [...] [S]ince this adventure in the dentist's chair, I feel a new confidence in myself (*OML* 92–93).

Later in Toomer's experience, he too heard a "voice," alerting him to the importance of the experience.[12] And Toomer also found himself as "detached" as Crane, explaining that he felt "decentred, off to the side as a spectator" (35). Unlike Toomer, though, Crane immediately makes the connection between his "higher consciousness" and his writing. This may be partly because by the time he wrote about his 1926 experience Toomer had become disenchanted with the literary world and was following – and subsequently teaching – the mystical philosophy of G.I. Gurdjieff.[13] It was also partly due to the fact that Crane had been under the influence of Waldo Frank, whose view that America was "a mystic Word" (10), was to correspond well with the views expressed by Ouspensky.[14]

Shortly after this experience, Crane read Ouspensky's *Tertium Organum*. The book, loaned to him by a friend in Cleveland, blends mathematics, philosophy, and mysticism to argue that man is capable of developing a higher state of consciousness in which he casts off ordinary logic and replaces it with "*intuitive* logic – the logic of infinity, the logic of ecstasy" (261). Casting around for a way in which to describe his own poetic process, such a term would have been attractive to Crane, and Tim Dean has suggested that Crane was indeed inspired by Ouspensky to coin his "logic of metaphor" when he wrote his 1925 essay "General Aims and Theories" (see Dean 86). In his "Introduction" to Ouspensky's book, Claude Bragdon claimed that "[s]uch a title says, in effect: 'Here is a book which will reorganize all knowledge'" (1). Ouspensky finds substance for his claims both in mathematics and in philosophy, contending that beyond the phenomenal world is to be found the noumenal world theorized by Kant. Ouspensky suggests that artists, including poets, are capable of understanding this, and that by developing and strengthening a "*poetical* understanding of the world" it is possible to perceive that "behind phenomena which appear to us similar, often stand noumena so different that only by our blindness is it possible to account for our idea of the similarity of those phenomena" (161).

When Crane wrote to Allen Tate about *Tertium Organum* – presumably referring to the events in the dentist's chair – he remarked that "[i]ts corroboration of several experiences in consciousness that I have had gave it particular interest" (*OML* 130).[15] But Crane came to see Ouspensky's writings as valuable in another way too. His reading of *Tertium Organum* coincided with his first encounter with *The Waste Land*, and his letters between 1922 and 1923 show how he is determined to address and challenge Eliot's work. To Tate he wrote that

> I have been facing him for four years, – and while I haven't discovered a weak spot yet in his armour, – I flatter myself a little lately that I have discovered a safe tangent to strike which, if I can possibly explain the position, – goes through him toward a different goal (*OML* 89).

And he told Munson that he regarded Eliot "as a point of departure toward an almost complete reverse of direction" (*OML* 117). The language which Crane uses already suggests the influence of fourth dimension writings, couched in the terms of geometry that were common in a philosophy that frequently observed how mathematics proved that the fourth dimension existed even if, ordinarily, people were not able to see it. Crane explained more about this "safe tangent" when he told Munson that

> I would apply as much of his erudition and technique as I can absorb and assemble toward a more positive, or (if [I] must put it so in a sceptical age) ecstatic goal. [...] I feel that Eliot ignores certain spiritual events and possibilities as real and powerful now as, say in the time of Blake (*OML* 117–18).

Citing Blake here confirms that Crane was considering mysticism when he referred to "certain spiritual events and possibilities," and Crane believed that he could "strike" Eliot because at the conclusion of "Tradition and the Individual Talent" (1919), Eliot said that his essay "propose[d] to halt at the frontier of metaphysics or mysticism, and confine itself to such practical conclusions as can be applied by the responsible person interested in poetry" (59).[16] Crane, therefore, sought to be "[ir]responsible." When he claimed that he would "go[..] through" Eliot, he saw that he must "absorb" the kind of knowledge ("erudition and technique") to which Eliot's work directed him, and then strike out in his own direction. Once again, Crane prioritized experience over knowledge. When he read in *Tertium Organum* that "[t]he sign of the growth of the emotions is the liberation of them from the *personal* element, and their sublimation on the higher planes" (221), he saw a clear connection with Eliot's notion that the bad poet was too "personal," and that "[p]oetry is not a turning loose of emotion, but an escape from emotion; it is not the expression of personality, but an escape from personality" ("Tradition and the Individual Talent" 58). Crane aligned himself with the emotional growth that Ouspensky described by using, rather than dismissing his experience, and yet he also acknowledged the worth of the "escape from personality" that Eliot advocated. In "General Aims and Theories," Crane wrote that he "would like to establish [the poem] as free from my own personality as from any chance evaluation on the reader's part. (This is of course an impossibility, but it is a characteristic worth mentioning)" (*CP* 220). Crane had read Ouspensky's assertion that "[i]n no case are emotions merely organs of feeling *for feeling's* sake: they are all organs of knowledge" (219), and in his determined attempts to reverse Eliot's pessimism, Crane aspired to use his own emotional knowledge. In this aspiration, and in his commitment to the kind of detachment (or impersonality) that he found in his experience of higher consciousness, Crane sought to uncover the "certain spiritual events and possibilities," which he said Eliot ignored. He realized that he could both adhere to Eliot and go "through" him. As Langdon Hammer has reasoned, "Crane's opposition to Eliot was essential to establish his difference, but also his similarity – his right to speak on the same platform, to address the same audience" (*Hart Crane and Allen Tate* 142).

"For the Marriage of Faustus and Helen," which Crane wrote between 1922 and 1923, was very much directed at the kind of audience that appreciated Eliot, just as in the poem Crane also tried to refute him. I suggested previously that the poem can be seen as offering a queered *vision* of the world, but Crane's affirmations in the poem are also endorsements of a queer materiality. R.W.B. Lewis is right to observe the irony in this respect of Crane's beginning the poem with a quotation from Ben Jonson, a writer whom Eliot had celebrated in *The Sacred Wood*, but also notes how the scene from *The Alchemist* in which this passage appears is one of deception, "a flamboyant parody of the meeting between Faustus and Helen in Marlowe's play" (91). The poem thereby gives the impression that it contains the kind of academic knowledge that is typical of Eliot. But this is not the case. In the first part of "Faustus and Helen" in particular, Crane employs his "emotional knowledge" in order to offer a fusion of the old and new materiality that he found in Ouspensky and used to work "through" Eliot. Ian F. A. Bell has contended that

> [a]t its most fundamental, the new materiality evades the idealist pitfall of eschewing the material world entirely by offering itself

as apprehendable and non-apprehendable simultaneously. Herein lies its attractiveness for Modernism's cultivation of fresh space and fresh languages, for an art needing the contemporaneity of scientific and psychical research and its opening up of the extra-sensory world while remaining discontented with the transcendental hues of its idealism (69).

In its use of Paterian aesthetics and engagement with the body, Part I of "Faustus and Helen" describes an experience that is both visible and invisible. Despite critics' assertions that Crane's poetry attempts to transcend into a higher dimension (see, for example, Winters 102–8), Bell's comments are instructive in suggesting that poetry like Crane's opens up to material difference, whilst also "remaining discontented with [...] idealism." In his fusion of the material and immaterial in this poem, Crane offers something illicit, the "correlative[s]" (*OML* 125), again sourcing his language from Eliot and his "objective correlative,"[17] that he finds between Helen's historical period and the present also paralleled with the connections between lovers of the same sex. In doing so, Crane was also adopting "the mythical method," which Eliot had termed the technique in *Ulysses*, by which he observed Joyce "manipulating a continuous parallel between contemporaneity and antiquity" ("*Ulysses*, Order, and Myth" 372–73).

When, in "For the Marriage of Faustus and Helen," Crane writes that *"[t]here is the world dimensional for/those untwisted by the love of things/ irreconcilable..."* (*CP* 26), he seems to foreclose the possibility of same-sex relations, but this is an assertion he subsequently challenges both with the ellipsis that follows "irreconcilable," and with the following line "And yet" and later "There is some way." Yet he is also suggesting that such illicit material connections should not occur in a "dimensional"/normative world. Sara Ahmed has described how the proximity of certain bodies – she describes a poem by Countee Cullen in which two boys, one white, one black, are seen walking arm in arm – "produces a queer effect" (169). Ahmed argues that

> queer tables and other queer objects support proximity between those who are supposed to live on parallel lines, *as points that should not meet*. A queer object hence makes contact possible. Or, to be more precise, a queer object would have a surface that supports such contact. The contact is bodily, and it unsettles that line that divides spaces as worlds, thereby creating other kinds of connections where unexpected things can happen (169).

In the case of "Faustus and Helen," the poem itself can be seen as the queer object, its linguistic surface the basis for a meeting of material and immaterial that also figures queer contact in the fourth and fifth stanzas of Part I (*CP* 27). The italicized lines that begin *"There is the world dimensional for those untwisted..."* mark a boundary between the material world and the immaterial one and the subsequent fusion of "the two worlds [...] at once," as Crane described his experience in the dentist's chair. The boundary "line" between the two is being, in Ahmed's terms, "unsettled" through a queerness that *twists* together the mythical method and the possibilities of the fourth dimension to result in a kind of material disorientation where contact occurs that "should not" happen. Crane suggests that the "undimensional" possibility of these two stanzas is the result of *forgetting* the fare and transfer, and getting to a place *without recall*, just as his own personal experience of a higher consciousness was also the result of forgetting or being "under the influence of aether and amnesia." The body of the Other is here in the form of eyes that are "[s]till flickering with those prefigurations," as if they have not yet taken on material form and are not fully apprehended. In my first chapter I showed how in this section of the poem the Paterian appreciation of beauty and the fleeting impression was related to same-sex attraction, and here too in his blending of immaterial and material and his emphasis upon a crucial moment figured by the description of clear arteries, Crane suggests the possibility of queer contact.

Helen will reappear later in the poem, but here – just as he would in "Voyages" (where it is the sea) and in "The Dance" in *The Bridge* (where it is Pocahontas) – Crane uses the female body as the basis for that queer contact. Helen is both the artistic object and the queer object. The clear arteries and "bartered blood" (where "bartered" means "exchanging one commodity for another (*WUD* 110)," and Helen is merely something to be bought and sold) refer not just to Helen's presence, but to that of the male lover. In his desire that "before its arteries turn dark/I would have you meet this bartered blood," the speaker alludes to the "diaphanous" nature of the world (as he refers to it later in the poem), which enables this encounter to take place. Crane makes subtle reference to Pater's homoerotic essay "Diaphaneitè," which celebrates the "clear crystal nature" of heroic individuals that appears both "like a sweet aroma in early manhood" and in "every man of genius" (139).[18] The final lines here, in which Crane presents "[t]he white wafer cheek of love" and the appearance of "words/Lightly as moonlight on the eaves meets snow," offers both a linguistic basis for this blending and a spiritual one. The presentation of these words continues the sense of the "crystal nature" whilst also connoting evanescence and drawing upon his mosaic empiricism, as the moonlight meets the eaves. In making a link to the wafer of Communion, Crane suggests thereby the transubstantiation of the Eucharist in Catholic Mass. Transubstantiation is the non-apprehendable transformation of one material into another, living material under spiritual conditions, and in connecting the image with the body of the lover, Crane concludes this section by suggesting again queer proximity: as in the Mass, where the priest "offers words," which bring about the transubstantiation, so here the poet's language brings about a body that is material and immaterial at once.[19]

A crisis of materiality, sexuality, and language

Crane's final poem, "The Broken Tower" (1932/1932) is problematic within the queer criticism of his work, since it is generally accepted to have been inspired by his sexual relationship with a woman, Peggy Cowley, a long-time friend with whom he began an affair in Mexico during 1931–1932. The relationship has allowed some critics to assure themselves that Crane was therefore either – as Allen Tate put it, "an unwilling homosexual" ("Crane: The Poet as Hero" 325) – or bisexual, as John Logan asserts in his foreword to a 1972 edition of *White Buildings*.[20] Their arguments seem dangerously close to one of the objections that Eve Kosofsky Sedgwick identifies as typical of critics who deny the need to read the work of writers against the background of their sexuality:

> The author under discussion is certified or rumored to have had an attachment to someone of the other sex – so their feelings about people of their own sex must have been completely meaningless (*Epistemology of the Closet* 52).

The poem actually presents a three-fold crisis: of sexuality, of materiality, and of language and textuality, thereby revealing the energy behind its creation to be a result of, as Allen Grossman has argued, *"the urgency of a problem to which only a poem (only poetry) can find a solution"* ("On Communicative Difficulty" 151). Grossman identifies this problem as the struggle to find a universal, secular language, but the problem is also deep-rooted in Crane's own presence in the world.

Judith Butler has acknowledged that

> [t]o problematize the matter of bodies may entail an initial loss of epistemological certainty, but a loss of certainty is not the same as

political nihilism. On the contrary, such a loss may well indicate a significant and promising shift in political thinking. This unsettling of "matter" can be understood as initiating new possibilities, new ways for bodies to matter (*Bodies that Matter* 30).

The speaker, who, as it will become clear, I identify as Crane himself, describes in the poem his preparation for the moment when he would "enter[...] the broken world/To trace the visionary company of love" (*CP* 160).[21] As becomes clear in the process of reading the poem, "the broken world" is the heteronormative world. The foregoing stanzas therefore describe how Crane is relinquishing his hold on the queer dimension. What follows is both "a loss of certainty" and an embrace of "new possibilities, new ways for bodies to matter."

In the background to the poem, "epistemological doubt" results from the challenge to Crane's understanding of his own sexualized body. The bells themselves bring about this unsettling of matter, aggressively challenging the speaker's current state. In the first stanza, "[t]he bell-rope that gathers God at dawn" also "[d]ispatches me," implying a means by which the speaker, or part of him, is being killed off. In this third stanza, the corporeality of the bells and the speaker's ignorance about their new location, as well as his ongoing change from one sexuality to another, offer parallel layers of doubt to the experience.

However, Crane is also unsure about the strength of his language. A number of critics have assumed that this kind of uncertainty is a commentary upon Crane's inability to work whilst in Mexico, and a real worry that he had lost the ability to write poetry. But this doubt needs to be read together with the doubts about materiality expressed here. The repetition in "[t]he bells, I say, the bells," is the sound of a speaker straining to be heard, whilst "I say" is a speech act that needs to draw attention to itself to have legitimacy. When the tongues "engrave/ Membrane through marrow," they enforce the presence of "membrane" ("[a] thin extended, soft, transparent tissue, formed by fibers interwoven like net-work" (*WUD* 827)) over "marrow" ("[a] soft, oleaginous substance [...]. The essence; the best part" (*WUD* 814)). As a metaphor for "[t]he essence" of himself, "marrow" recalls a letter from Crane at this time to a gay friend, Wilbur Underwood, in which he admitted

> I have the sad news to relate that for the first time in my life I have broken ranks with the "brotherhood" and extended my sexual dominions to some extent at least. I don't know how long this affair will last (I have engaged in no promises of any sort) but I think it has

done me considerable good. The old beauty still claims me, however, and my eyes roam as much as ever. I doubt if I'll ever change very fundamentally (*OML* 507).

"The Broken Tower" examines the concerns in evidence here, and this stanza figures the "doubt": the replacement of Crane's "marrow" or "fundamental[...]" part with something that acts only as a cover or "tissue," an idea continued in the fifth stanza where he describes how he will "trace the visionary company of love": tracing suggesting that he will merely "copy" (*WUD* 1398) it, rather than create a new path for himself. In describing the marrow as "my long-scattered score/Of broken intervals," Crane reveals his essence to be found not in the notes that make up a score, but in the "broken intervals," a figuration of an alternative sexual presence that recalls the transitions of his mosaic strategy in evidence in "Passage." The stanza therefore describes the shape of the conflict going on in Crane, for regardless of the continuing place of his "marrow," he has to acknowledge that he is responsible for that conflict: "And I, their sexton slave!" is an ironic comment upon his own role in the "dispatching" of his queerness, and like a sexton taking charge of his own "en-grav[e]ing." He is of course complicit in the "extend[ing of his] sexual dominions."

Into this new world, Crane brings language. Even from the start it seems diminished: this is his "word," not the "imaged Word" of "Voyages" or the "multitudinous Verb" of "Atlantis." It is at this juncture that the three parts of the crisis described in the poem join together, and as so often with Crane, understanding the multiple meanings of his diction grants access to the world he is describing. Crane's concern that his word might not be "cognate" betrays a concern about its relationality, which *Webster's* helps to untangle. Firstly, is it "connected with another by ties of kindred" (*WUD* 248)? This is a question about language: is it as powerful as his word has been in the past? Secondly, is it "related to another on the female side" (*WUD* 248)? This is a question about sexuality and language: can this word be part of a language that describes the materiality of a heterosexual relationship now "scored" by the same divine, judgmental power that "dispatche[d]" his queer identity? This power is determined to destroy the "crystal Word" (denoting a Paterian aesthetic that is always on the search for "[t]he old beauty"), which was the bedrock of Crane's queer poetics. That "[t]he steep encroachments of my blood" seem to provide no answer to these questions actually does provide Crane with the very answer he seeks. The presence of the "encroachments" as "unlawful intrusion[s]"

(*WUD* 445) signify the body's inability to conform to the laws of the "tribunal monarch." Butler has reasoned that "[t]o posit by way of language a materiality outside of language is still to posit that materiality, and the materiality so posited will retain that positing as its constitutive condition. [...] To have the concept of matter is to lose the exteriority that the concept is suppose[d] to secure" (*Bodies that Matter* 31). Caught between an "old" language and body that is "unlawful," and a new language to which the body can never be "cognate," Crane asserts a different kind of materiality, one that thereby "lose[s] the exteriority," and which asserts a partial return to the sexual self by means of textuality, by going inside the "body" of his work.

Just as he did in "Faustus and Helen," in "Voyages," and in "The Dance," Crane uses the body of the divine female in "The Broken Tower" as the location to reassert queerness. It is through the Virgin Mary, acknowledged in the "angelus,"[22] that he is able to be "revived and sure." Yet it is also clear that the return to this motif is only partly responsible for the form of the reaffirmation that Crane offers in the final stanzas. The "angelus" itself recalls the line from "Ave Maria": "Some Angelus environs the cordage tree" (*CP* 48). By itself, this repetition would be no surprise, since Crane frequently reuses phrases from or parts of incomplete poems in later work. But "The Broken Tower" contains far more echoes than usual. For instance: "[a]ntiphonal" ("Atlantis"), "carillon[...]" ("The Wine Menagerie," "Virginia"), "hived" ("The Hive"), "[...-]scattered" ("At Melville's Tomb"), and just as the phrase "[t]he steep encroachments of my blood [...]/As flings the question true" recalls the line from "Voyages III," "[u]pon the steep floor flung from dawn to dawn," so too the moment in "To Brooklyn Bridge" where "[t]he seagull's wings [...] dip and pivot him,/Shedding white rings of tumult" (*CP* 43) suggests the "slip/Of pebbles, – visible wings of silence sown/In azure circles, widening as they dip [...]." This latter example offers confirmation that Crane's self-referential strategy was a conscious one. On one of the manuscript pages for "The Broken Tower" on which Crane was drafting the poem, he wrote out an earlier form of the line:

> but drop a stone
> Into a pool – and hear the silence ~~widen~~
> In rings of emerald, azure, widen til they [ring] (C45 verso of second sheet)[23]

Then above his drafting Crane also included the first four lines of "Virginia" from *The Bridge*, another poem that includes a Mary and a tower with bells. Judith Butler has asserted that "matter is founded through a set of violations" (*Bodies that Matter* 29), and Crane shows here that whilst one element of that set is his self-imposed challenge to his sexuality and his body – the violation of the terms of his "brotherhood" – another element is in bringing his language to a point of crisis, of violating the "crystal Word." In doing so, Crane sought therefore to resolve the crisis in "The Broken Tower" by asserting the authenticity of his own textual history in poems, which had helped to shape his queer identity, believing that the (now printed) lines from "Virginia" gave legitimacy to his present work, and also by introducing a different kind of materiality, a "tower that is not stone."

As is clear from the manuscript page above, Crane intended "slip" in the penultimate stanza to mean the slipping of a stone or pebbles from a hand into a pool, causing the "visible wings of silence [to be] sown/In azure circles." In this way, the new "tower" to be constructed "within" the body has no materiality at all, for it is in a permanent state of free-fall, endorsing what Crane had written in 1925: "Language has built towers and bridges, but itself is inevitably as fluid as always" ("General Aims and Theories," *CP* 223). This process of free-fall is continued in the need to "lift down the eye" and meet "[t]he matrix of the heart." As Lee Edelman has concluded, the "lift[ing] down [of] the eye" describes the action of looking down at the printed page (*Transmemberment of Song* 270–71), a kind of free-fall, whilst *Webster's* defines the "matrix" as "that which gives form or modifies any thing [...] a mold, as, the matrix of a type" (*WUD* 819). One image details a process, the other implies a process. Just as the "lift[ing] down" is equivalent to the "slip/Of pebbles" from which the new material tower is constructed inside the body, so the "matrix" is "of the heart," meaning both that it is internalized and that it is bound up with the identity of the poet himself – emphasized by the pun on "eye"/"I." But Crane's use of "commodious," "[a]dapted to its use or purpose" (*WUD* 257), shows that he intends the poem to go beyond just a concern with interiority. Langdon Hammer and others have noted how this poem is "a retrospective reflection on the shape of Crane's career" (*Hart Crane and Allen Tate* 154), and given the examples above, it is clear that the poem provides a textual history of that career. The poem's "use" for Crane therefore is in the way that it provides a reminder of what Edelman calls "the provisional nature of all his poetic constructions" (271), that process is all, and that he is constantly seeking "decorum," another word in the penultimate line of the poem, that is to say "grace arising from suitableness of speech and behavior to one's own character" (*WUD* 342). The poem provides a record of how Crane has tried to fit his language to his queer "character." In this way, Crane's intention to go beyond the material and prioritize the process or immaterial is inevitable, for the need to do this is ongoing. The "shower" with which the poem concludes is an affirmation of just that, being continuously in free-fall and promising plenty. Given Crane's constant awareness of Eliot, the shower may be his last retort to him, representing the rain that never falls in *The Waste Land*. Rather than being a conclusion of his writing career, "The Broken Tower" indicates Crane's desire to continue the search for the right words to describe experience.

"Hauntology" of the body

"The Broken Tower" challenges the notion that the material body is required to ensure intelligibility and legitimacy for the queer subject. Instead, Crane insists upon something more shadowy or fluid. The figuration of death in the poem, constantly in the background before the sexual/textual resurrection of the final three stanzas, recalls Heidegger's concept of "being-toward-its-end" discussed in the book's previous chapter: the speaker's identity in the poem only makes sense when its very existence is challenged. Christopher Peterson has discussed the possibilities of such a problem in his discussion of both Heidegger and Jacques Derrida, and Derrida's notion of the "spectral." Observing that marginalized figures such as those who are victims of homophobic or racist abuse have often been linked with death and spectrality, Peterson observes:

> Naming a process of originary mourning that animates corporeal life, spectrality has no beginning or end. The abjection that sexual and racial minorities endure might be better understood as a mode of *redoubled ghostliness* that harnesses the spectrality inherent to all life and attaches it to those on the margins of sociality (155–56).

Spectrality can be seen, therefore, as a tactic of oppression from which there appears to be no escape for the "socially dead" (157). However, Peterson continues:

> Although the possibility of the specter requires a certain return to the body, that body never fully returns to itself. Indeed, the return of the body to itself is forever deferred by its "hauntological' condition. Following Derrida, we might consider that all bodies live in the "shadowy regions of ontology," all bodies are *hauntological*, not ontological (157).

Whilst this "hauntological" condition might be regarded as a stigma, further marginalizing those on the edges of society, I want to suggest that Crane embraces it, and that bodies that appear in his work are subject to it. Each hauntological character is representative of an empowered queerness: present but not present; in the position of having a body which changed and "never fully return[ed] to itself." Its hauntological status means that the queer body cannot be pinned down, rendering it continually resistant to "abjection."

"The Broken Tower" partly charts the passage of "that corps/Of shadows in the tower," the use of corps ("[a] body of men" (*WUD* 296)) representing the "brotherhood" to which Crane belongs. The death-in-life status of this "corps[e]" is transferred to the penultimate stanza, where the "corps," a word that carries a hint of the corporeal, becomes the "slip/Of pebbles," which, as discussed above, also implies the body, as the pebbles slip from the hand. Here, the shadowy body of men, whilst still retaining its immateriality, forms one of the elements that constitute the new kind of material tower. Since "The Broken Tower" is also a palimpsest, it is also hauntological, and "haunted" by the previous writings of its author. Its urgency to move forward at the end of the poem ensures that it will not return "fully" to itself and proceed retrogressively.

The hauntological is also evident in "At Melville's Tomb" (1925/1926). A form of elegy for the author of *Moby-Dick*, it offers various ways in which the bodies of Melville and the sailors about whom he wrote are transformed: "[t]he dice of drowned men's bones he saw bequeath/An embassy" (*CP* 33).[24] Elsewhere in the poem, the bodies of the sailors are "obscured," the shipwreck becomes "[a] scattered chapter, livid hieroglyph," and these complex corporeal changes (since a ship is typically gendered "she") conclude with reference to "[t]his fabulous shadow only the sea keeps." This "shadow" is representative of Melville the writer, evident in the etymological association between "fabulous" and "fables." These material bodies in the poem never, to use Peterson's terms, come back to themselves, and they are presented as difficult to view or interpret. Like the ship which, being wrecked, is difficult to understand any longer as a material object, the other bodies are "livid hieroglyph[s]": representative images that resist immediate recognition.

A heteronormative society, however, demands the materiality of the body, as Lee Edelman's "homographesis" has demonstrated. This concept is founded on the idea that a heterosexual society requires the queer body to be legible, for without the ability to "read" him, it is otherwise impossible to tell the difference between a queer man and a heterosexual one. Edelman explains that

[l]ike writing, homographesis would name a double operation: one serving the ideological purposes of a conservative social order intent on codifying identities in its labor of disciplinary inscription, and the other resistant to that categorization, intent on *de*-scribing the identities that order has so oppressively *in*scribed. (10)

One key element of Edelman's argument is his use of the term "homograph," which refers to words that are spelled identically to one another but which have no etymological or other connection between them, such as "bear" (the animal) and "to bear" (to carry). According to Edelman, "[h]omographs insist upon the multiple histories informing graphic 'identities'" (13), for to do so posits both the visual similarity between men, but also connotes their (unmarked) difference. This description also reinforces the way in which the hauntological has a spectral background and recalls Jean Toomer's mystical experience in the train, when his fellow passenger's view of him was limited by their attachment to a material self. It also adds a further dimension to Toomer's understanding that because of the mismatch in perceptions, "whether he meant to or not, he would mistreat you, and himself" ("The Experience" 49).

In his use of shadows, immaterial characters, and textual memory, Crane thus seeks to make his poems resistant to categorization, and to being marginalized or mistreated. His use of shadows in "The Broken Tower," "At Melville's Tomb," and elsewhere, demonstrates the dangers to the queer body, but also a fierce resistance to its extinction. Rather than suffer that body to be "[d]ispatch[ed]," Crane has it transform into something immaterial, a gesture akin to liberation, rendering it no longer under threat from to the normative power and discourse that would seek to closet, damage, or even destroy it. In "At Melville's Tomb," "only the sea keeps" the umbral body, and the sea is figured here as it often appears in "Voyages," as an atopic space of security.

6
Queer Technology, Failure, and a Return to the Hand

When Hart Crane incorporated technology into his long 1930 poem *The Bridge*, he was engaging with a debate within American modernist culture that had been going on for more than a decade. Many writers proclaimed the period between the two World Wars to be "the Machine Age," and Crane was hardly alone in acknowledging that the increasing presence of machinery and other elements of apparent scientific progress in everyday life had to be reflected in visual and verbal art if these artists were to give a vital and realistic portrayal of the way people lived in the modern world. However, Crane's engagement with the Machine and technology in *The Bridge* is unconventional, for rather than celebrate the Machine Age as so many of his contemporaries did, he describes situations in which technology fails. What is more, that failure is an essential element of his poetic and queer practices. Reading Crane's failure as a deliberate aesthetic choice provides a necessary way to challenge a prevailing assumption about Crane, and particularly about *The Bridge*, that it and he were failures, an assumption which, as I have indicated elsewhere in the book, unhelpfully conflates his lifestyle (his alcoholism and queer sexuality) with a supposed breakdown in his work. If failure is read as a positive energy, however, it becomes a way of understanding how Crane develops a sense of a queer community, of reinvigorating language for his queer project, and also how that failure enables a return to older forms of technology and a rejection of the Machine.

In the 1920s and 1930s, the concept of modernity seemed to be synonymous with technology. During this time, the Machine Age was reaching a crescendo of grinding gears and humming of dynamos in little magazines, newspapers, art, and literature. On the one hand, this invasion of the human world by technology was perceived at the time as a great threat to humanity – partly because of its unknown potential. This was a transatlantic concern. The German historian Oswald Spengler, whose influential book *The Decline of the West* Crane had read in 1926,[1] noted with alarm in 1932 that civilization was watching "[t]he creature [...] rising up against the creator," and warned that "[a]s once the microcosm Man against Nature, so now the microcosm Machine is revolting against Nordic Man" (63). Spengler's use of "Nordic" illustrated his narrow and racist definition of which societies he regarded sufficiently advanced to be at risk from the Machine, and in this he usually confined his remarks to Europe and North America. But in the United States, the danger was frequently seen as being more subtle and insinuating, and American clergyman and author Gerald Stanley Lee, wondered "what is it in the new Machine-made World which, in spite of the splendid joy, a rough new, wild religion there is in it, keeps daily filling me as I go past machines with this contradictory obstinate dread of them?"(34). Whilst Lee and others cannot help but admire the thrilling new possibilities of the Machine, they also identify it as a "wild religion," using the same kind of terminology that critics used when drawing attention to the dangerous relationship, or, in Spengler's terms, a Faustian pact into which Americans were entering. According to Michael Pupin, the Serbian electrical inventor and physicist who did much of his research in America,

> [m]achine civilization has, it is true, reached its highest development in this country, and we are, therefore, accused of sordid materialism, of a worship of the machine. It is the worship of a heathen idol, our European critics tell us, and they hold our scientists and engineers responsible for the spread of this heathen worship (27–28).

Describing the Machine in these terms: as a replacement for God, and as a particularly American problem, is characteristic of much discussion about technology in the 1920s and early 1930s. In a 1921 review of Sherwood Anderson's novel about small-town Ohio, *Poor White*, Crane praised Anderson for creating key episodes in the novel to demonstrate the effects of technology upon his characters. Crane argued that:

> [n]o one who treats however slightly of the lives of the poor or middle classes can escape the issue of its present hold on us. It has seduced the strongest from the land to the cities, and in most cases made empty and meaningless their lives. It has cheapened the worth of all human commodities and even the value of human lives. It has

destroyed the pride and pleasure of the craftsman in his work (*CPSL* 210).

Another typical feature of Machine-Age comment is this assertion that people at all levels of society and all over the country are affected. The contrast between the "splendid joy" and "obstinate dread," which Gerald Stanley Lee identifies as "filling" him when he sees machinery, is represented in Crane's review by the opposing forces of seduction on the one hand and nihilism on the other in the feeling that technology will nonetheless create "empty and meaningless" lives. Crane's critique is also notable for its attention to questions of "value," as if to suggest that the kinds of Taylorist and Fordist techniques employed in factories and production lines focused too much upon the financial value of labor and not upon the human cost of a society obsessed with the Machine. Crane echoes the alarm that came to be felt across the nation that the monstrous Machine would make people less human, penetrating their bodies and very selves, and presumably thereby stifling the creativity of artists and writers who endeavor to describe them. But despite its threatening nature, Crane here and elsewhere identifies the necessity of dealing with the Machine, and holds up art as a way of interacting with, perhaps even subjugating, this overwhelming force.

Not long after this review was published in 1921, Crane became less sympathetic to Sherwood Anderson's work, partly for the reasons I outlined in my second chapter in respect to William Sommer, and he shifted his aesthetic concerns away from a preoccupation with a modernism that located itself in the semi-rural Midwest towards an urban, specifically New York-based avant-garde. This shift coincided with Crane's new-found enthusiasm for the work of Waldo Frank, who argued that it was necessary to absorb the Machine into culture.[2] Writer-friends of Crane like Frank, Matthew Josephson, and Gorham Munson (who wrote a study of Frank's work in 1923), acknowledged the importance of the Futurists in this regard, particularly F.T. Marinetti in Italy, and whilst they were suspicious of the tendency of the Futurists towards violence and apparently chaotic, even irrational use of language, they did accept them as what Munson called "the agents of a new recognition" (*Waldo Frank* 24). Rather than concern itself with the traditional dimensions of man and nature, Munson contended, culture must now make a place for technology and, in his words, "bring the Machine into the scope of the human spirit" (*Waldo Frank* 24).

Yet even with such a conceptual shift accomplished, there was still the question of the demands that the incorporation of technology would place upon style. Would a poem involving the Machine have to look and sound like a work by avant-garde experimenters such as Marinetti or, beyond Futurism, like Guillaume Apollinaire, or Dadaists such as Tristan Tzara – all poets whose appeal Crane could not understand? Any attempt to represent the Machine in poetry was risky, Crane and his peers knew, not just because of what they thought of as the stylistic chaos coming from Europe, but also because they had experienced *The Waste Land* in 1922. Here, Eliot's use of technology brings a very negative coloring to the work, especially when the typist, after being "assault[ed]" by her supposed lover, the young man carbuncular, "[p]aces about her room again, alone,/[...] smoothes her hair with automatic hand,/And puts a record on the gramophone." Sexuality is presented through the perceived violence of the Machine, and the typist, a woman who deals with a machine all day, becomes one, in her repetitive movement and the way in which she seems to sacrifice her bodily and mental agencies first to the "small house agent's clerk," and then to the machinery around her. For Crane, Eliot's poem must have merely confirmed the threat he had seen identified in Sherwood Anderson's novel – a sense in which the human body had been invaded by technology, and – in the case of the typist – replacement of the human body with a mechanical one. Crane was disturbed by the negativity of *The Waste Land*, and so he knew that if he were to involve technology in his work, he would have to treat it carefully.

In addition, was the integration of technology into writing no more than a fad? Certainly this was Crane's impression in 1922, when he asked Munson: "[w]ill radios, flying machines, and cinemas have such a great effect on poetry in the end? All this talk of [Josephson]'s is quite stimulating, but it's like coffee – twenty-four hours afterward not much remains to work with" (*Hart Crane: Complete Poems and Selected Letters* 82). One of Crane's objectives in 1922 was to formulate a suitable and substantial response to *The Waste Land*, and he was thus wary of anything in terms of content or style that might distract his serious message. And yet by 1923, Crane had significantly changed tack, writing to Munson that he felt himself "quite fit to become a suitable Pindar for the dawn of the machine age, so called" (*OML* 137) and making it clear that Munson himself was responsible for his reassessment of the Machine, telling him that he was

> grateful for your very rich suggestions best stated in your Frank study on the treatment of mechanical manifestations of today as subject for lyrical, dramatic, and even epic poetry. [...] The field of

possibilities literally glitters all around one with the perception and vocabulary to pick out significant details and digest them into something emotional (*OML* 132).

In his role as a verbal magpie and in his proposed use of "mechanical manifestations," Crane seems to maintain a certain skeptical, even ironic detachment from the Machine, but be nonetheless committed to make use of it.

The first conclusion that can be drawn about Crane's involvement with technology then is that he is not, as early critics of *The Bridge* suggested, a zealous prophet of technology. In 1948, Karl Shapiro described part of "Cape Hatteras" as "the well-known paean to machinery" ("Cape Hatteras" 40). In addition, as will become clear in the rest of this chapter, he does not employ technology in an uncomplicated way. In fact, Crane's use of technology in *The Bridge* dramatizes the ongoing tension in American modernism regarding the potential dangers of the Machine to humanity that I have sketched out here, as well as the risks and benefits of incorporating it into artistic work.

Technology and failure

This tension is most obvious in the fourth section of the poem, "Cape Hatteras," which begins by evoking the formation of the landmass of the American continent. Crane then describes in spectacular detail the new technologies being created in the country, and offers up two episodes featuring the aeroplane as an example of that new technology, first through the Wright brothers and then through a military-style "Falcon-Ace" whose plane crashes into Cape Hatteras itself. The final part of this section immediately after the crash describes the speaker's relationship with his literary and queer antecedent, Walt Whitman, situating him as a poet who speaks through nature rather than through the Machine. It is thus a crucial moment in the poem as a whole for its endorsement of a certain kind of language and for the maintaining of the poem's queer aesthetic.

This section contains the poem's most sustained engagement with ideas of the Machine, and here the technology fails spectacularly in the section beginning: "But first, here at this height receive," and concluding with: "By Hatteras bunched the beached heap of high bravery!" (*CP* 81). Albert Gelpi calls this part of the poem "the most extreme and successful attempt at Futurist poetry in America" (413), and since Crane rarely experiments in this way with form, it seems likely that he was modelling his treatment of the aeroplane on the more typographically experimental Futurist poetry or similar avant-garde work from Europe, such as that of Jean Cocteau.[3] But, as I have suggested, Crane was suspicious of the Futurists, and this excerpt from "Cape Hatteras" demonstrates his critique of Futurism as it was proposed by Marinetti.

Certainly the poem echoes parts of Marinetti's document "The Founding and Manifesto of Futurism 1909." Marinetti relates how "like young lions we ran after Death, its dark pelt blotched with pale crosses as it escaped down the vast violet living and throbbing sky" (250), a description that recalls the descent down the sky by the Falcon-Ace. In the "Manifesto of Futurism," Marinetti writes of the need to cultivate "the enthusiastic fervour of the primordial elements," and Crane taps into this too by offering at the beginning of "Cape Hatteras" a vision of the creation of the American continent that eventually marries up the prehistoric beginnings of the country with the new technological advances in architecture, radio, and vision. The verbal and typographical presentation of the aeroplane at this point also seems to endorse Marinetti's promotion of energy and speed, which will undoubtedly lead to warfare. Yet there are also ways in which Crane offers a different view of technology. In his introduction to the Manifesto, Marinetti relates how he crashes his car into a ditch, but presents the experience as a moment of revelation in which the car itself emerges relatively unscathed. In Crane's poem, the plane is utterly destroyed. The lineation of the poem at this point too, even though it may echo a Futurist style, creates a kind of inevitable linguistic and material vortex that must lead to the aeroplane's destruction. It is almost as if the poem collapses into itself, into a vortex, which drags the words and the page down to crash – and to failure. Moreover, whereas Marinetti demands: "Why should we look back, when what we want is to break down the mysterious doors of the Impossible?" (251), the figurative language Crane employs situates the aeroplane's demise simultaneously in the past and in the present. Throughout this section, Crane makes use of imagery associated with heraldry, jousting, and falconry: the wings of the plane become "escutcheoned" (referring to a shield bearing a coat of arms); the plane is described first as "tilting" (a term used in jousting for the thrusting of a lance) and then as if it were a gauntlet in the act of being thrown down; and the "eagle-bright" aircraft becomes its own prey, "quarry-hid" in the next line. The falconry imagery is augmented by an allusion to W.B. Yeats's 1919 poem "The Second Coming," by which Crane connects the postwar anarchy alluded to in Yeats's poem to the dangers of a mechanical civilization. In his use of such historical imagery, which explicitly contradicts the Futurist aesthetic, as well as a critique that suggests that Futurism will prey upon itself and bring about its own aesthetic collapse, Crane offers a picture of technological failure.

In order to suggest some reasons for Crane's inclusion of failed technology, I want to broaden out the concept of failure to include links that have been made between failure and Crane's poem as a whole. Ever since its publication, critics have considered *The Bridge* to be a failure. Allen Tate, for example, whose criticisms I address throughout this chapter, labelled Crane as the last of the Romantic poets, and in comparing him to Keats, suggested that *"The Bridge* is a failure in the sense that 'Hyperion' is a failure, and with comparable magnificence" (qtd. in Clark, *Studies in the Bridge* 123). R.P. Blackmur concluded his 1935 essay on Crane with the assertion that "there is about him [...] – such were his gifts for the hearts of words, such the vitality of his intelligence – the distraught but exciting splendor of a great failure" (316). In an early review of *The Bridge*, Crane's friend Yvor Winters criticized Crane for his embrace of "the Whitmanian inspiration," noting that "[n]o writer of comparable ability has struggled with it before, and, with Mr. Crane's wreckage in view, it seems highly unlikely that any writer of comparable genius will struggle with it again" (31). And in his recent selection of Crane's poems, Maurice Riordan (seeming to follow Tate and Winters), claims that *"The Bridge* is a failure. It can accurately be called a 'heroic' failure because of its Romantic aim" (xi).

But what if Crane actually sought to embrace failure? And what if failure, read as an integral part of Crane's queer project in *The Bridge*, could actually be constructive? Crane himself had an understanding of failure that was not straightforward. Writing about the poem in a letter of 1926 to his friends Charlotte and Richard Rychtarik, he observed that "[a]t times the project seems hopeless, horribly so; and then suddenly something happens inside one, and the theme and the substance of the conception seem brilliantly real, more so than ever! At least, *at worst*, the poem will be a *huge* failure! If you get what I mean" (*OML* 229). Crane's assessment of failure is a positive one – there is a grandness about failure; it has its own kind of significance, Crane contends. And, as I argue, the failure of the Machine in particular was a necessity for the success of Crane's poem. Failure of this increasingly normative technology allows the poet to reveal how the alternative is in fact built into the dominant. In particular, such destruction releases the queer qualities of the poem at a critical moment, and these are both figurative (represented through the body of Walt Whitman), and linguistic (a recasting of language which allows for a reassessment of the way in which we see the world). This attention to language resulting from mechanical destruction also allows Crane to move the poem away from modern technologies back towards "handiness": language as material and poetry as a form of craft, which is fashioned by the hand, rather than by the machine, thus positioning his work in the early stages of a narrative that was, in the mid-to-late 1920s, rejecting the Machine aesthetic altogether.

Failed technology and queer community

In his 1937 appraisal of Crane's work, written soon after the poet's death, Allen Tate concluded that

> [t]he finest passages in [Crane's] work are single moments in the stream of sensation; beyond the moment he goes at his peril; for beyond it lies the discrepancy between the sensuous fact, the perception, and its organizing symbol – a discrepancy that plunges him into sentimentality and chaos. […] Beyond the quest of pure sensation and its ordering symbolism lies the total destruction of art ("Hart Crane" 322).

Tate argues that Crane has no guiding narrative for his long poem, no coherent set of symbols that tie the poem together. If a symbol used in the poem cannot be linked perceptibly to a clear emotion (an idea that recalls Eliot's "objective correlative"), the effect of the poem will be vague and sentimental. I will return to the concept of the "beyond" later in the chapter, since it represents a further dimension of Crane's use of technology that was deliberately set against Tate and others' understanding of what art can do. Tate's unequivocal assertion, however, that Crane's poem offered nothing less than a "total destruction of art" was right, in a way, since, as I have argued, Crane was intent on presenting a poem that endorsed destruction on levels of both form and content.

In the ninth stanza of "Cape Hatteras," Crane describes the way in which destruction is both a necessity and an inevitability. The very speed of the aeroplane has overtaken the pilot so that he is made blind by it. By consciously overreaching, attaining heights that mean he seems to duel for space with bolts of lightning ("the levin's lance"), the pilot "sowest[s] doom," an image that indicates that he causes his own downfall, and which also alludes to the phrase "they who sow the wind, reap the whirlwind." This line from the *Book of Hosea* 8:7, which warns Israel about setting up false gods for worship rather than God himself, also echoes that criticism recorded by Michael Pupin and others that mankind had come to consider the machine as a replacement for God. Just as the pilot's ambition seems to bring about his own ruin, so his body seems fatally marked: his "stilly eyes" are both the result of speed and contain a pun on "still," a vessel in which alcohol is made, which contributes to the sense that these eyes are inextricably linked with the dangerously intoxicating skies. And finally, the "Falcon-Ace" is reminded by the poet that his body has been inscribed with its destiny, whether we interpret "thy wrist" to mean that he will write it out and be an author of his own destruction, or whether it suggests his control of the levers to fly the plane and cause a crash. Crane's aims are summed up in the word "conjugate," which can be understood here to mean two different, linked things. In the first place, and in the context of the "Sanskrit charge," Crane understands "conjugate" to mean: "[t]o distribute the parts or inflections [of a verb] into the several voices, modes, tenses, numbers, and persons" (*WUD* 275). This understanding of the word indicates an attempt to create order out of "infinity's dim marge," to bring order to chaos. But this kind of organization brings about, as can be seen from the aeroplane's crash, a rather different form of order. It encourages instead multiplicity – conjugate suggests the creation of something multiple out of one thing – a process that brings about diversity and difference, and in the crash of the aeroplane – the curious word used is "dispersion" – Crane suggests a kind of ordered destruction. In addition, Crane suggests that this multiplicity will be one of language, the Falcon-Ace's demise will bring about new "voices, modes, tenses, numbers, and persons." This leads to the second understanding of "conjugate" that Crane has in mind: "to unite in marriage; to join" or "[u]nited in pairs; yoked together" (*WUD* 275). What Crane has in mind is a literary marriage with his queer antecedent, Walt Whitman, so that the "dim marge" to be conjugated is not simply filled with language, but with bodies as well: his and Whitman's. To unite his body and mind with Whitman, as he will do in the final lines of the poem, is for Crane a way of reconstructing that "dim marge," in order to re-negotiate a place on the margins and bring his queer project into the light. All of this serves to reinforce Crane's intention that technology must fail here: so that Whitman can appear and spur the poem's queer aesthetic onwards, and so that the language of the poem can be reaffirmed.

The reference to "a Sanskrit charge" alludes to Whitman's poem "Passage to India," with which "Cape Hatteras" is constantly in dialogue, and from which the epigraph to this section of *The Bridge* is taken. It is a poem that begins by "[s]inging the great achievements of the present," (531) the possibility that modern science and technology might conquer space, and concludes with the idea that we must be concerned with "[p]assage to more than India!" – a spiritual exhortation from Whitman to dive even deeper than "the Sanscrit and the Vedas," (539) the ancient language and literature of the Hindus. Since Sanskrit is thought to be the closest we can find to the source of all classical and European languages, this is consequently a return to a purer kind of language from which poetic creation can begin anew.

In these lines and in the moment after the Falcon-Ace has sacrificed himself and his aeroplane, Crane seeks the release of what might be termed "queer qualities." This is a critical moment in *The Bridge* as a whole, and Crane himself described it himself as "the very 'center' of the book, both physically and symbolically" (*OML* 421). With the destruction of the aeroplane, Crane creates a dramatic moment in the poem in which he requires a reaffirmation of faith in his project, and he succeeds in finding it when he joins his poetic voice to the queer poetics of Walt Whitman. But the destruction of the Machine and the appearance of Whitman in the poem are inextricably linked. Susan Schultz has argued that Crane is demonstrating here how Whitman's vision for America and the world has been destroyed by World War I. For Crane, she suggests, "this destruction – of the plane and of the myth of flight – is part of a redemptive process [...] because that destruction allows for rebirth, reascension" (61). Whitman represents this idea of "reascension." Yet Crane's engagement with technology goes beyond merely its use as a symbol or shorthand for myth, and demonstrates a desire to seek out the essence of what the Machine means for writers such as himself and Frank, keen to interrogate its status within American society. At the moment when the plane crashes, Whitman emerges from the land, phoenix-like, taking the place of the Falcon-Ace, whose motion "down" to the land is set in opposition to Whitman's appearance: "upward from the dead/Thou bringest tally, and a pact, new bound/Of living brotherhood!" It is technology that makes this possible, and in his destruction of it, Crane begins to fashion a queer community, that "living brotherhood" whose figurehead is Whitman, who brings with him, in contrast to the exotic elements of modern technology, "[t]he competent loam, the probable grass."[4]

Crane's original conception for this part of *The Bridge* was not concerned with the Machine at all, but with a much older technology, and examining Crane's notes for this section can help to make sense of the striving for community that runs through the second half of "Cape

Hatteras." Originally, "Cape Hatteras" was to feature a scene in which Walt Whitman tended to a Southern soldier in a Washington hospital during the Civil War. The soldier, realizing that he is close to death, asks Whitman to find a priest so he can seek absolution for his sin of the murder of Northern soldiers on the battlefield, but almost as soon as Whitman has left he calls him back. The planned scene would end before Whitman had returned. In his notes, Crane wrote:

> The irony is, of course, in the complete absolution which Whitman's words have already given the dying man, before the priest is called for. This, alternated with the eloquence of the dying man, is the substance of the dialogue – the emphasis being on the symbolism of the soldier's body having been used as a <u>forge</u> toward a state of Unity (B29).

In the first place, the essential image of the forge is a form of old technology, and this makes its way into the final version of "Cape Hatteras": the forge and the body are replaced by the combustion of the plane and the Falcon-Ace's body, whilst the absolution lives on in the "benediction" and "reprieve" that are given to the pilot. In addition, in the final version Crane fuses together his early plan for Whitman's role (to help bring about Unity in America) with the thoughts of Waldo Frank, who enabled him to see the possibilities for community and collective identity behind modern technology. Frank writes that

> [i]n the machine are adumbrated the will of the inventor, the will of the owner, the will of many workers, the will, indeed, of an age and of a world. Only when the individual worker experiences that these wills are not alien to him; that these elements of life contained in the machine fuse, in a higher synthesis, together with his own, into a unitary act – only then will his spirit in participation be able to go out through the machine, so that it and the whole mechanized world may once again, in his joy, in his beauty, in his human pride, express him ("The Machine and Metaphysics" 157).

In his incorporation of Whitman, someone who constantly tried to present himself as an ordinary working American, and in the moment of Unity described in the unused Civil War scene, Crane suggests that behind all technology there are these "wills": a community in which he might participate. By destroying the technology, Crane seeks to release this community out into the world.

Frank also draws attention to the idea that it is only through the fashioning of this community, the creation of this "unitary act," that his expression – in other words his ability to use language creatively – can once again be true. And yet at this moment when community is forged, Crane speaks once again of failure, commenting that:

> The competent loam, the probable grass, – travail
> Of tides awash the pedestal of Everest, fail
> Not less than thou in pure impulse inbred
> To answer deepest soundings! (*CP* 81)

Behind this part once again is Crane's original plan: the fact that the section with the soldier ends before Whitman's return is, I suggest, the model for this failure to answer. However, as I indicated earlier, Crane's sense of failure is not a negative one. As Crane explained, Whitman's words have already provided the soldier with the absolution that he requires, and here, in responding to Whitman's poem "Passage to India," Crane acknowledges that his mentor also failed to answer his own question: "Soundest below the Sanscrit and the Vedas?" By having in the background to the text a failure to answer the soldier, and in the foreground an acknowledgement that he is failing to answer this question, Crane creates a challenge to language. What has the "Sanskrit charge" of the Falcon-Ace brought about? What is the relationship between the failure of technology and language?

Language and difference

In his commentary upon the role of entities in *Being and Time*, Martin Heidegger offers some ways to consider this relationship, offering a direct connection between broken technology and the revealing of language's potential. Heidegger describes how objects are usually seen as separate from man, merely as *vorhanden*, "present-to-hand." This renders all objects on the same level: they are all *vorhanden*. However, Heidegger argues that objects – here he describes his ideas in terms of an elementary form of technology, a hammer – would be correctly seen in respect to their use (*zuhanden*, "ready-to-hand"), and that, importantly, such a change also alters the way in which we speak about them:

> Something *at hand with which* we have to do or perform something, turns into something "about which" the statement points it out is

made. Fore-sight aims at something objectively present in what is at hand. Both *by* and *for* the way of looking, what is at hand is veiled as something at hand. Within this discovering of objective presence which covers over handiness, what is encountered as objectively present is determined in its being objectively present in such and such a way. Now the access is first available for something like *qualities* (*Being and Time*, division I, chapter V, 152–53).

As Sara Ahmed has noted, it is only when the object is considered in respect to man's use of it, for instance, if the hammer is broken and thus cannot be used, that the true "qualities" of the object are revealed. Ahmed observes:

> I become aware of the hammer as an object-in-itself, rather than as an object, which refers beyond itself to an action that I intend to perform. So at this moment of "failure" the hammer is perceived as having properties; as being, for instance "too heavy" (48).

As I have indicated, the failure of technology in "Cape Hatteras" results in "access [...to] qualities": the queer quality that is Whitman himself and an opportunity to join a community forged out of the Machine's demise. But Heidegger's observations also show how a failure of machinery also leads to a redefinition of language and how we use it. He suggests that the "ready-to-hand" nature of an object is a way of determining difference, and more significantly, shows how a revelation about a piece of technology through its failure can inscribe a difference into the discussion of the object itself: from "at hand with which" to "about which." In his analysis of this passage, Michael Inwood has observed that Heidegger is resisting the notion that all objects are the same: "a surreptitious homogenization of being" (19), and this resistance is a parallel to Crane's queer project, which seeks to suggest alterity: both of sexuality and of language. When the "Falcon Ace" "conjugate[s] infinity's dim marge –/Anew..!" through material self-destruction, he is not simply pushing beyond the boundaries of space, but also bringing forth a revelation in language and a reassessment of the way in which the world can be perceived and described. And just as the "Sanskrit charge" (the imperative to crash and bring us back to what Whitman and Crane understood to be a primitive, and thus refreshing, understanding of language) was built into the Falcon-Ace's body, so what Crane is drawing attention to is the presence of the alternative within the dominant, where the dominant is the increasingly powerful role that the machine plays in everyday lives. As Judith Halberstam has observed in her discussion of queer failure,

> [w]e can [...] recognize failure as a way of refusing to acquiesce to dominant logics of power and discipline and as a form of critique. As a practice, failure recognizes that alternatives are embedded already in the dominant and that power is never total or consistent; indeed failure can exploit the unpredictability of ideology and its indeterminate qualities (*The Queer Art of Failure* 88).

So Crane offers the machine literally and figuratively as a manifestation of the dominant, and creates a space in which the queer alternative can emerge. As I have already outlined in the comments from Gerald Stanley Lee, throughout the "Machine Age" there is a sense in which the Machine is inherently unstable and unpredictable, that it cannot be trusted (it is *too* efficient, *too* prominent now across the land), and recognizing this, Crane seeks to exploit the instability at the heart of the Machine in order to open it up for scrutiny, and fashion spaces in which an aesthetic that resists the dominant might thrive.

Technology's threat

But this version of the Machine's failure by which technology is inherently responsible for its own demise, which points towards the sociological criticisms of figures like Spengler, hints at something dark and threatening in technology's character. In his 1953 lecture, "The Question Concerning Technology," Heidegger offered an analysis of this danger. He argued that the essence of technology was the attempt to control or order mankind, something Heidegger termed "enframing": "the gathering together of the setting-upon that sets upon man, i.e. challenges him forth, to reveal the actual, in the mode of ordering, as standing-reserve" (227). To be "standing-reserve" describes how humankind would be ready to be in the service of technology, in the ways which those critics of technology, suspicious of its increasing prominence, explained. And here the real risk to Crane's queer project becomes clear: by adopting technology, his poetics might be perceived as subservient to something else, thereby diluting or compromising the very principle of queer resistance embedded in Crane's work.

However, Heidegger goes on to relate how in the past, technology, poetry, and art all had the same name, *technē*. He explains this by saying that art was "a revealing that brought forth and made present, and therefore belonged within *poiēsis*" (237). Heidegger notes that *"poiēsis"* refers to "[n]ot only handicraft manufacture, not only artistic and poetical bringing into appearance and concrete imagery" (221). In this respect then, technology has an alternative history, and it is this alternative nature that Crane seeks to access in *The Bridge*. Notwithstanding his use of the jousting and heraldry imagery, and the significance of the body as forge in the background to the text, Crane himself acknowledged that behind modern technology there was a history to be accessed. Writing to Waldo Frank in 1926, he observed that "to realize suddenly, as I seem to, how much of the past is living under only slightly altered forms, even in machinery and such-like, is extremely exciting" (*OML* 272). Perceived in these terms, the use of technology can be understood in "Cape Hatteras" and the final section of the poem, "Atlantis," to be a queer strategy. As I have suggested, it is the "revealing" of a real figure, Whitman, in "Cape Hatteras" that creates the possibility of a queer community, whilst the release of a new understanding of language offers a chance to reassess the world in and beyond the poem.[5] In the last part of *The Bridge*, "Atlantis," Crane uses technology/*technē*'s power to reveal and make present by enabling the Bridge itself to grant passage to Atlantis, a place, after all, considered to be impossibly present. Crane addresses the Brooklyn Bridge itself but also addresses it as the mythical structure he has created through the course of the poem, and he figures this possible re-emergence of the lost city as a fusion of materiality and temporality and of art, particularly in the form of song, and technology.

> From gulfs unfolding, terrible of drums,
> Tall Vision-of-the-Voyage, tensely spare –
> Bridge, lifting night to cycloramic crest
> Of deepest day – O Choir, translating time
> Into what multitudinous Verb the suns
> And synergy of waters ever fuse, recast
> In myriad syllables, – Psalm of Cathay!
> O Love, thy white, pervasive Paradigm...! (*CP* 106)[6]

The tension presented here is between an opening up or revealing (the "unfolding"), and an impulse towards synthesis: the desire to retain the possibility of linguistic multiplicity (in "myriad syllables") or alterity (in the suggestive ellipsis at the end of the stanza), whilst simultaneously empowering the verbal art to bring about a singularity of purpose, including one "Vision," one "Verb," and one "Paradigm" – in sum, one "Bridge" that is "tensely spare" – held in tension, as the bridge structure itself can be said to be – as a result of this contrast between multiplicity and synthesis.

Nature and the primitive

Both "Atlantis" and "Cape Hatteras" present a further friction, this time between the mechanized and the natural worlds, which indicates another way in which Crane seeks to resist the dominance of technology. Towards the conclusion of "Cape Hatteras," the presence of Whitman in the poem also leads to the presentation of rural landscape. As critics have suggested, the first line of this stanza, which asks "[p]ropulsions toward what capes?" could be read ironically. Having presented the dangers of modern technology, Crane could also be questioning the value and risk of the machinery that propels humanity towards an unknown end, or, worse, the inevitability that the development of technology might merely result in humanity's demise, as Spengler insists. Instead, Whitman seems to offer an alternative that is grounded, quite literally, in the American earth. Rather than be concerned about the possibilities of what science and technology might magically "open up" – in one meaning of "sesame" – Crane prefers to emphasize the more ordinary meaning of sesame, the seed, and associate it with the "spear of summer grass," which gives Whitman's major work, *Leaves of Grass*, its title and its representative idea. All can recognize and relate to a blade of grass, Whitman believed, and this familiarity allows him (and Crane) to suggest the possibility that the American might become a "[n]ew integer," develop a wholeness of identity (based on the meaning of "integer" as a whole number) derived from the landscape that could in time be recognized alongside those of Roman, Viking, and Celt.

In *The Machine in the Garden*, Leo Marx identifies a significant pattern within nineteenth- and twentieth-century American literature: the prominence given to the pastoral landscape. This impulse, he says, "is generated by an urge to withdraw from civilization's growing power and complexity," and he goes on to suggest that:

> Movement toward such a symbolic landscape […] may be understood as movement away from an "artificial" world, a world identified with "art," using this word in its broadest sense to mean the disciplined habits of mind or arts developed by organized communities. In other words, this impulse gives rise to a symbolic motion away from centers of civilization towards their opposite, nature, away from sophistication toward simplicity, or, to introduce the cardinal metaphor of the literary mode, away from the city toward the country (9-10).

As the reference to Whitman's *Leaves of Grass* shows, "Cape Hatteras" engages directly with this movement away from the sophisticated towards the simple, and even toward the primitive or primordial. This section of *The Bridge* offers a journey from the "hushed land" of prehistoric America, represented by the dinosaur and the "[c]ombustion at the astral core" as the land is itself being created, in the opening stanza, through to a situation in which things can begin all over again in the company of Whitman. It is a process that Crane represents typographically by having that opening and closing of this part appear as movement forward and down across the page:

> Imponderable the dinosaur
>   sinks slow,
>   the mammoth saurian
>   ghoul, the eastern
>   Cape...

and

> Afoot again, and onward without halt, –
> Not soon, not suddenly, – no, never to let go
>   My hand
>   in yours,
>   Walt Whitman –
>   so –

With the return to the primitive, Crane implies the necessity for a return to the primitive ways of living. The aeroplane or locomotive or automobile are rejected (the typography here can also act as an ironic replacement for the spiraling text that represented the aeroplane's crash) in favor of being "[a]foot," and the violence and unpredictability of the Machine is replaced by a temporal description more appropriate for a man venturing out onto the "Open Road": "[n]ot soon, not suddenly." But I want to suggest that it is Crane's use of the hand that is most significant, because it offers a radical alternative to the dominant Machine culture. Certainly Crane alludes to Whitman's poem "Whoever You Are Holding Me Now in Hand," (270–71) a homoerotic lyric in which Whitman proposes his book to be an affective tool by which he can connect with his reader. Whitman offers himself as a Christ-like figure and gives the reader the chance to become a disciple, to enter into an affective bond with him if they are willing to commit themselves entirely to his words and beliefs. As the reader holds the book, so they also hold onto the body of Whitman.

But the reference to the hand also suggests an emphasis upon craft, a return to low or old technologies using what might be termed primitive tools. So whilst he does strive towards simplicity rather than sophistication, Crane does not intend to relinquish art or artifice in the way that Leo Marx suggests many twentieth-century American writers did when they shifted their focus away from civilization towards nature. In fact, in a way that recalls James Joyce's *A Portrait of the Artist as a Young Man* (a novel which he reviewed and celebrated in the pages of the *Little Review* in 1918), Crane shows himself to be very conscious of modernism's concern with artifice – an early draft of "Cape Hatteras," B24, even referred explicitly to "Deadelus" [sic], the surname of Joyce's protagonist, and the repeated references in the final version of this part to the "labyrinth" indicate that Daedalus, the craftsman of the Minotaur's prison, remains in the background.

Making things: The ordinary and a return to craft

But if in Joyce's novel Stephen Daedalus promotes himself as an exceptional figure and ends the book by committing himself to exile from his country, Crane by contrast seeks to prioritize the ordinary just as he incorporates a sense of the simple. As I have been suggesting, the natural world forms a backdrop for this presentation of the ordinary, as Whitman is Crane's partner in fashioning an understanding of – as Crane puts it – the "familiar." When Crane wrote about the Machine in his 1930 essay "Modern Poetry," it was to explain the importance of a strategy that rendered technology ordinary:

> Machinery will tend to lose its sensational glamour and appear in its true subsidiary order in human life as use and continual poetic allusion subdue its novelty. For, contrary to general prejudice, the wonderment experienced in watching nose dives is of less immediate creative promise to poetry than the familiar gesture of a motorist in the modest act of shifting gears. I mean to say that mere romantic speculation on the power and beauty of machinery keeps it at a continual remove; it can not act creatively in our lives until, like the unconscious nervous responses of our bodies, its connotations emanate from within – forming as spontaneous a terminology of poetic reference as the bucolic world of pasture, plow, and barn (*CPSL* 262).

Crane's aim, then, is to ensure that, what Perry Miller (in his 1965 book *The Life of the Mind in America*) has termed "the technological sublime," is brought into the realm of the quotidian through continuous use. It is noticeable that Crane's method is both linguistic and corporeal: not only will "continual poetic allusion" serve to subjugate the Machine (a concern that brings to mind Heidegger's warnings about the threat from technology), but so too will the process of bringing technology close to, even into, the body in a way that is quite different to the automatic hand of Eliot's typist. Crane's assertion of the presence of the ordinary in his work is consistent with other modernist writers. Liesl Olson has described how works by Joyce, Woolf, Stein, and others are part of "modernism's commitment to the ordinary, to experiences that are not heightened" (3–4), and Crane's interest here in "subdu[ing] novelty," the "modest act of shifting gears," and "unconscious nervous responses" all suggest that his work has something like the same commitment. However, Crane departs from his contemporaries (and the concerns of modernist criticism in this area) firstly by not showing to the same extent a fascination with the everyday as they do, and also by paying attention much more to a *process by which* the extraordinary is made ordinary, rather than just presenting an ordinary life or set of objects. In this way, Crane demonstrates once again – as I have discussed throughout the book, but particularly Chapters 4 and 5 – his interest in describing processes.

As Crane indicates in his essay, the process of making ordinary is grounded in the body. In "Cape Hatteras," after the "sensational" moment of the aeroplane's crash and the queer qualities being released through the appearance of Walt Whitman, Whitman himself is described as "[f]amiliar," and as having "set breath in steel." When the Bridge is celebrated again in the final part of the poem, "Atlantis," it is with the onlooker's eyes being constantly aware of the body "[p]ick biting up towering looms that press/Sidelong with flight of blade on tendon blade," and by using more terms that make the body and the technology one, a kind of *mechanomorphism*:[7] "like an organ, Thou, with sound of doom –/Sight, sound and flesh Thou leadest from time's realm"; "intrinsic Myth/[...]iridescently unborne/Through the bright drench and fabric of our veins"; "Inventions that cobblestone the heart." Each of these examples suggest ways in which the Machine has been made to "emanate from within," and if – as I have been arguing – technology was being considered as a dominant and normative force, here Crane also succeeds in absorbing that otherness into his non-normative poetics.

His doing so indicates another reason why that technology had to fail in "Cape Hatteras." As Tim Armstrong has observed, "[m]odernity [...] brings both a fragmentation and augmentation of the body in relation to technology; it offers the body as lack, at the same time as it offers technological compensation" (3). This too would be a threat to Crane's poetics because if the normative body is seen to lack, then the queer one would be perceived as even more deficient. Not to render technology ordinary by drawing it closer to the body and absorbing it would be to risk the possibility that the queer body and identity[8] within the poem might be overwhelmed by a socio-cultural engagement with technology that seeks enhancement, but only in the direction of normativity. Sara Ahmed has explained how

> [w]hat is other than me is also what allows me to extend the reach of my body. Rather than othering being simply a form of negation, it can also be described *as a form of extension*. The body extends its reach by taking in that which is "not" it, where the "not" involves the acquisition of new capacities and directions – becoming, in other words, "not" simply what I am "not" but what I can "have" and "do." The "not me" is incorporated into the body, extending its reach (115).

Instead of being mastered, the fusing of technology and body posits a "more," which ultimately allows Crane to bring elements of normative technology into the queer body and extend the poem, just as the ever-present image of the Bridge itself mimics a leap or extension into the world.

This extension represents a significant statement in Crane's queer project. Challenged by the editor Harriet Monroe to explain one of the images from his earlier poem, "At Melville's Tomb": "[c]ompass, quadrant and sextant contrive/No farther tides," Crane wrote:

> Hasn't it often occurred that instruments originally invented for record and computation have inadvertently so extended the concepts of the entity they were invented to measure (concepts of space, etc.) in the mind and imagination that employed them, that they may metaphorically be said to have extended the original boundaries of the entity measured? (Monroe and Crane 39).

In declaring that his image – and poetry itself – can "be said to have extended the original boundaries of an entity," Crane offers a queering of those boundaries. Instead of showing what Edelman has described as "the persistence of lack" in his work (*Transmemberment of Song* 241), Crane's idea posits a "more," something beyond the material entity, exemplifying what José Esteban Muñoz calls the "not-yet" of queer potential (1).

By extending itself in this way, Crane draws attention to the poem's potential for use beyond the confines of its pages. Frank identified this as a possibility for the poem when he observed that

> *The Bridge* is not a particularised being to be popularly sung; it is a conceptual symbol to be *used*. [...] From being a machine of body, it becomes an instrument of spirit. *The Bridge is matter made into human action* ("An Introduction" xxxv).

When Frank suggests that the poem's main purpose is to be an object or instrument of use, he offers a radical reassessment of its meaning. By being in a position of use, the poem itself is, in Heidegger's terms, "ready-to-hand," but as Liesl Olson has observed, "[t]he common logic about modernism [...] is that this state of being-ness, what Heidegger calls 'ready-to-hand,' must be radically shaken up; it must be re-seen or seen anew" (4). Instead, Crane's alternative modernism is located in a poem that resists the nosedives and somersaults of the increasingly dominant Machine, and redirects the focus upon the ordinary and handmade, as being something that is capable of acting for humankind. Roy Harvey Pearce has suggested that

> Crane admired Brooklyn Bridge as a machine whereby a man might ascend to complete self-knowledge and complete self-realization, thence to a complete community made up of men like himself who had ascended as he had. *The Bridge*, as poem, is meant to be such a machine [...] (109)

If the poem is itself "a small (or large) machine made of words," to use William Carlos Williams's famous expression ("Author's Introduction [to *The Wedge*]" 54), then the spun cables of *The Bridge* make up, what Crane calls in "Atlantis," a "telepathy of wires," a way of registering – even having access to – a definite shift in reality away from the heightened and fantastical world of modernist technology and towards a world that is tangible and grounded and human. In its extension outwards beyond the page, and in its potential for "use," Crane's work can be said to intervene in a debate between the world wars that crosses disciplines – from literature to design to architecture – which advocates a return to handicraft and a rejection of the Machine. It was a movement encouraged by such a prominent cultural critic as Lewis Mumford, who observed as early as 1924 that "[o]n the human side, the prime distinction overlooked by the mechanists is that machine work is primarily toil: handicraft, on the other hand, is a form of living" (103). Mumford makes it clear why Crane and his fellow writers should be concerned with this issue: machine work stifles the imagination, he claims, making the machine operator servile, devoted merely to the reproduction of identical objects rather than to the joy of creation. Several years before Mumford was writing, however, and before his composition of "Cape Hatteras," Crane showed a concern with the role of the Machine. "Episode of Hands," the 1920 poem that was discussed at the very beginning of this book, proposes the hand as a way of resisting the dominance of the Machine, and as a form of queer living. It is the relational contact through hands that negates the influence and danger of the Machine, as the "factory owner's son" binds up the wound of a factory worker injured, we assume, by machinery. The emphasis upon the hands of both the owner's son and the factory worker is a way of suggesting the world beyond the moment, beyond the poem. The hands of the owner's son "knew a grip for books and tennis/As well as one for iron and leather," whilst the worker's hand had "knots and notches, – many in the wide/Deep hand that lay in his," and these "seemed beautiful." It is as if Crane is describing a work of art handcarved in wood. And this hand-to-hand contact enables "factory sounds and factory thoughts/[to be] banished from him" as the two men enter into an intersubjective moment by which they are completely removed from their environment. Indeed the pronoun "him" throughout the poem is deliberately made ambiguous by Crane – we are not always sure which man is being described – in a way that mimics that intersubjectivity in the touching of hands, and an entering into an alternative, queer reality. The injury to the worker's hand is another example of technology's failure, but once again Crane's return to "handiness," which recalls the way in which Heidegger suggests we re-conceptualize the world, grants us access to that reality.

Conclusion: Towards a Queer Community

Unexpected interest

The opening line of "Episode of Hands" (*CP* 173) describes an "unexpected interest," a queer moment of connection that is set up against the normative background. Throughout this chapter and throughout the book I have been arguing that the key principle behind Crane's queer aesthetic is relationality and a desire for community; impulses that are often quite at odds with the majority of criticism about Crane which seeks to emphasize his obscurity and difficulty – a kind of expected unexpectedness if he is to be considered to be a modernist writer. In this final section I want to draw together those ideas by suggesting that the recent turn towards affect and reparative reading practices within queer theory can help to understand the type of unexpectedness in Crane's work that I have been highlighting. Such a reading acknowledges queer criticism about Sapphic modernism, but also situates Crane within a queer modernist community in a way that has not yet been made apparent in contemporary modernist studies. Considering these new developments within queer theory can therefore provide a valuable way of reflecting upon the queer reading practices within my discussion, and suggest ways in which my analysis of Crane's work might offer different possibilities for understanding literary modernism. Just as the book has shown that Crane's work challenges structures of modernism, particularly High Modernism, so attention to the affective can indicate why other queer modernists approach and erode these same structures and develop an aesthetic which, as I have demonstrated, includes rather than excludes. For Crane and for other queer modernists, this is an aesthetic that seeks to find common ground with a reader: in the perception of objects, in the negotiation of spatial forms, and in linguistic connotation. It goes beyond the normative to offer new times, new spaces, and new material through which sexualized currents can flow, and thus extends modernism's boundaries.

The fact that there is still a limited amount of academic writing addressing the intersection of queerness and modernism is surprising, given that there are a number of prominent modernist writers who wrote about queer or alternative forms of sexuality, such as Gertrude Stein, Virginia Woolf, Djuna Barnes, E. M. Forster, and Marcel Proust. In addition, given Foucault's dating of the beginnings of discourse about homosexuality to 1870 ("[t]he sodomite had been a temporary aberration; the homosexual was now a species" (*The Will to Knowledge* 43)), it might be expected that much greater attention would be paid to ways in which late Victorian and early modernist writers portrayed their sexualities. The prominence given to the trials of Oscar Wilde and then, later in the 1920s, the censorship of Radclyffe Hall's *The Well of Loneliness*, suggest important ways to consider what a queer aesthetic might look like. However, there have been very few studies of queer modernism, and even the publication of Joseph Allen Boone's *Libidinal Currents: Sexuality and the Shaping of Modernism* in 1998 did not result in an increased number of books and articles on the subject. Despite all the material available, and despite Heather Love proposing in the "Introduction" to a 2009 issue of *PMLA*, which featured a cluster of essays on queer modernism, that "of all the forms of marginal modernism that have surfaced in the past couple of decades, queer modernism seems particularly likely to merge into modernism proper," queer modernism still somehow seems to lack an identity (744). A special issue of *Modernism/modernity* (17.3 (September 2010)) collected essays on Forster and Liberace, homoerotic desire in the Middle East, Bryher and Marianne Moore, and Virginia Woolf, but the reader was left to make the connections between these only distantly-related texts and writers themselves. There was no contextual grounding for this section of the issue as there had been, for instance, in the special issue of "Decadent Aestheticism and Modernism" (15.3 (September 2008)), which was introduced by Cassandra Laity. Presented in this piecemeal, disjointed way, it seems that queer modernism is no more than an umbrella term to apply to writing that is by or about queer individuals, rather than a useful theoretical frame. Only the group of critics writing about Sapphic modernism have been successful in this regard, and as I suggested earlier in the book, these critics' sole focus upon women fails to take into account queer male modernism.[1]

Queer reading

Queer modernism's gradual emergence in the late 1990s and early 2000s coincided with what some critics have asserted to be the exhaustion of queer theory itself. This development could go some way to explaining the lack of progress in identifying and assessing the contribution of queer modernism to modernist aesthetics. In 2004 Stephen Shapiro argued that

> Queer Theory is less an ongoing event, than a periodisable moment, a relatively defunct agenda that can be safely syllabised and packaged for digestion through a shrink-wrapped assortment of contained debates (essentialism versus social construction, the politics of outing, transgendering, etc.) (77).

For Shapiro, Queer Theory no longer corresponded to Eve Kosofsky Sedgwick's definition of queer as a "continuing moment, movement, motive" (*Tendencies* xii), and worse still it had sacrificed its radical qualities for a position of safety. Although Shapiro did offer the "economic turn" as a way by which queer theory might rediscover its meaning, he was not able to perceive the much greater impact that Sedgwick's own 2003 book *Touching Feeling: Affectivity, Pedagogy, Performativity* would have upon the field. In that book, Sedgwick identified a prevalent strain of "paranoid" reading within queer theory, and sought to counteract this kind of negative affect by adopting a reparative reading practice. According to Sedgwick, some queer thinkers had adopted

> an anticipatory mimetic strategy whereby a certain, stylized violence of sexual differentiation must always be *presumed* or *self-assumed* even, where necessary, imposed – simply on the ground that it can never be finally *ruled out*. [...] The contingent possibilities of thinking otherwise than through "sexual difference" are subordinated to the paranoid imperative that, if the violence of such gender reification cannot be definitively halted in advance, it must at least never arrive on any conceptual sense *as a surprise*. In a paranoid view, it is more dangerous for such reification ever to be unanticipated than often to be unchallenged (*Touching Feeling* 132–33).

Sedgwick suggests here that the power of queerness in certain work is diluted by what she refers to elsewhere, borrowing a phrase from Paul Ricoeur, as its "hermeneutics of suspicion" (*Touching Feeling* 124) and a tendency not to be specific enough ("can never be finally *ruled out*"). In reacting defensively against what Sedgwick once called "homophobic criticism," queer critics have sometimes over-read situations and texts, reading everything through the lens of sexuality and disregarding the other possibilities of queer theory.

It is these other possibilities of queer theory that are most useful in accounting for Crane's unique contribution to modernism. Although my argument throughout this book has been fundamentally based upon an interpretation of the effects of sexuality, I have also frequently employed the wider implications of "queer" in order to show how Crane challenges the normative structures of mainstream modernism, as well as the dominant components of modernity, such as technology. In effect, my reading of Crane's work is closer to the "reparative" process that Sedgwick proposes in place of a "hermeneutics of suspicion":

> to read from a reparative position is to surrender the knowing, anxious paranoid determination that no horror, however apparently unthinkable, shall ever come to the reader *as new*; to a reparatively positioned reader, it can seem realistic and necessary to experience surprise. Because there can be terrible surprises, however, there can also be good ones. Hope, often a fracturing, even a traumatic thing to experience, is among the energies by which the reparatively positioned reader tries to organize the fragments and part-objects she encounters or creates (*Touching Feeling* 146).

The reading of Crane's work that I adopt draws attention to the way in which queerness creates a multiplicity in his poetry. As I showed in Chapters 3 and 4, Crane's writing and his techniques offers the possibility of multiple voices and the possibility of going beyond the normative to find a new position outside space and time. Reading Crane from this position emphasizes the newness of his work, the "surprise," and shows how he accepts the risk attached to his aesthetic: despite his efforts to make his work clear, it is possible that a reader may not "get" his work. In this respect, my book resists another influential critical approach that I consider to be a paranoid form of reading. This approach, exemplified in the criticism of Thomas E. Yingling and Tim Dean, is based on the idea that Crane's work is somehow inaccessible or private. If paranoia assumes more than is actually intended, the interpretation of Crane's work as encoded text suggests an exaggerated form of analysis that shows how any reading of Crane's sexuality "can never be finally *ruled out*," because every word can be an encoded one. Rather than delivering an open-ended reading of Crane, full of potential, this kind of paranoid reading ends up closing down the possibilities of Crane's writing. As Eric Ormsby has noted, commenting on Thomas Yingling's reading of "Voyages III," "Yingling is so intent on his Procrustean interpretation that he even misses the word play in 'oar' ('ore' as well as 'or') and suggests what I suppose will now be called a 'hermaphrotextual' approach both to poor Crane and his hapless lover" (38). Ormsby therefore suggests that Yingling limits his interpretation of Crane to one based only on sexuality and not on what Sedgwick calls "[t]he contingent possibilities of thinking otherwise than through 'sexual difference.'" A queer reading of Crane, as I have shown, need not disregard or subvert the meaning of the poetry. It can instead address the dimensionality of Crane's aesthetic, that is to say the visual, spatial, temporal, and material modernist contexts for his work, taking into account both the sexual currents of the writing and a close attention to Crane's use of language.

Reading strategies

The queer mode of reading presented in this book adopts the methods of close reading and genetic criticism; two approaches that might be considered as contradictory in their aims, especially if close reading is traced back to the practical criticism of a New Critical approach. As Dirk Van Hulle observes, "[g]enetic criticism presents an alternative to the New Critical machismo that refuses all extratextual help to interpret a work of literature" (6). But these methods have been complementary rather than contrary in my reading of Crane's poetry, since they both seek to make Crane's work more transparent. If, as I have been arguing, a reading of Crane's work that presents it as encoded ultimately limits interpretation, genetic criticism – in Van Hulle's words – "provides a context that does not only surround the work and delimit its meaning; it also opens it up" (6). In doing so, it adheres to the aesthetic of Crane's that I have been outlining, particularly in Chapter 3: an aesthetics of transience that is concerned with gaps and spaces between objects and ideas as a way of resisting and avoiding heteronormative temporal and spatial pressures, but suggesting an accordance with some of the interests of literary modernism. In addition, genetic criticism opens up Crane's work for an analysis of its affective qualities.

As I demonstrated in Chapter 4, tracking the changes made through the drafting process of "Voyages II" helps to show the particularly strong affective background for this sequence and to suggest ways in which the genesis of Crane's aesthetic can be reconsidered. His experimentation with shifting tenses exemplifies his thought process as Crane attempts to give appropriate weight to a particularly strong emotional moment of loss, whilst the emphasis given to the body, and in particular the way in which the queer body is oppressed by the world around it, helps a reader to understand and interpret the roles that both the human body and the body of the sea play in the published version of the poem. In particular, as I have demonstrated, a genetic analysis of the sequence allied to close reading of the published version of the poems and the poet's letters, indicate how far Crane was basing the work on his own biography, and the extent to which it prioritized experience, since early drafts show Crane seemingly writing down events almost as they happen. This is not a writer who is attempting to close off his experience of the world in code. In addition, those manuscripts of "Voyages II," which describe the oppression of the speaker or his assertion "I ask/ wreak hell or worse into this step" (A32), reveal a Crane who actively proposes to resist oppression, a socio-political Crane who is normally more visible in his letters than in his poetry. These examples show that there needs to be a reassessment of the shame and guilt with which Crane is associated by critics.

Embracing surprise

Considering a reparative reading of Crane can also help to develop an understanding of what I have been referring to as the "unexpectedness" of his writing. If, as Sedgwick argues, a paranoid reading forecloses the possibility of surprise, "to a reparatively positioned reader, it can seem realistic and necessary to experience surprise" (*Touching Feeling* 146). On the one hand, such "surprise" can be experienced in the content of Crane's work. The queer negativity of his aesthetic, in which the speaker of his poems relinquishes agency or challenges reproductive futurity so as to create alternative spatial and temporal dimensions, is jarring for the reader, but so too is the demand that Crane makes of his reader when getting to grips with his style. As Allen Grossman has argued, "it is the strangeness, the radical unfamiliarity of the thought, the unexpectedness of the cognitive demand that makes Crane 'difficult'" ("On Communicative Difficulty" 156). (Grossman offers another reason here to make use of genetic criticism: if the "thought" is so unfamiliar, a reader and critic will benefit from seeking out the genesis of that thought in earlier drafts of the poetry.)

The source of this "unexpectedness" is Crane's logic of metaphor, the connotative process which is, as I outlined, improper and disorderly.

But what is perhaps most queer and unexpected about it is that, more than any other modernist poet, Crane accords his reader tremendous independence of thought. Crane's "ontology of accidental attributes" (Butler, *Gender Trouble* 32–33), which, drawing on Judith Butler, I identified at the end of Chapter 3 as representative of his logic of metaphor, proposes an engagement with the text that is unlike other reader–poet relationships. The very particular stress that Crane places upon connotation and the extent to which he asserts that "[t]he reader's sensibility simply responds by identifying this inflection of experience with some event in his own history or perceptions – or rejects it altogether" (*CP* 235), demonstrate the "unexpectedness of the cognitive demand" (Grossman, "On Communicative Difficulty" 156). Rather than being asked to merely read the poem, the reader is invited to take part in it, as if the intervention of their own "event" might somehow change it. Crane therefore sets up an affectivity of connotation, a relationship that I have been identifying as intersubjectivity, and which can also be termed relationality. However, the emphasis Crane places upon the relational does not just apply to the relationship between reader and speaker; it can be considered in terms of modernism more generally, and suggests the creation of a queer community of modernist writers.

A queer modernist community: Crane, H.D., and the reader

Interviewed in 1981, Michel Foucault proposed that

> [h]omosexuality is a historic occasion to reopen affective and relational virtualities, not so much through the intrinsic qualities of the homosexual but because the "slantwise" position of the latter, as it were, the diagonal lines he can lay out in the social fabric allow these virtualities to come to light (*Ethics: Subjectivity and Truth* 138).

Foucault's notion of "affective and relational virtualities" and the possibilities that come from "the diagonal lines [...] in the social fabric" suggest that unexpected connections between queer writers might be drawn, and furthermore that shared queer concerns can offer a way of seeing queer aesthetics as an integral part of literary modernism. Brian Reed has attempted to position Crane in respect to his queer contemporaries, most particularly Djuna Barnes, with whom Crane was well acquainted, in order to "discern the contours of a period-specific queer response to more mainstream literary developments" (Reed 43). However, in keeping with Foucault's idea of a more indirect and virtual relationality, with the angle of the book that considers Crane as having a transatlantic queer identity, and in keeping too with the sense of queerness that I have been proposing as bound up with the immaterial, I want to argue that a queer modernist community might not be located in a specific place (as Joseph Allen Boone suggests when he analyses the queer sites of Harlem, the Left Bank in Paris, and Greenwich Village[2]) nor even between queer writers who actually knew each other, like Crane and Barnes. Instead, like his early virtual community of Oscar Wilde and Walter Pater, Crane's strongest queer community lies in a Foucauldian "affective and relational virtualit[y]" with the poet H.D., a connection I foregrounded in my opening chapter by suggesting both writers' associations with Decadence.[3]

Even before examining their poetry in tandem, and quite apart from their links to Decadence, there are a number of other parallels between the two writers. Both H.D. and Crane had their work defined for them by their peers. Pound, after all, labelled H.D. the first "Imagiste," whilst Crane was branded a failure by his contemporaries Yvor Winters and Allen Tate. Partly because of these critics or their associations with them, both Crane and H.D. encountered hostility later in their writing careers when they produced sequences of poems with an underlying narrative structure rather than single lyrics. Crane wrote *The Bridge*, and H.D. completed her 1940s *Trilogy*: *The Walls Do Not Fall, Tribute to the Angels*, and *The Flowering of the Rod*, but critics regarded the development of these poetic sequences to be retrograde steps. Both writers also wrote "'slantwise'" to the "social fabric" of mainstream modernism, and in particular at a tangent to the androcentric modernism of Pound and Eliot. Diana Collecott has shown that because of Pound's "discovery" of Eliot in 1914, "H.D.'s poetry was effectively displaced by Eliot's in the annals of Anglo-American modernism," forcing H.D. "underground" ("The Poetry of H.D." 362). Crane's own friction with Eliot, which I detailed earlier in my discussion, was made explicit when Crane wrote of a "safe tangent [at which] to strike" Eliot (*OML* 89), and it is through a shared geometrical imagery that both H.D. and Crane consider an aesthetic resistance to other modernist writers. Images of slant lines are associated with alternative forms of desire in Crane, and are found in "Garden Abstract" (1920/1926), in which a woman, metamorphosing into a tree, finds that her voice, "[d]umbly articulate in the slant and rise/Of branch on branch above her, blurs her eyes" (*CP* 9). In a similar way, "The Bridge of Estador" (c.1920–1921/unpublished), deals with "the love/Of things irreconcilable, –/The slant moon with the slanting hill" (*CP* 174). In the case of H.D., as Miranda B. Hickman has shown, the poet's experiences of visions in 1919–1920 whilst travelling with her partner Bryher were dominated by the geometric figures she had seen on a wall, and these informed her poetry and thought during the 1920s, although she only developed them at length when she wrote about her experience of being analyzed by Sigmund Freud. Comparing H.D.'s "mystical geometry" with that of W.B. Yeats's, Hickman shows how "H.D. connected her geometric visionary experiences with a forceful gesture of disobedience" (244),[4] and as I demonstrated in Chapter 5, it is clear from his own adopting of a mystical, geometric discourse that Crane sought not only to enter into dialogue with, but also speak *against*, the dominant modernist voice of Eliot.

In addition to the corresponding interest in mystical thought from which they derive imagery to articulate alternative voices and desires, I suggest that the "affective and relational" queer community produced by H.D. and Crane is also based upon the breaking down of the boundaries of the self in order to invite the reader to make intersubjective connections with the poets. This exemplifies not only the affective continuities that exist between the two writers, but also their attempts to reach outwards and draw readers into their community.

The writings of H.D. and Crane are notable for their detachment from the material world, a process that frequently involves a breaking up or dissolution of the self. This process, which Peter Nicholls has identified as a form of "psychic violence" (198), is evident in a poem from H.D.'s *Sea Garden* such as "Mid-day":

>   The light beats upon me.
>   I am startled –
>   a split leaf crackles on the paved floor –
>   I am anguished – defeated. (10)[5]

H.D. sets up a close parallel between the first person speaker and the natural world around: the crackling of the "split leaf" registers acutely as a fracturing of the self and seems to suggest complete psychic collapse. This imagery of violence is also a characteristic of Crane's poetry, the "cleaving and [...] burning" of a poem like "Legend" (*CP* 3), which had previously seemed to assert a stable and definite self, or in the contemplation in "Repose of Rivers" (1926/1926) of "the city that I finally passed/With scalding unguents spread and smoking darts" (*CP* 16). Yet in both writers this impulse towards destruction is frequently a preface to re-formation. In "Legend," the self is painfully restored when "drop by caustic drop, a perfect cry/Shall string some constant harmony."

In H.D.'s "Mid-day," although the self is "scattered like/the hot shrivelled seeds," it is juxtaposed with the image of the poplar tree: "bright on the hill,/the poplar spreads out, deep-rooted among trees." Rather than presenting the self in realistic terms, both poets employ abstraction, which is often set against the background of the natural world, in order to present this fragmented self. As Nicholls suggests in his discussion of H.D., "poetry becomes the medium in which the 'I' constitutes and reconstitutes itself" (198). However, this process is an affective one, and not restricted to the words on the page or to the experience of the first person speaker. The possibility of reconstitution that both poets present can be perceived as a form of hope, and the process by which the speaker (and reader) find that reconstitution is a genuine possibility can be seen as an attempt to fashion a queer place for the individual in the world. Hope can be, as Sedgwick has described it, "a fracturing, even a traumatic thing to experience" (*Touching Feeling* 146), but through their juxtaposition of images of destruction and reconstruction, both Crane and H.D. adopt hope as one of "the energies by which [they try] to organize the fragments and part-objects" (*Touching Feeling* 146) they create. As I argued in my discussion of Crane's relationship with Alfred Stieglitz, Crane employed a process of abstraction because it drew the reader into an intersubjective relationship with the poet. Through their use of abstract imagery and broken syntax, Crane and H.D. invite their readers to make an affective connection with them as they delineate the gradual emergence of hope in their poetry. As Michael Snediker has observed, "Crane's attempt to save affirmation from the demands of skepticism counts as one of the most singularly important and as yet unacknowledged contributions made by Crane, to both poetry and criticism" (48).

The queer community that I am proposing between Crane and H.D., and which could be extended to include other writers, offers new ways of thinking both about modernism and queer theory. The range of queer theory's engagement with literary texts would be widened by examining those modernist texts that speak to some of its key concerns, including those interests that have only recently appeared as part of critical developments in the turn towards affect and reparative reading. Examining the work of modernist writers like Crane and H.D. would fruitfully challenge and revitalize those areas of queer theory that were perceived to be too safe or predictable. The creation of a queer community also removes Crane from the critical discourse that treats his work as coded or inaccessible, since it makes very clear links outward and suggests ways in which his poetry might be read through other queer modernists, throwing light upon both his work and theirs. It can also help to address Crane's style and demonstrate the ways in which it can be simultaneously difficult and relational. I have attempted to show throughout the book how considering modernism and queerness alongside each other helps to demonstrate modernism's complexity and diversity, how reading Crane's work like this offers a challenge to the ways in which visual and literary strands of modernist art are perceived and connected, and how that reassessment can lead to greater attention being paid to the ways in which modernist poets try to reach beyond the page. Considering Crane as part of a queer community also adds to the debate, to which the book contributes, regarding the extent to which Crane accepts or resists the spaces of the heteronormative world, and how it is possible for him, through a challenge to futurity and forms of completion, to occupy his own distinctly queer position within a modernist conception of time that already contests the value of linear time as a representation of subjective experience. I have also been keen to address the kind of epistemological doubt that Crane's poetry encourages through its presentation of the material world, and offer the possibility that the modernism that a queer community might share could be based upon the desire to remain uncategorized.

At a time when there is greater attention being paid to the "unfolding of different, interacting responses to the predicament of modernity" (Boehmer and Matthews 285), such analysis builds upon existing modernist and queer criticism to open up Crane's work still further, realigning his influences, demonstrating how his example shaped the work of others, and drawing attention to his crucial role as a dominant figure within the overlying social fabrics of modernism.

Notes

Introduction: Relationality

1. All subsequent references to "Episode of Hands" are from *CP* 173. All first references to poems give the year(s) of writing and revision, followed by the year(s) of publication, separated by a slash. Dates are as given in Marc Simon's 1986 edition of *The Complete Poems of Hart Crane*.
2. In *Transatlantic Avant-Gardes: Little Magazines and Localist Modernism*, Eric B. White has explored the successes and failures of this striving for synthesis in his discussion of the relationship between the Young Americans and the expatriate avant-garde as it appeared in the pages of little magazines such as *Secession* and *S4N*. See, in particular, 140–54.
3. The best guide to Crane's appearances in various little magazines is *The Oxford Critical and Cultural History of Modernist Magazines. Volume II, North America 1894–1960*, which discusses many of the publications I mention during the book. A number of these magazines have been digitized by the Modernist Journals Project, directed by Robert Scholes and Sean Latham, and they can be consulted online: http://modjourn.org/index.html
4. Although he does not name it as such, Edward J. Brunner provides a genetic reading of the "Voyages" sequence (and a more detailed one of the development of *The Bridge*) in *Splendid Failure: Hart Crane and the Making of "The Bridge"* (35–55). Brunner makes no reference to Crane's sexuality, and refers instead to an ungendered lover.
5. Giles makes extensive use of dictionaries to develop his argument that the guiding principle behind *The Bridge* is the pun. He uses a slightly different edition of the 1909 dictionary, the *New International Dictionary of the English Language*, whereas the edition I use, *Webster's Unabridged Dictionary: An American Dictionary of the English Language*, was published "for the trade" in 1909.
6. It is not clear which edition Crane used, though Cowley's comment that Crane referred to '*Webster's Unabridged*,' suggests that Crane might have used the same edition from which I am quoting. In addition, since this edition was published for the trade, it is possible that Crane might have encountered it in the course of his advertising career. Indeed, Cowley places his recollection, which Clive Fisher locates in the summer of 1924, in the context of the workplace where Crane worked as a copywriter (Fisher 229).

1 American Decadence and the Creation of a Queer Modernist Aesthetic

1. There is some debate over which label, "Aestheticism" or "Decadence," to place on the work of the writers of this period, particularly those of the

1890s. Previous critics have used aestheticism and decadence as synonyms, as Karl Beckson chooses to do in his anthology *Aesthetes and Decadents of the 1890s: An Anthology of British Poetry and Prose*, or alternately placed a forward slash between "Decadent/Aestheticism" and combined the two terms in "Decadent Aestheticism" as Laity does ("Editor's Introduction" 427). In her valuable "Introduction" to the anthology *Decadent Poetry from Wilde to Naidu*, Lisa Rodensky suggests that "[t]o handle such confusion, perhaps one could separate late-century decadence from late-century aestheticism, such that the former would concern itself with the lurid subject matter and the latter with questions of form and style. One could, after all, reduce 'decadence' so that as a term it would take in only the most perverse work" (xxiii–xlviii). I choose to use Decadence as a term to describe Crane's influences because, unlike Aestheticism, it encompasses a number of the key ideas that most affected Crane: the concept of decay as it was attributed to the decline of classical periods of history and culture, and the concept of perversity or alternative sexuality from the normative. Yet it also denotes, as Rodensky observes, "an unexpected discipline and rigour, an obsessive refinement – of language, of sensation; it attempts to capture a fleeting impression in exact and exacting language" ("Introduction" xxiv). As the chapter goes on to suggest, these Decadent concerns were prominent in shaping Crane's aesthetic.
2. John Unterecker, in his description of Laukhuff's store, explains how important the shop was, not just to patrons, but to local artists and writers: "it was evident from the beginning that the bookstore had in it the makings of an informal educational institution. Any time of day one could drop in on what became a kind of continuing seminar. The chairs at the back of the store were always occupied, though the occupants varied from hour to hour. Here literature became a living force as ideas were debated and styles of writers analyzed" (47). For more details about Laukhuff's store and Crane's links to it, see Gladys Haddad, "Laukhuff's Book Store: Cleveland's Literary and Artistic Landmark."
3. The connections between Crane's work and French Symbolism are well known, particularly his links with Arthur Rimbaud, Charles Baudelaire, and Stéphane Mallarmé, and I do not rehearse them during this chapter. For the most recent of these, see Irwin, 371–83.
4. See "Plea of Justification Filed by the Defendant in *Regina (Wilde) v. Queensbury*" in Appendix A of H. Montgomery Hyde, *The Trials of Oscar Wilde*, 323–27.
5. For examples of the kind of responses to Wilde's trials, see Greenberg, 392–93.
6. All subsequent references to "The Moth that God Made Blind" are from *CP* 167–69.
7. The image of "sea-daisies" also suggests the flower and sea imagery of H.D., whose connection with Swinburne Cassandra Laity has discussed at length in *H.D. and the Victorian Fin de Siècle: Gender, Modernism, Decadence*. See, for example, 48–51.
8. Although he told Yvor Winters in 1928 (*OML* 359) that he had not encountered Gerard Manley Hopkins's work previously, Crane's poetry does bear similarities to that of the Victorian poet, especially in its use of sound patterning and surprising diction. See Brian Reed 21–23 for an exploration of this connection.

9. The line appears in Book VI, line 743. In the Commentary to his edition of the *Aeneid*, R. G. Austin offers this translation: "we endure, each of us, a personal ghostly treatment" (228).
10. This and all subsequent references to "Modern Craft" are from *CP* 142.
11. Both poems originally published in *Silhouettes* (1892), and reprinted in Rodensky, *Decadent Poetry*, 40.
12. As just one example among several cited by David F. Greenberg in *The Construction of Modern Homosexuality*, Ferdinand and Isabella of Spain "confirmed the thirteenth-century death penalty for male homosexuality, but brought the sanction into line with Roman precedent by changing the penalty from castration followed by stoning to burning at the stake" (302). Ferdinand and Isabella, the patrons of Columbus's 1492 trip across the Atlantic, appear prominently in the "Ave Maria" section of *The Bridge*.
13. Originally published in the *Chameleon* (December 1894), and reprinted in Rodensky, *Decadent Poetry*, 190–92. In the poem, the character of the "Love that dare not speak its name" is set alongside the character of "'true Love, [who] fill[s]/The hearts of boy and girl with mutual flame.'" (192). In "Modern Craft," Crane plays on the idea of there being "two loves," questions the idea of "true Love," and adopts the imagery of flame.
14. Sinfield argues that in fact, "it was in late 1894, only a few months before the trials, according to Holbrook Jackson, that 'serious rumours about [Wilde's] private life and habits became more persistent in both London and Paris'. And still not everyone believed them. W.B. Yeats, who knew Wilde well, thought he was unjustly accused when the trials began" (2).
15. Although the warder's narrative was certainly published in *Bruno's Weekly*, it is not clear from the subsequent reprint of the document that Freeman-Ishill's "Tribute" prefaced it or not.
16. This and all subsequent references to "C33" are from *CP* 135.
17. Crane is also making ingenious use of the "femme fatale," which Cassandra Laity suggests is a key trope of Decadent writing (see *H.D. and the Victorian Fin de Siècle*, 115–49). Here, this figure – as a trope of his writing or as his muse – has betrayed Wilde, becoming his jailer.
18. In reading the Wilde trials in this way I follow Alan Sinfield, who argues that "the trials helped to produce a major shift in perceptions of the scope of same-sex passion. At that point, the entire, vaguely disconcerting nexus of effeminacy, leisure, idleness, immorality, luxury, insouciance, decadence and aestheticism, which Wilde was perceived, variously, as instantiating, was transformed into a brilliantly precise image. [...] The principal twentieth-century stereotype entered our cultures: not just the homosexual, as the lawyers and medics would have it, but the queer" (3).
19. Crane's enthusiasm for *Ulysses* was tremendous: he was an early subscriber of the copies printed in Paris in 1921, but when the *Little Review* was taken to court in 1920 under obscenity laws and the book's publication banned in the United States, he was forced to ask his friend Gorham Munson to smuggle his copy into America, telling him "I must have this book!" (*OML* 73).
20. "Joyce and Ethics" is reprinted in *CPSL* 199–200.
21. In an article from his continuing series about Nietzsche in the *Little Review*, George Burman Foster asserted that "[a]t bottom, the decadent seeks to escape the diremption of the modern man between the individual and the social, by

affirming the former and negating the latter. The individual, the social cell, detaches itself from the whole organization, from the social body, without considering that he thereby dooms himself to death. The cell can just as little exists without the organism, as the organism without the cell. Decadence is the last word which anti-social individualism has to say to our time" (43). Such a definition, derived from Nietzsche, parallels criticism of the queer individual's perversity: since he cannot reproduce, he is unnatural. I explore this idea in more detail in Chapter 4, which examines Crane's work against the backdrop of recent theoretical discussions in queer theory about the antisocial thesis.

22. According to Dennis Denisoff, "[b]y the century's end, people were using the terms 'decadent' and 'aestheticist' to condemn almost any artwork that displayed innovations in aesthetic philosophy, subject or style – including realist stories, New Woman writing, and Impressionist art" (31).

23. The phrase appears a number of times in Pound's work, for example in "Canto LIII" (*The Cantos of Ezra Pound* 265).

24. Langdon Hammer makes a related point when he observes how Crane's letters to his queer friend Wilbur Underwood frequently show a "rapid shuttle [...] between intellectual and sexual enthusiasms." (*Hart Crane and Allen Tate* 126). Hammer goes on to argue that there are similarities of style and vocabulary between Crane's letters to his queer friends and those to his "straight" friends.

25. All references to "Impression. Le Reveillon" are quoted from Rodensky, *Decadent Poetry*, 7. In writing this series, Wilde was particularly influenced by Claude Monet, whose canvas *Impression, soleil levant*, had given rise to the term "Impressionism" in 1874 and the movement's preoccupation with quality of light and how best to represent it. Another significant visual influence was James McNeill Whistler from whom, as Karl Beckson and Bobby Fong observe, Wilde borrowed musical phrases ("nocturne" and "harmony") that had appeared in the titles of some of Whistler's paintings (64).

26. Pound urged writers to "[g]o in fear of abstractions" in his "A Few Don'ts by an Imagiste," originally published in *Poetry* 1.6 (1913) and reprinted as "A Retrospect" in Cook, *Poetry in Theory*, 85. All subsequent references to this essay will refer to the Cook text.

27. This and all subsequent references to "October–November" are from *CP* 136.

28. Collecott quotes from "Pursuit" (11) and part XIV of "Sigil," a section of "In Our Town" from *A Dead Priestess Speaks* (414), both of which appear in *H.D.: Collected Poems, 1912–1944* (Doolittle).

29. Pound complained in a letter to Alice Corbin Henderson, associate editor of *Poetry*: "Hellenism and *vers libre* have nothing to do with it." *Poetry*'s description of Aldington and Pound's letter are both quoted in Jacob Korg's essay "Imagism" (131).

30. Originally from Pound's letter to the editor, published as "The Caressibility of the Greeks," *Egoist* 1.6 (1914).

31. See chapter 4 of Collecott, and in particular part 6 of that chapter, "Greek Ecstasy," 130–34.

32. Untermeyer's article was published as "The New Patricians" in the *New Republic* (1922), 41–42.

33. In Crane's edition, the poems were translated by John Addington Symonds. It was published by Thomas B. Mosher in Portland, Maine, in 1909. Crane

inscribed his name and the date in the front of his copy: "Cleveland, '21." Kenneth A. Lohf reproduces a photocopy of the page with the two sonnets and Crane's copy of Sappho's poem in "The Library of Hart Crane" (303). All quotations from the Sappho poem are derived from there.
34. Crane mentions Pater in a letter to a gay friend, Wilbur Underwood, in December 1922, telling Underwood that he hoped a raise in his advertising salary would result in "more and decent people to work with who enjoy Joyce, Cabell, Pater and the best things of life" (*OML* 113). Although Crane does not explicitly mention *The Renaissance* here – and as later letters show, Crane read other works by Pater such as *Marius the Epicurean* and *Plato and Platonism* – my ongoing discussion will make it clear that this must have been the volume that Crane read at this point. Whilst I suggest below that other sections of *The Renaissance* were important in shaping "Faustus and Helen," I certainly agree with John T. Irwin (328) that Pater's essay on Winckelmann was a significant influence upon his poetry in the 1920s.
35. Hereafter cited as "Faustus and Helen." All subsequent references are from *CP* 26–32.
36. In his discussion of "Faustus and Helen," John Irwin notes that Pater's essay on Winckelmann addresses precisely the question which Crane was grappling with in his poem (328). As Pater puts it: "Can we bring down that ideal [of Hellenic culture] into the gaudy, perplexed light of modern life?" (*The Renaissance* 148). Irwin sees this question being addressed by Crane in Part III of "Faustus and Helen."
37. As is the case for a number of the volumes in his extant library, Crane read the text critically, with the aim not just to comprehend, but also to determine how the text might be useful for his own work. In his copy of *The Renaissance*, Crane made a number of annotations in the chapters about "The Poetry of Michelangelo," "Joachim du Bellay," and "Winckelmann," annotating the latter in three places.

2 Abstraction and Intersubjectivity in *White Buildings*

1. Crane described the excitement of reading at the party in a letter to his mother on November 30, 1924 (Lewis 377–79).
2. The essay was originally published in *Revolt in the Arts: A Survey of the Creation, Distribution and Appreciation of the Art in America*, edited by Oliver M. Sayer.
3. The Kokoon Arts Klub, modelled on New York's Kit Kat Club as an artistic and social meeting place, met with considerable resistance from Clevelanders, who were outraged at their social gatherings and artistic choices: one member organized a local display of ten cubist and futurist works from Paris in 1913. Given that the Armory Show had only just taken place, this was a startlingly bold move. For more on the various controversies associated with the Klub, see Holly Rarick Witchey's article "The Battle of the Early Moderns: The Kokoon Club [sic] and the Cleveland Society of Artists."
4. For more details on William Sommer's life, see Philip Kaplan, "'Look for the Miracle!' Some Early Memories of William Sommer, From 1924–1936." Gladys Haddad situates Sommer within his Cleveland milieu in her article

"Interpreters of the Western Reserve. William Sommer, Henry Keller, Frank Wilcox."
5. The work in question was Jean Cocteau's long poem "The Cape of Good Hope," translated by Jean Hugo, and published in the *Little Review* 8.1, Brancusi Number (Autumn 1921): 43–95. It was originally published as *Le Cap de Bonne-Espérance* in 1919.
6. In a letter to Gorham Munson in August 1922, Crane said that, unusually for him, he wrote the poem in one sitting on August 6, 1922 (Crane, *The Letters of Hart Crane, 1916–1932*, 96).
7. First published in *1924* (July 1924). Later published in *White Buildings* in 1926. This and all subsequent references to "Sunday Morning Apples" are from *CP* 7.
8. Crane responded through visual art with a telling caricature of Rosenfeld in the Winter 1922 issue of the *Little Review*. Enclosing the drawing, Crane commented ironically that it was "a bit of real 'significant form'" (qtd. in Fisher 167), thereby recalling Clive Bell's phrase in *Art:* "when I speak of significant form, I mean a combination of lines and colours (counting white and black as colours) that moves me aesthetically" (19). *Art* was originally published in 1914. The fact that it was Sommer who had introduced Crane to Bell's work would have made this reference all the more pointed.
9. For a representative selection of Sommer's paintings, see William H. Milliken, Frances Meriam Francis, Henry Sayles Francis, and others, eds. *The William Sommer Memorial Exhibition Catalogue*.
10. All subsequent references to "Interludium" are from *CP* 158.
11. Martin finds a number of clear parallels between Crane's essays and poetry and the work of Clive Bell and Roger Fry in his article "Painting and Primitivism: Hart Crane and the Development of an American Expressionist Esthetic." See in particular 50–53.
12. This was volume 68, January–June 1920. Originally begun as a Transcendentalist magazine in 1840, the *Dial* was re-launched under various editors.
13. This photograph of *La Montagne*, by Charles Sheeler, was printed in the *Dial* 70.3 (March 1921). Further images of Lachaise's work can be seen at the Lachaise Foundation website: http://www.lachaisefoundation.org.
14. Crane created Cubist portraits of his friends Susan Jenkins Brown in 1923 and Waldo Frank in 1924. For the Brown portrait, see Herendeen and Parker, eds., *The Visionary Company* 168. The sketch of Frank was originally published in *S4N*, and was reprinted in Cook, ed., 201.
15. This was part of an unpublished essay about Stieglitz's work by Crane, included in a letter to the photographer in 1923.
16. Sommer's cover for *Secession* (Number Four, January 1923) featured two pears, presented in a Cubist style. For a full narrative of Crane's attempts to promote Sommer's work, see John Unterecker's account in *Voyager*, 205–8.
17. Composed between October, 1923 and approximately March, 1924. First published in the *Little Review* (Spring 1924): 19, in a different form. This and all subsequent references to "Recitative" are from *CP* 25.
18. Crane's ideas here recall Pater's notions in "The School of Giorgione," in which he suggested that "the ideal examples of poetry and painting [are] those in which the constituent elements of the composition are so welded together that the material or subject no longer strikes the intellect only; nor

the form, the eye or the ear only; but form and matter, in their union or identity, present one single effect to the 'imaginative reason,' that complex faculty for which every thought and feeling is twin-born with its sensible analogue or symbol" (*The Renaissance* 92).
19. In the same letter to Tate in which he explained his conception of "Recitative," Crane emphasized the connection between visual obscurity and linguistic obscurity, noting how "'[m]ake my dark poem light, and light', [...] is the text I chose from Donne some time ago as my direction. I have always been working hard for a more perfect lucidity, and it never pleases me to be taken as wilfully obscure or esoteric" (*OML* 183).
20. Crane dated this poem in his own collection of his poems "Oct. '24." It was first published in the *Fugitive* magazine in September, 1925.
21. This and all subsequent references to "Legend" are from *CP* 3.

3 Spatiality, Movement, and the Logic of Metaphor

1. The Isle of Pines (Isla de Pinos) was renamed Isla de la Juventud (Isle of Youth) in 1978.
2. Stockinger concludes his essay by suggesting that "only recently have homosexuals realized that, as writers, readers, or critics, they were expected to conform to majority projections of minority sexuality. The rules of that game can now be revised. 'Homotextuality' is not so much a way to read texts as a way to reread them and to measure once again the disparity between the reactions that were implied or imposed and the substance that is really there" (148).
3. The poem was composed during the period October 1925–April 1926. It was published in May 1926 in the *Dial*, albeit in an almost unrecognizable form since the editor, Marianne Moore, would only accept the poem if she be allowed to make certain changes to it. Crane, desperate for money, agreed, but after Moore had rewritten the poem and retitled it "Again," Crane disowned it. For a detailed examination of Moore's changes and the possible implications of them, see John Emil Vincent, *Queer Lyrics: Difficulty and Closure in American Poetry*, especially chapter 4, "A Mirror at the End of a Long Corridor: Moore, Crane, Closure," 59–88.
4. All subsequent references to "The Wine Menagerie" are from *CP* 23–24.
5. In his consideration of Jeremy Bentham's concept of the Panopticon, Foucault speculates that there may have been a connection between Bentham's ideas and [Louis] Le Vaux's menagerie at the Palace of Versailles in Paris: "[a]t the centre was an octagonal pavilion, which, on the first floor, consisted of only a single room, the king's *salon*; on every side large windows looked out onto seven cages (the eighth was reserved for the entrance) containing different species of animals. [...] One finds in the programme of the Panopticon a similar concern with individualizing observation, with characterization and classification, with the analytical arrangement of space" (*Discipline and Punish*, 203). There is no way of knowing whether Crane too knew of the menagerie, but his reference to "[o]ctagon, sapphire transepts round the eyes" may suggest at the least a sense of this "analytical arrangement of space."

6. All subsequent references to "The Wine Menagerie" are from *CP* 23–24.
7. Gordon Tapper convincingly links Crane's reading of Pound's edition of *The Natural Philosophy of Love* by Remy de Gourmont with the use of sexual and animal imagery in this poem (53–67).
8. All references to the published version of "Voyages" are from *CP* 34–40.
9. Crane's manuscripts have been extensively catalogued by Kenneth A. Lohf in *The Literary Manuscripts of Hart Crane*. I refer to each manuscript by the number that Lohf gives it in his catalogue; so this early draft of "Voyages II" is cited as A42. For further details and credit lines, readers should refer to the "Abbreviations and Notes on Sources" page at the beginning of this book. In my transcriptions of all drafts, I use a ~~single strikethrough~~ to denote where Crane has deleted a word; **bold type** to show where he has made an addition; and a ~~double strikethrough~~ to show where he has made a change and then deleted it. If a word is unclear, I place it in [square brackets]. There are fifteen extant drafts of "Voyages II" in all, numbered in Lohf as A32–A46.
10. Although Baudelaire never used the term "flâneur," it has frequently been used to describe the figure and the behavior of the artist in Baudelaire's essay "The Painter of Modern Life." Whilst I use the term as it was applied by Walter Benjamin, I do quote directly from Baudelaire, thereby avoiding the problems of attributing assertions about the character which are in fact Benjamin's interpretations of Baudelaire's ideas, rather than Baudelaire's own notions.
11. These poems are "The Second Anniversary" and "The Expiration."
12. In a letter of early July 1921, Crane explained to Gorham Munson that he did not intend the poem to have a particular message about "the negro question." See "To Gorham Munson [probably early July 1921," *OML*, 64.
13. There is a parallel here with early twentieth-century views of the constituency of space. Stephen Kern describes how "[t]he traditional view that space was an inert void in which objects existed gave way to a new view of it as active and full. A multitude of discoveries and inventions, buildings and urban place, paintings and sculptures, novels and dramas, philosophical and psychological theories, attested to the constituent function of space." Kern refers to this concept as "positive negative space," which "implies that the background itself is a positive element, of equal importance with all others [...]. [I]t implies that what was formerly regarded as negative now has a positive, constitutive function" (152–153).
14. Commenting upon one account of nineteenth-century cruising in which two men meet by shop windows, Neil Bartlett suggests that "shopping and cruising become interchangeable activities in the city [...] Cruising is like window shopping. The boy, like a purchase, begs to be chosen and taken home" (253).
15. All subsequent references to "Possessions" are from *CP* 18.
16. Chauncey actually provides evidence to show that Bleecker Street, mentioned as the site for the cruise in the poem, could be a dangerous place to pick up men. Apart from clubs and tearooms like The Black Rabbit (on MacDougal Street), the area around it contained a number of male-only boarding houses, such as the Mills Houses, and residents of these were arrested during the 1920s for queer sexual activity (155).
17. In fact, Crane found it no easier abroad. In "Cruising with Hart Crane," Edouard Roditi recalled his unwilling cruise with Crane in Paris in 1929,

during which the poet came to blows with some local sailors (200–8). Not long after that evening, Crane was imprisoned for six days for "outrages violences ivresse" and fined 800 francs, only escaping further punishment thanks to the assistance of various American and European writers, such as Jean Cocteau, Andre Gide, Jane Heap, and Jean Paulhan, editor of the influential *Nouvelle Revue Française* (Fisher 406–7).
18. The poem was written between November and December, 1919, and published in the *Dial* 68.4 (1920). This and all subsequent references to "My Grandmother's Love Letters" are from *CP* 6.
19. This and all subsequent references to "Stark Major" are from *CP* 10.
20. These lines first appear in Job 1.8, and are repeated at 2.3. (*The Holy Bible* 464 and 464–65).
21. Job 1.6 and 2.2 (*The Holy Bible* 464). In the Oxford University Press New Revised Standard Version the lines are both translated as "Where have you come from?"
22. This and all subsequent references to "Cutty Sark" are from *CP* 71–74.
23. Crane clearly did not regard the Brooklyn Bridge as a piece of modern technology. Completed in 1883, the Bridge was already forty-seven years old when Crane published *The Bridge*, but because of the allusions to myth and history in the poem, it frequently seems older.
24. This and all subsequent references to "Cape Hatteras" are from *CP* 77–84.
25. "Recorders Ages Hence" appears in the Calamus section of *Leaves of Grass* (1891–1892 edition).
26. This epigraph is translated in Kramer 8. Crane's use of these lines is also ironic since the section's protagonist, Columbus, thought that he had reached Asia, but would never actually set foot on her shores.
27. All subsequent references to "Atlantis" are from *CP* 105–8.

4 Temporality, Futurity, and the Body

1. Brian M. Reed, for example, pays attention to the way in which Crane would spend hours typing verses whilst listening to his Victrola turned up loud, sometimes listening to the same piece of music over and over again, and alternating typing with yelling out a phrase or line from the poem he was composing. "Voyages," according to Reed, "delights in its half-intelligibility and its inconsistencies," and he argues that we should view the suite as Crane's attempt to write a sequence that "avoids teleology and favors the creation of a timeless, ecstatic state [...] Love is no longer an episode in a biography but an ahistorical state and a way of speaking into which the poet enters at will" (98–99 and 114).
2. This Ad Council public service campaign from March 1997 featured Bill, Hillary, and Chelsea Clinton, and encouraged viewers/readers to uphold children's rights.
3. These comments are not clear since Tate's letter has been lost, but given Crane's comments in the letter, Tate must have related his awestruck admiration of Eliot's work.
4. "The Bottom of the Sea is Cruel" was sent by Crane in a letter to Gorham Munson on October 1, 1921 (*OML* 66). It is catalogued by Lohf as A31a.

Crane left a significant number of drafts for "Voyages" behind: twenty-eight in manuscript, three in letters, and three in little magazines ("Voyages I" appeared in *Secession*, no. 4 in January 1923, "Voyages IV" was printed in the pages of *1924* in December of 1924, and sections II, III, V, and VI featured in the *Little Review* in the Spring-Summer issue of 1926).
5. All subsequent references to the published version of "Voyages" include all sections from I–VI and are from *CP* 34–40.
6. All subsequent references to "The Dance" are from *CP* 62–65.
7. All subsequent references to "Van Winkle" are from *CP* 55–56.
8. Although I discussed drafting in the previous chapter, since I shall be dealing more extensively with the drafts of "Voyages" here, it is worth reiterating the details of Crane's drafting and the way I transcribe it. In my transcriptions, I use a ~~single strikethrough~~ to denote where Crane has deleted a word; **bold type** to show where he has made an addition; and a ~~double strikethrough~~ to show where he has made a change and then deleted it. If a word is unclear, I place it in [square brackets].
9. A similar technique is employed by Crane in "Voyages V," but there the question of doubt is even more obviously raised.
10. In his drafts for "Voyages III" Crane explores this sense of homophobic oppression more explicitly, referring to an "obstacle" that comes between him and his lover.
11. It also calls to mind Crane's letter of 1926 to Wilbur Underwood in which he claimed: "Let my lusts be my ruin, then, since all else is a fake and mockery" (*OML* 261).
12. All subsequent references to "Indiana" are from *CP* 66–68.
13. "Passage to India" first appeared in the fifth edition of *Leaves of Grass*, dated 1871 but published in 1870.
14. For more details see Kramer 28.
15. All subsequent references to "The River" are from *CP* 57–61.
16. All subsequent references to "Quaker Hill" are from *CP* 92–94.
17. All subsequent references to "The Tunnel" are from *CP* 97–101.
18. Lee Edelman points out that "in its root sense ['inflections' implies] the 'bendings' of the lovers" (*Transmemberment of Song* 137).
19. Edward Brunner has observed how Crane appropriated these lines from the poem "Life" by Samuel Greenberg (*Splendid Failure* 39). As numerous critics have explained, Crane's poem "Emblems of Conduct," published in *White Buildings*, is largely a collation of various lines from Greenberg's work.
20. All subsequent references to "Cape Hatteras" are from *CP* 77–84.
21. It is notable that in its final form, "Voyages II" is the only poem in the sequence not to use the first person "I," as if the Other has been rendered meaningless, as the lovers become one being; "we" and "our." Whilst this seems like a crucial assertion to affirm the potency of this desire, it is important also to recall the "transmemberment of song" of "Voyages III," and acknowledge that the urgency to repeat or reinscribe meaning is also a form of memorialization.
22. In French, "s'abîmer" also means "to deface oneself," a highly appropriate image for this section of "Voyages," with its emphases upon the body as text and the "superscription" or "writing over" of one body with another.

Notes 193

5 Empiricism, Mysticism, and a Queer Form of Knowledge

1. "The Experience" was excerpted by Rusch from the first 102 pages of Part II of Toomer's unpublished autobiography, "From Exile into Being." Hereafter cited as "The Experience."
2. Toomer was elusive, sometimes hostile about his racial identity, and he was famously resistant to Horace Liveright's suggestion that details of Toomer's "colored blood" should be contained in the publicity materials for *Cane* (1923). Toomer was particularly disappointed that Waldo Frank's introduction to *Cane* suggested that its author had managed to go beyond his race in the writing of the work, and Toomer subsequently resisted any associations with the Harlem Renaissance and any attempts to label the book "Negro" fiction. For more details on Toomer's concerns, see Whalan, "Introduction," xvii–xli, particularly xix–xxiv. References to Toomer's letters are hereafter cited as *The Letters of Jean Toomer*.
3. Although the word "queer" was in currency in the 1910s and 1920s as a term of sexual identity, I do not suggest here that Toomer is knowingly using it in this way, but rather he is suggesting something that is out-of-the-ordinary or jarring.
4. In a letter to Munson in 1923, Crane responded to Munson's question about whether he should tell others of Crane's sexuality: "I discover that I have been all-too easy all along in letting out announcements of my sexual predilections. Not that anything unpleasant has happened or is imminent. But it does put me into obligatory relations to a certain extent with 'those who are in the know,' and this irks me to think of sometimes" (*OML* 138).
5. In his letter responding to Munson's essay, Crane wrote of his "suspicion that you have allowed too many extra-literary impressions of me to enter your essay, sometimes for better, sometimes for worse" (*OML* 234).
6. That Crane saw this move by Munson as an acknowledgement of his own "threat" is clear earlier in the letter where Crane observes: "No wonder Plato considered the banishment of poets; – their reorganizations of chaos on bases perhaps divergent from his own threatened the logic of his system, itself founded on assumptions that demanded the very defense of poetic construction which he was fortunately able to provide" (*OML* 233).
7. As Michel Foucault has noted, in the (lack of) discussion of sex and sexuality "[t]here is not one but many silences, and they are an integral part of the strategies that underlie and permeate discourses" (*The Will to Knowledge: The History of Sexuality, Volume 1* 27). Particularly noticeable in Crane's response is the idea that Munson is trying to silence his work by making him continue to speak – but as if through dictation. Paradoxically, one of the "silences' to which Foucault alludes can be speech.
8. James's essay "A World of Pure Experience" was first published in the *Journal of Philosophy, Psychology and Scientific Methods*, September 29 and October 13, 1904.
9. "Passage" was written between August and December 1925 and first published with "Praise for an Urn" and "At Melville's Tomb" in *Calendar* (July 1926).
10. All subsequent references to "Passage" are from *CP* 15–16.

11. William Carlos Williams spoke of Moore's own poetry in similar terms to the way he described Crane's, commenting in a 1925 review of Moore's *Observations* about how Moore's methods of composition lacked cement and involved the connection of edges (see Buxton 531–51).
12. Toomer wrote: "This is *it* was said in me with undeniable authority by the action itself. What *it* might be I could not imagine" ("The Experience" 34).
13. Toomer left New York in 1924 to become one of Gurdjieff's disciples at Château Le Prieuré at Fontainebleau-Avon in France. Toomer's correspondence with Crane stopped around this point, although Mark Whalan dates his first significant break from the New York group of Crane, Munson, and Frank to mid-1923 (xxxiv). In a letter to Gorham Munson just before his departure in July 1924, Toomer wrote that "[a]s a means to life as I desire to live it, as an end-in-itself, I have given up art – as we have practiced it" (*The Letters of Jean Toomer* 209). When Crane saw a demonstration in 1924 in New York by Gurdjieff's touring group, he was impressed with the "astonishing dances and psychic feats" of his group, but found some of the rhetoric and much of the presentation (especially by Gurdjieff's spokesman A.R. Orage) difficult to take seriously (*OML* 181).
14. As Steve H. Cook has observed, Frank's comments later on in *Our America* (which Crane read very closely both at its publication in 1919 and later) seem to prefigure Ouspensky (28). Prefacing his remarks about Whitman, Frank writes that "[s]ome men's knowing holds three dimensions. [...] But there are souls whose consciousness is higher. They partake of this global, three-dimensional world, but know it too for a mere moving surface, moving beyond itself into dimensions that are truer, and that cease from motion as they become more true" (*Our America* 202).
15. By establishing the route through friends by which Crane came to first see a copy of *Tertium Organum*, Brom Weber has asserted that "Crane read the book before the end of 1921 at the very latest, if not earlier" (153). Since Crane is writing about it to Tate in early 1923, it seems likely that Crane did not finish reading the book until 1922.
16. Eliot's essay was first published in 1919 in the *Egoist*: part I in 6.4 (September 1919) and parts II & III in 6.5 (December 1919). This sentence, which begins the third and final section of the essay, is prefaced by a quotation from Aristotle's *De Anima*, 1.4: "The mind is doubtless something more divine and unimpressionable." The use of such a quotation, suggesting aspects of the mind hitherto unexplored, show again how Eliot seemed to touch upon and then avoid the unknown elements that Crane was so keen to investigate.
17. Eliot discusses the "objective correlative' in "Hamlet and His Problems," naming it "a set of objects, a situation, a chain of events which shall be the formula of that *particular* emotion; such that when the external facts, which must terminate in sensory experience, are given, that emotion is immediately evoked" (100).
18. The essay was originally read to the Old Mortality Society at Oxford University in July 1864, and first published in *Miscellaneous Studies*, ed. C.L. Shadwell, 1895.
19. This recalls Poe's 1850 story "The Power of Words," in which Agathos educates his fellow angel Oinos about "the physical power of words' (825). Particularly emotional about passing a planet on their journey, Agathos

reveals how "with clasped hands, and with streaming eyes, at the feet of my beloved – I spoke it – with a few passionate sentences – into birth" (825). The connection made here between the erotic impulses of the lovers and the materiality of language provides a non-modernist source for Crane's concept of language's potentiality.
20. Logan uses his certainty about Crane's bisexuality to argue for the universality of Crane's lyrics in his balancing of male and female aspects of the human personality (xvii–xxxiii).
21. All references to "The Broken Tower" are from *CP* 106-7.
22. "A prayer to the Virgin, used by Roman Catholics" (*WUD* 52). The Angelus is traditionally said at the stroke of a bell once in the morning, at noon, and in the evening.
23. On one of the other pages attached to this, Crane had typed out his location and the date ("March 14th, 1932"), apparently beginning a letter.
24. This and all subsequent references to "At Melville's Tomb" are from *CP* 24.

6 Queer Technology, Failure, and a Return to the Hand

1. The influence of Spengler's book upon Crane is plain in his letters to Waldo Frank in 1926 (see *OML* 256-61). Initially he found Spengler's analysis of the dangers of technology and a Faustian decline of Western civilization to be pessimistic and depressing, and even suggested that it might render the artist's role meaningless, but after suddenly being re-energized in his writing of *The Bridge* in late July 1926, Crane was more circumspect, even crediting Spengler with assisting him in developing some of the themes of the poem.
2. Eric B. White has observed how Frank, Munson, and Jean Toomer all sought to develop a place in America for *unanimisme*, a movement begun by Jules Romains in France in the early 1900s. As White notes, this "drew on ancient folk cultures to synergise urban environments" (149), and "[t]o the Young Americans especially, *unanimisme* proved to be a remarkably resilient transatlantic model for infusing metropolitan populations with a pan-American sense of 'mystical synthesis'" (150). Such urban environments are also spaces implicitly connected with technology. Even if in the end, as White suggests, Frank did not feel that the principles of *unanimisme* could be adapted for America (because he could not point to the kinds of folk traditions which were an essential part of its meaning), these debates must have been explored by Crane, Frank, Munson and others, and Crane certainly read *S4N*'s "Homage to Waldo Frank" issue in which, as White notes, Frank was often linked with *unanimisme*. If Crane was not part of this nascent movement, I would suggest that such discussions would have provided Crane with a way of thinking about how a synthesis of America might occur in literature (and such a synthesis was, of course, Crane's stated aim for *The Bridge*). Certainly the sense of a folk tradition would have been of great interest to him, and in his use of Pocahontas, Rip Van Winkle, and the several writers and cultural figures who are included in *The Bridge*, Crane might be said to be constructing his own kind of "native" American folklore. In addition, as I will go on to argue, the conclusion to "Cape Hatteras" shows a need to return to the simple and handmade, marks of a folk tradition.

3. As I indicated in my second chapter, Crane indicated that he was no fan of Cocteau, resisting what he thought of as "impressionism" as it was exemplified in Cocteau's poem "The Cape of Good Hope." However, that poem, which celebrates the French aviator and fighter pilot Roland Garros, also clearly had an effect on Crane's presentation of the aeroplane, whether in terms of Crane's diction or the poem's fragmented or staggered lineation, as it explores a sense of the infinite space which the plane conquers, as well as the risk of the flight: in a section entitled "Invitation to Death," Cocteau describes his own experience of flying with Garros in 1913. In the first section of the poem, Cocteau, in a way that recalls the "Falcon-Ace"'s "Sanskrit charge" to bring about a new kind of poetic language, compares Garros's aerodynamics with his own "loopings/my records of high altitude" (44). Although Cocteau's poem is a celebration and lament for his friend (Garros was shot down in 1918), Cocteau does describe himself and the pilot in terms of "Dante and Vergil" [sic], echoing Crane's use of Whitman as a guide through and beyond the world of the Machine.
4. In a reading which also suggests the necessity of the aeroplane's destruction, Dickran Tashjian, commenting upon the inevitable misuse of technology in warfare, suggests that "[g]iven this course of civilization, the narrator implies that spiritual knowledge can be gained only through tragic descent, through the destruction of the airplane in combat" (162).
5. In their 2010 study, *Modernist Avant-Garde Aesthetics and Contemporary Military Technology: Technicities of Perception*, Ryan Bishop and John Phillips argue that the developing relationship of visual art to visual technology in the early twentieth-century presented a conflict between what could be seen and what could not, and that the artist had a role in representing this struggle. This is what they term a "hinge logic," by which "the reality behind visible things can be made visible *or* the making visible of that reality behind visible things reveals that it cannot be made visible" (9). Bishop and Phillips go on to argue that a significant power constituted within modernity is that of division, and that the military "is manifestly capable of enforcing and making the many divisions essential to the modern milieu, in addition to its functioning as a hinge. The hinge provides a techne [sic] – without giving itself up *as* a techne – through which divisions are made. Consequently, such divisions would never be entirely accomplished. The logic of the hinge nonetheless allows this simultaneous linking and de-linking to occur, and thus allows the military as the crucial hinge between *praxis* and *poiesis* [sic] – now recast as operations and intelligence – to prosper in its ascendance. The hinge would therefore be the most basic component of the military body itself as well as its primary mode of operation" (15-16). This conflict between the aesthetic and the technological is one with which Crane is engaged in "Cape Hatteras" and "Atlantis" (particularly in the destruction of the aeroplane). In addition, Bishop and Phillips' identification of the military as a key site where the invisible is or is not made visible suggests that Crane's use of a poetic which enables military technology to "release" or make present elements of his poem (in this case Whitman and queer qualities of language) was consistent with an ongoing development within modernist art. The analysis of the military's function as a hinge between *praxis* and *poiesis* also indicates that Crane's use of the fighter plane can be understood

as a mode of understanding by which those earlier understandings of *technē*, as outlined by Heidegger, might be accessed.
6. This and all subsequent references to "Atlantis" are from *CP* 105-08.
7. Tim Armstrong discusses the possibilities of *mechanomorphism*, a term first coined by Gerald Heard in 1939, in his book *Modernism, technology, and the body: a cultural study* (78).
8. In his discussion of the possibilities for the technological body, Armstrong, drawing upon Freud's 1930 book *Civilization and its Discontents*, identifies two different types of prosthesis which are present in modernist literature and culture: "a 'negative' prosthesis involves the replacing of a bodily part, covering a lack. [...] A 'positive' prosthesis involves a more utopian vision of technology, in which human capacities are extrapolated" (78). Ordinarily, the fighter plane might be seen as a prosthesis which augments human capabilities, but as I have argued, Crane's identifies this kind of technology as a normative, dominant form which needs to be destroyed to make way for queer qualities. However, in "Atlantis" we might consider the extension of the Bridge to be a type of prosthesis which allows for extension beyond the human world and reality of the body into the world of "Atlantis," which might indicate a form of utopia.

Conclusion: Towards a Queer Community

1. A panel at the 2012 Modernist Studies Association conference ("Queer Modernism/Modernism Queered") considered "the history of scholarly discussions about sexuality in modernist studies and explore[d] new directions for study." Rather than move discussion about queer modernism forward, the panel's title seems to suggest a re-introduction after a false start. The description hints at a lack of certainty about modernism's relationship with sexuality studies and a need to re-assess where modernism stands in respect to queerness. See the call for papers on cfplist.com <http://www.cfplist.com/CFP.aspx?CID=302> [accessed October 11, 2014].
2. See chapter 4, "Theaters of the Mind II: Queer Sites in Modernism: Harlem/The Left Bank/Greenwich Village in the 1920s and 1930s," in *Libidinal Currents* (204–87).
3. There are parallels here between the notion of a virtual community and the kind of imagined community that Benedict Anderson identifies as being instrumental in the formation of national identity. Anderson suggests that such a community "is *imagined* because the members of even the smallest nation will never know most of their fellow-members, meet them, or even hear of them, yet in the minds of each lives the image of their communion" (6).
4. Hickman argues that H.D.'s use of a geometric mystical language was designed to challenge Freud (see Hickman 232–34).
5. "Mid-day" was first published in *Sea Garden* (1916).

Bibliography

Ahmed, Sara. *Queer Phenomenology: Orientations, Objects, Others*. Durham: Duke University Press, 2006.
Altieri, Charles. *Painterly Abstraction in Modernist American Poetry*. Cambridge: Cambridge University Press, 1989.
Anderson, Benedict. *Imagined Communities: Reflections on the Origin and Spread of Nationalism*. 1983. London: Verso, 2006.
Apollinaire, Guillaume. "The Cubist Painters [excerpt]." 1913. Trans. Lionel Abel. *Modernism: An Anthology of Sources and Documents*. 1998. Eds. Vassiliki Kolocotroni, Jane Goldman and Olga Taxidou. Edinburgh: University of Edinburgh Press, 2009. 262–67.
Armstrong, Tim. *Modernism, Technology, and the Body: A Cultural Study*. Cambridge: Cambridge University Press, 1998.
Bachelard, Gaston. *The Poetics of Space*. 1958. Trans. Maria Jolas. 1964. Boston: Beacon, 1994.
Baldwin, Thomas. [Introduction to "The Intertwining – The Chiasm"]. *Maurice Merleau-Ponty: Basic Writings*. Ed. Thomas Baldwin. London: Routledge, 2004. 247–48.
Barber, Stephen M. and David L. Clark. "Introduction." *Regarding Sedgwick: Essays on Queer Culture and Critical Theory*. Eds. Stephen M. Barber and David L. Clark. London: Routledge, 2002. 1–56.
Barthes, Roland. *The Pleasure of the Text*. 1973. Trans. Richard Miller. New York: Hill and Wang, 1975.
Barthes, Roland. *A Lover's Discourse: Fragments*. 1977. Trans. Richard Howard. 1978. London: Vintage, 2002.
Bartlett, Neil. *Who Was That Man?: A Present for Mr Oscar Wilde*. London: Serpent's Tail, 1988.
Baudelaire, Charles. *Selected Writings on Art and Literature*. Trans. P. E. Charvet. 1972. London: Penguin, 2006.
Beaver, Harold. "Homosexual Signs (In Memory of Roland Barthes)." *Critical Inquiry* 8.1 (1981): 99–119.
Bech, Henning. *When Men Meet: Homosexuality and Modernity*. 1987. Trans. Teresa Mesquit and Tim Davies. Cambridge: Polity, 1997.
Beckson, Karl. *Aesthetes and Decadents of the 1890s: An Anthology of British Poetry and Prose*. 1966. Chicago: Academy Chicago, 1993.
Beckson, Karl and Bobby Fong. "Wilde as Poet." *The Cambridge Companion to Oscar Wilde*. Ed. Peter Raby. Cambridge: Cambridge University Press, 1997. 57–68.
Beer, Thomas. *Hanna, Crane and the Mauve Decade*. New York: A.A. Knopf, 1941.
Bell, Clive, *Art*. 1914. New York: BiblioBazaar, 2007.
Bell, Clive, *Since Cézanne*. London: Chatto & Windus, 1922.
Bell, Ian F. A. "The Poundian Fourth Dimension." *Symbiosis: A Journal of Anglo-American Literary Relations* 11.2 (2007): 61–84.

Bell, Ian F. A. and Merial Lland. "Silence and Solidity in Early Anglo-American Modernism: Nietzsche, the Fourth Dimension, and Ezra Pound, Part One." *Symbiosis: A Journal of Anglo-American Literary Relations* 10.1 (2006): 47–61.
Bell, Ian F. A. and Merial Lland. "Silence and Solidity in Early Anglo-American Modernism: Nietzsche, the Fourth Dimension, and Ezra Pound, Part Two." *Symbiosis: A Journal of Anglo-American Literary Relations* 10.2 (2006): 115–31.
Benjamin, Walter. "The Flâneur." *The Arcades Project.* Trans. Howard Eiland and Kevin McLaughlin. Cambridge, MA: Belknap Press of Harvard University Press, 1999. 416–55.
Berger, John. *Ways of Seeing.* London: BBC and Penguin, 1972.
Berlant, Lauren and Lee Edelman. *Sex, or the Unbearable.* Durham and London: Duke University Press, 2014.
Bersani, Leo. "Is the Rectum a Grave?" *October* 43 (1987): 197–222.
Bersani, Leo. *Homos.* Cambridge: Harvard University Press, 1995.
Bishop, Ryan and John Phillips. *Modernist Avant-garde Aesthetics and Contemporary Military Technology: Technicities of Perception.* Edinburgh: Edinburgh University Press, 2010.
Blackmur, R. P. "New Thresholds, New Anatomies: Notes on a Text of Hart Crane." *Language as Gesture: Essays in Poetry.* 1954. London: George Allen & Unwin, 1961. 301–16.
Bloom, Harold, Ed. *Hart Crane: Modern Critical Views.* New York: Chelsea House Publishers, 1986.
Bloom, Harold, ed. *Hart Crane: Comprehensive Research and Study Guide.* Philadelphia, PA: Chelsea House, 2003.
Boehmer, Elleke and Steven Matthews. "Modernism and colonialism." *The Cambridge Companion to Modernism.* 2nd Edition. Ed. Michael Levenson. Cambridge: Cambridge University Press, 2011. 284–300.
Boone, Joseph Allen. *Libidinal Currents: Sexuality and the Shaping of Modernism.* Chicago: University of Chicago Press, 1998.
Bradshaw, David and Kevin J. H. Dettmar, Eds. *A Companion to Modernist Literature and Culture.* Oxford: Blackwell, 2006.
Bragdon, Claude. "Introduction to the English Translation." *Tertium Organum, 2nd American Edition.* Trans. Nicholas Bessaraboff and Claude Bragdon. New York: Knopf, 1924. 1–7.
Bromwich, David. *Skeptical Music: Essays on Modern Poetry.* Chicago: University of Chicago Press, 2001.
Brooker, Peter and Andrew Thacker, Eds. *The Oxford Critical and Cultural History of Modernist Magazines. Volume II, North America 1894–1960.* Oxford: Oxford University Press, 2012.
Brunner, Edward. *Splendid Failure: Hart Crane and the Making of* The Bridge. Urbana: University of Illinois Press, 1985.
Buelens, Gert. "The American Poet and His City: Crane, Williams, and Olson, Perceptions of Reality in American Poetry (1930–1960)." *English Studies* 73.3 (1992): 248–63.
Butler, Judith. *Gender Trouble: Feminism and the Subversion of Identity.* 1990. London: Routledge Classics, 2006.
Butler, Judith. *Bodies That Matter: On the Discursive Limits of 'Sex.'* London: Routledge, 1993.

Butterfield, R.W. *The Broken Arc: A Study of Hart Crane*. Edinburgh: Oliver & Boyd, 1969.
Buxton, Rachel. "Marianne Moore and the Poetics of Pragmatism." *Review of English Studies* 58.236 (2007): 531–51.
Calinescu, Matei. *Five Faces of Modernity: Modernism, Avant-Garde, Decadence, Kitsch, Postmodernism*. 1977. Durham, NC: Duke University Press, 1987.
Carr, Helen. *The Verse Revolutionaries: Ezra Pound, H.D. and The Imagists*. London: Jonathan Cape, 2009.
Chauncey, George. *Gay New York: Gender, Urban Culture, and the Making of the Gay Male World, 1890–1940*. New York: Basic Books, 1994.
Chisholm, Dianne. *Queer Constellations: Subcultural Space in the Wake of the City*. Minneapolis: University of Minnesota Press, 2005.
Clark, David R., Ed. *Studies in* The Bridge. Columbus: Charles E. Merrill, 1970.
Clark, David R., Ed. *Critical Essays on Hart Crane*. Boston: G. K. Hall, 1982.
Cocteau, Jean. "The Cape of Good Hope." Trans. Jean Hugo. *Little Review* 8.1, Brancusi Number (Autumn 1921): 43–95.
Cole, Merrill. *The Other Orpheus: A Poetics of Modern Homosexuality*. London: Routledge, 2003.
Collecott, Diana. *H.D. and Sapphic Modernism: 1910–1950*. Cambridge: Cambridge University Press, 1999.
Collecott, Diana. "The Poetry of H.D." *A Companion to Modernist Literature and Culture*. Eds. David Bradshaw and Kevin J.H. Dettmar. Oxford: Blackwell, 2006. 358–66.
Cook, Jon., Ed. *Poetry in Theory: An Anthology 1900–2000*. Oxford: Blackwell Publishing, 2004.
Cook, Steve H., Ed. *The Correspondence between Hart Crane and Waldo Frank*. Troy, NY: Whitston, 1998.
Cowley, Malcolm. *Exile's Return: A Literary Odyssey of the 1920s*. 1951. New York: Viking, 1969.
Cowley, Malcolm. *A Second Flowering: Works and Days of the Lost Generation*. 1973. London: Penguin, 1980.
Crane, Hart. "Joyce and Ethics." *Little Review* 3 (July 1918): 65.
Crane, Hart. "Sherwood Anderson." *The Double Dealer* 2.7 (July 1921): 42–45. Rpt. in *Hart Crane: Complete Poems and Selected Letters*. Ed. Langdon Hammer. New York: Library of America, 2006. 154–58.
Crane, Hart. "General Aims and Theories." Unpublished (1925). *Hart Crane: Complete Poems and Selected Letters*. Ed. Langdon Hammer. New York: Library of America, 2006. 160–64.
Crane, Hart. "Modern Poetry." *Revolt in the Arts: A Survey of the Creation, Distribution and Appreciation of Art in America*. Ed. Oliver M. Sayler. New York: Bretano's, 1930. 294–98. Rpt. in *Hart Crane: Complete Poems and Selected Letters*. Ed. Langdon Hammer. New York: Library of America, 2006. 170–73.
Crane, Hart. *The Letters of Hart Crane, 1916–1932*. 1952. Ed. Brom Weber. Berkeley: University of California Press, 1965.
Crane, Hart. *The Complete Poems and Selected Letters and Prose of Hart Crane*. Ed. Brom Weber. London: Oxford University Press, 1968.
Crane, Hart. *White Buildings*. New York: Liveright, 1972.
Crane, Hart. *The Complete Poems of Hart Crane*. Ed. Marc Simon. New York: Liveright, 1986.
Crane, Hart. *O My Land, My Friends: The Selected Letters of Hart Crane*. Eds. Langdon Hammer and Brom Weber. London: Four Walls Eight Windows, 1997.

Crane, Hart. *Hart Crane: Complete Poems and Selected Letters.* Ed. Langdon Hammer. New York: Library of America, 2006.
Crane, Hart. *Hart Crane – Poems Selected by Maurice Riordan.* Ed. Maurice Riordan. London: Faber and Faber, 2008.
Crane, Hart, and others. *Letters of Hart Crane and his Family.* Ed. Thomas S. W. Lewis. New York: Columbia University Press, 1974.
Culler, Jonathan. *Barthes: A Very Short Introduction.* 1983. Oxford: Oxford University Press, 2002.
Currell, Susan. *American Culture in the 1920s.* Edinburgh: Edinburgh University Press, 2009.
Davison, Richard Allan. "Hart Crane, Louis Untermeyer, and T.S. Eliot: A New Crane Letter." *American Literature* 44.1 (1972): 143–46.
Dean, Tim. "Hart Crane's Poetics of Privacy." *American Literary History* 8.1 (1996): 83–109.
De Certeau, Michel. *The Practice of Everyday Life.* 1980. Trans. Steven Rendall. Berkeley: University of California Press, 1984.
Delany, Samuel R. *Longer Views: Extended Essays.* Hanover, NH: University Press of New England, 1996.
Denisoff, Dennis. "Decadence and aestheticism." *The Cambridge Companion to the Fin de Siècle.* Ed. Gail Marshall. Cambridge: Cambridge University Press, 2007. 31–52.
Doan, Laura and Jane Garrity. "Modernism Queered." *A Companion to Modernist Literature and Culture.* Eds. David Bradshaw and Kevin J.H. Dettmar. Oxford: Blackwell, 2006. 542–50.
Doeren, Suzanne Clark. "Theory of Culture, Brooklyn Bridge, and Hart Crane's Rhetoric of Memory." *Bulletin of the Midwest Modern Language Association* 15.1 (1982): 18–28.
Dollimore, Jonathan. *Sexual Dissidence: Augustine to Wilde, Freud to Foucault.* Oxford: Clarendon, 1991.
Doolittle, Hilda [H.D.]. *H.D.: Collected Poems, 1912–1944.* Ed. Louis L. Martz. New York: New Directions, 1986.
Edelman, Lee. *Transmemberment of Song: Hart Crane's Anatomies of Rhetoric and Desire.* Stanford: Stanford University Press, 1987.
Edelman, Lee. *Homographesis: Essays in Gay Literary and Cultural Theory.* London: Routledge, 1994.
Edelman, Lee. *No Future: Queer Theory and the Death Drive.* Durham, NC: Duke University Press, 2004.
Eliot, T.S. "Hamlet and His Problems." *The Sacred Wood: Essays on Poetry and Criticism.* 1920. London: Methuen, 1967. 95–103.
Eliot, T.S. *The Sacred Wood: Essays on Poetry and Criticism.* 1920. London: Methuen, 1967.
Eliot, T.S. "Swinburne as Poet." *The Sacred Wood: Essays on Poetry and Criticism.* 1920. London: Methuen, 1967. 144–50.
Eliot, T.S. "Tradition and the Individual Talent." *The Sacred Wood: Essays on Poetry and Criticism.* 1920. London: Methuen, 1967. 47–59.
Eliot, T.S. "The Metaphysical Poets." *Times Literary Supplement* 1031 (October 20, 1921): 669–70. Rpt. in *Selected Essays.* New York: Harcourt Brace, 1950. 241–50.
Eliot, T.S. "London Letter." *Dial* 71.2 (1921): 213–17.
Eliot, T.S. "*Ulysses*, Order, and Myth." *Dial* 75.5 (November 1923). Rpt. in *Modernism: An Anthology of Sources and Documents.* Eds. Vassiliki Kolocotroni,

Jane Goldman and Olga Taxidou. 1998. Edinburgh: Edinburgh University Press, 2009. 371–73.
Eliot, T.S. *Collected Poems, 1909–1962.* 1963. London: Faber and Faber, 1974.
Eliot, T.S. *The Waste Land: A Facsimile and Transcript of the Original Drafts.* Ed. Valerie Eliot. London: Faber and Faber, 1971.
Ferrer, Daniel and Michael Groden. "Introduction: A Genesis of French Genetic Criticism." *Genetic Criticism: Texts and Avant-textes.* Eds. Jed Deppman, Daniel Ferrer and Michael Groden. Philadelphia: University of Pennsylvania Press, 2004. 1–16.
Fisher, Clive. *Hart Crane: A Life.* New Haven, CT: Yale University Press, 2002.
Foster, George Burman. "Personality." *Little Review* 1.9 (1914): 40–45.
Foucault, Michel. *Discipline and Punish: The Birth of the Prison.* 1975. Trans. Alan Sheridan. 1977. London: Penguin, 1991.
Foucault, Michel. *The Will to Knowledge: The History of Sexuality, Volume 1.* 1976. Trans. Robert Hurley. London: Penguin, 1998.
Foucault, Michel. *Ethics: Subjectivity and Truth. Essential Works of Michel Foucault, 1954–1984, Volume 1.* Ed. Paul Rabinow. London: Penguin Books Ltd., 2000.
Frank, Waldo. *Our America.* New York: Boni & Liveright, 1919.
Frank, Waldo. "The Machine and Metaphysics." *The New Republic* (November 18, 1925): 330. Rpt. in *In the American Jungle [1925–1936].* New York and Toronto: Farrar & Reinhart Incorporated, 1937. 153–57.
Frank, Waldo. "An Introduction by Waldo Frank." *The Bridge: A Poem by Hart Crane.* By Hart Crane. New York: Liveright, 1958. xvii–xxxvi.
Freeman, Elizabeth. "Introduction." *GLQ: A Journal of Lesbian and Gay Studies* 13.2–3 (2007): 159–76.
Freeman, Elizabeth and others. "Theorizing Queer Temporalities: A Roundtable Discussion." *GLQ: A Journal of Lesbian and Gay Studies* 13.2–3 (2007): 177–95.
Freeman-Ishill, Rose. "Tribute." *The Story of Oscar Wilde's Life & Experience in Reading Gaol by his warder: Published in Bruno's Weekly, Jan 22, 1916, incl. a tribute by Rose Freeman-Ishill.* Berkeley Heights, NJ: Oriole, 1963.
Gabriel, Daniel. *Hart Crane and the Modernist Epic: Canon and Genre Formation in Crane, Pound, Eliot, and Williams.* New York and Basingstoke: Palgrave Macmillan, 2007.
Gardner, Jared. "'Our Native Clay': Racial and Sexual Identity and the Making of Americans in *The Bridge.*" *American Quarterly* 44.1 (1992): 24–50.
Gelpi, Albert. *A Coherent Splendor: The American Poetic Renaissance, 1910–1950.* Cambridge: Cambridge University Press, 1987.
Giles, Paul. *Hart Crane: The Contexts of 'The Bridge.'* Cambridge: Cambridge University Press, 1986.
Goody, Alex. *Technology, Literature and Culture.* Cambridge: Polity, 2011.
Greenberg, David F. *The Construction of Homosexuality.* Chicago: University of Chicago Press, 1988.
Grossman, Allen. "Hart Crane and Poetry: A Consideration of Crane's Intense Poetics with Reference to 'The Return.'" *Critical Essays on Hart Crane.* Ed. David R. Clark. Boston: G. K. Hall, 1982. 221–54.
Grossman, Allen. "On Communicative Difficulty in General and 'Difficult' Poetry in Particular: The Example of Hart Crane's 'The Broken Tower.'" *Chicago Review* 53.2–3 (2007): 140–61.

Guiguet, Jean. *The Poetic Universe of Hart Crane*. Trans. Jean Guiguet. Orono, ME: Puckerbrush Press, 1993.
Haddad, Gladys. "Interpreters of the Western Reserve: William Sommer, Henry Keller, Frank Wilcox." *Cleveland as a Center of Regional Art*. Ed. Sandy Richert. Cleveland: Cleveland Artists Foundation, 1993. 48–54. <http://academic.csuohio.edu/tah/regional_arts/Cleveland_as_a_Center/p48interpreters.pdf> [accessed October 13, 2014]
Haddad, Gladys. "Laukhuff's Book Store: Cleveland's Literary and Artistic Landmark." Midwest Art History Society (March 1996). <http://academic.csuohio.edu/tah/regional_arts/artsheritage/p45laukhuffs.pdf> [accessed October 13, 2014]
Halberstam, Judith. *In a Queer Time and Place: Transgender Bodies, Subcultural Lives*. New York: New York University Press, 2005.
Halberstam, Judith. *The Queer Art of Failure*. Durham, NC: Duke University Press, 2011.
Hammer, Langdon. *Hart Crane and Allen Tate: Janus-Faced Modernism*. Princeton: Princeton University Press, 1993.
Hammer, Langdon. "Stieglitz, Hart Crane, and Abstract Form." Unpublished essay, 1999.
Heidegger, Martin. *Being and Time*. 1958. Trans. Joan Stambaugh. Albany: University of New York Press, 2010.
Heidegger, Martin. "The Question Concerning Technology." *Basic Writings*. Ed. David Farrell Krell. 1977. London: Routledge Classics, 2011. 217–38.
Heidegger, Martin. *Nietzsche: Volumes One and Two*. Trans. David Farrell Krell. New York: HarperCollins, 1991.
Herendeen, Warren and Donald G. Parker, Eds. *Hart Crane Newsletter* 1.1 (1977).
Herendeen, Warren and Donald G. Parker, Eds. *The Visionary Company: A Magazine of the Twenties: Hart Crane Memorial Issue* 1.2 and 2.1 (1982).
Hickman, Miranda B. *The Geometry of Modernism: The Vorticist Idiom in Lewis, Pound, H.D., and Yeats*. Austin: University of Texas Press, 2005.
Hocquenghem, Guy. *Homosexual Desire*. Trans. Daniella Dangoor. Durham, NC: Duke University Press, 1993.
The Holy Bible: Containing the Old and New Testaments, New Revised Standard Version. 1989. Oxford: Oxford University Press, 1995.
Horton, Philip. *Hart Crane: The Life of an American Poet*. 1937. New York: Viking, 1957.
Hulme, T.E. "A Lecture on Modern Poetry." *Further Speculations*. Ed. Samuel Hynes. Minneapolis: University of Minnesota Press, 1955. 67–76.
Hyde, H. Montgomery. *The Trials of Oscar Wilde*. New York: Dover, 1973.
Inwood, Michael. *Heidegger: A Very Short Introduction*. 1997. Oxford: Oxford University Press, 2000.
Irwin, John T. *Hart Crane's Poetry: "Appollinaire lived in Paris, I live in Cleveland, Ohio."* Baltimore, MD: Johns Hopkins University Press, 2011.
James, William. *Writings 1902–1910*. Ed. Bruce Kuklick. New York: Library of America, 1987.
Kant, Immanuel. *Critique of Pure Reason*. Leipzig: Reclam, 1781.
Kaplan, Philip. "'Look for the Miracle!': Some Early Memories of William Sommer, From 1924 to 1936." *Serif* 8.2 (1971): 3–8.

Kaufmann, Walter, Ed. and Trans. *The Portable Nietzsche*. 1954. London: Penguin, 1976.

Kern, Stephen. *The Culture of Time and Space, 1880–1918*. 1983. Cambridge, MA: Harvard University Press, 2003.

Kochis, Matthew. Call for papers for "Queer Modernism/Modernism Queered" panel at MSA conference, October 2012. <http://www.cfplist.com/CFP. aspx?CID=302> [accessed October 13, 2014]

Kolocotroni, Vassiliki, Jane Goldman and Olga Taxidou, Eds. *Modernism: An Anthology of Sources and Documents*. 1998. Edinburgh: University of Edinburgh Press, 2009.

Korg, Jacob. "Imagism." *A Companion to Twentieth-Century Poetry*. Ed. Neil Roberts. Oxford: Blackwell, 2011. 127–37.

Kramer, Lawrence, Ed. *Hart Crane's 'The Bridge': An Annotated Edition*. New York: Fordham University Press, 2011.

Krieger, Murray. "The Problem of *Ekphrasis*: Image and Words, Space and Time – and the Literary Work." *Pictures into Words: Theoretical and Descriptive Approaches to Ekphrasis*. Eds. Valerie Robillard and Els Jongeneel. Amsterdam: University Press, 1998. 3–20.

Laity, Cassandra. *H.D. and the Victorian Fin de Siècle: Gender, Modernism, Decadence*. Cambridge: Cambridge University Press, 1996.

Laity, Cassandra. "Editor's Introduction: Beyond Baudelaire, Decadent Aestheticism and Modernity." *Modernism/modernity* 15.3 (2008): 427–30.

Lane, Gary, Ed. *A Concordance to the Poems of Hart Crane*. New York: Haskell House, 1972.

Lee, Gerald Stanley. *Crowds: A Moving Picture of Democracy*. Garden City, NY: Doubleday, Page & Company, 1913.

Lefebvre, Henri. *The Production of Space*. 1974. Trans. Donald Nicholson-Smith. Oxford: Blackwell, 1991.

Levenson, Michael, Ed. *The Cambridge Companion to Modernism*, 2nd edition. Cambridge: Cambridge University Press, 2011.

Lewis, R.W.B. *The Poetry of Hart Crane: A Critical Study*. Princeton: Princeton University Press, 1967.

Logan, John. "Foreword." *White Buildings*. By Hart Crane. New York: Liveright, 1972. xvii–xxxiii.

Lohf, Kenneth A. *The Literary Manuscripts of Hart Crane*. Columbus: Ohio State University Press, 1967.

Lohf, Kenneth A. "The Prose Manuscripts of Hart Crane: An Editorial Portfolio." *Proof* 2 (1970): 1–60.

Lohf, Kenneth A. "The Library of Hart Crane." *Proof: Yearbook of American Bibliographical and Textual Studies*. Vol. 3. Ed. Joseph Katz. Columbia: University of South Carolina, 1973. 283–333.

Love, Heather K. *Feeling Backward: Loss and the Politics of Queer History*. Cambridge, MA: Harvard University Press, 2007.

Love, Heather K. "Introduction: Modernism at Night." *PMLA* 124:3 (2009). 744–48.

Mack, Stephen John. "A Theory of Organic Democracy." *A Companion to Walt Whitman*. 2006. Ed. Donald D. Kummings. Oxford: Blackwell, 2009. 136–50.

Mariani, Paul. *The Broken Tower: A Life of Hart Crane*. New York: Norton, 1999.

Marinetti, Filippo Tommaso. "The Founding and Manifesto of Futurism 1909." Rpt. in *Modernism: An Anthology of Sources and Documents*. Eds. Vassiliki

Kolocotroni, Jane Goldman and Olga Taxidou. 1998. Edinburgh: Edinburgh University Press, 2009. 249–53.
Martin, Robert K. *The Homosexual Tradition in American Poetry*. Austin: University of Texas Press, 1979.
Martin, Robert K. "Painting and Primitivism: Hart Crane and the Development of an American Expressionist Ethic." *Mosaic* 14.3 (1981): 49–62.
Martin, Robert K. "Roland Barthes: Toward an '*Écriture Gaie*.'" *Camp Grounds: Style and Homosexuality*. Ed. David Bergman. Amherst: University of Massachusetts Press, 1993. 282–98.
Marx, Leo. *The Machine in the Garden: Technology and the Pastoral Ideal in America*. 2nd edition. Cary, NC: Oxford University Press, 1967.
Matthews, Steven. *Yeats as Precursor: Readings in Irish, British and American Poetry*. Basingstoke: Macmillan, 2000.
Matthews, Steven. *Modernism*. London: Arnold, 2004.
Matz, Jesse. *Literary Impressionism and Modernist Aesthetics*. Cambridge: Cambridge University Press, 2001.
McM, R. "James Joyce." *Little Review* 5.2 (1918): 55–57.
Meese, Elizabeth A. *(Sem)Erotics: Theorizing Lesbian Writing*. New York: New York University Press, 1992.
Merleau-Ponty, Maurice. *Basic Writings*. Ed. Thomas Baldwin. London: Routledge, 2004.
Miller, Neil. *Out of the Past: Gay and Lesbian History from 1869 to the present*. 1995. New York: Alyson, 2006.
Milliken, William H., Frances Meriam Francis, Henry Sayles Francis, et al., Eds. *The William Sommer Memorial Exhibition Catalogue*. Cleveland: Cleveland Museum of Art, 1950.
Monroe, Harriet and Hart Crane. "A Discussion with Hart Crane." *Poetry* (October 1926): 34–41. <http://www.poetryfoundation.org/poetrymagazine/browse/29/1#/20575761/0> [accessed October 13, 2014]
Morley, Catherine and Alex Goody, Eds. *American Modernism: Cultural Transactions*. Newcastle upon Tyne: Cambridge Scholars Publishing, 2009.
Mumford, Lewis. *Sticks and Stones: A Study of American Architecture and Civilization*. 1924. Second revised edition. New York: Dover Publications, 1955.
Muñoz, José Esteban. *Cruising Utopia: The Then and There of Queer Futurity*. New York: New York University Press, 2009.
Munro, Niall. "Hart Crane's American Decadence." *American Modernism: Cultural Transactions*. Eds. Catherine Morley and Alex Goody. Newcastle upon Tyne: Cambridge Scholars Publishing, 2009. 93–116.
Munson, Gorham. *Waldo Frank: A Study*. New York: Boni and Liveright, 1923.
Munson, Gorham. "Hart Crane: Young Titan in the Sacred Wood." *Destinations: A Canvas of American Literature since 1900*. By Gorham Munson. New York: J.H. Sears, 1928. Rpt. in *Critical Essays on Hart Crane*. Ed. David R. Clark. Boston: G.K. Hall, 1982. 43–51.
Nealon, Christopher. *Foundlings: Lesbian and Gay Historical Emotion Before Stonewall*. Durham, NC: Duke University Press, 2001.
Nicholls, Peter. *Modernisms: A Literary Guide*. Basingstoke: Palgrave Macmillan, 1995.
Nickowitz, Peter. *Rhetoric and Sexuality: The Poetry of Hart Crane, Elizabeth Bishop, and James Merrill*. Basingstoke: Palgrave Macmillan, 2006.

Norton-Smith, John. *A Reader's Guide to Hart Crane's 'White Buildings.'* Lewiston, NY: Edwin Mellen, 1993.

Olson, Liesl. *Modernism and the Ordinary*. Oxford: Oxford University Press, 2009.

Ormsby, Eric. *Facsimiles of Time: Essays on Poetry and Translation*. Erin, Ontario: The Porcupine's Quill, 2001.

Ouspensky, P. D. *Tertium Organum, 2nd American Edition*. Trans. Nicholas Bessaraboff and Claude Bragdon. New York: Knopf, 1924.

Parkinson, Thomas. *Hart Crane & Yvor Winters: Their Literary Correspondence*. Berkeley: University of California Press, 1978.

Pater, Walter. *The Renaissance: Studies in Art and Poetry*. 4th edition. 1893. Mineola, NY: Dover, 2005.

Pater, Walter. "Diaphaneitè." *Studies in the History of the Renaissance*. New edition. Ed. Matthew Beaumont. Oxford: Oxford University Press, 2010. 136–40.

Paul, Sherman. *Hart's Bridge*. Urbana: University of Illinois Press, 1972.

Pearce, Roy Harvey. *The Continuity of American Poetry*. 1961. Princeton: Princeton University Press, 1977.

Pearson, Keith Ansell and Duncan Large. "Introduction." *The Nietzsche Reader*. Eds. Keith Ansell Pearson and Duncan Large. Oxford: Wiley-Blackwell, 2005. 3–11.

Pease, Donald. "Hart Crane and the Tradition of Epic Prophecy." *Critical Essays on Hart Crane*. Ed. David R. Clark. Boston: G. K. Hall, 1982. 255–74.

Pemberton, Vivian. "Hart Crane's Heritage." *Artful Thunder: Versions of the Romantic Tradition in American Literature in Honor of Howard P. Vincent*. Eds. Robert J. DeMott and Sanford E. Marovitz. Kent, OH: The Kent State University Press, 1975. 221–40.

Perry, Robert L. *The Shared Vision of Waldo Frank and Hart Crane*. Lincoln: University of Nebraska, 1966.

Peterson, Christopher. "The Return of the Body: Judith Butler's Dialectical Corporealism." *Discourse* 28.2–3 (2006): 153–77.

Poe, Edgar Allan. "The Power of Words." *Edgar Allan Poe: Poetry and Tales*. Ed. Patrick F. Quinn. New York: Library of America, 1984. 822–25.

Pound, Ezra. "A Few Don'ts by an Imagiste." *Poetry* 1.6 (1913). Rpt. as "A Retrospect." *Poetry in Theory: An Anthology, 1900–2000*. Ed. Jon Cook. Oxford: Blackwell, 2004. 83–90.

Pound, Ezra. "A Pact." Part of the selection "Contemporanea." *Poetry: A Magazine of Verse* 2.1 (April 1913): 6. Rpt. in *Ezra Pound: Poems and Translations*. Ed. Richard Sieburth. New York: Library of America, 2003. 269.

Pound, Ezra. "Preface." *Poetical Works of Lionel Johnson*. London: Elkin Mathews, 1915. Rpt. As "Lionel Johnson." *Literary Essays of Ezra Pound*. Ed. T.S. Eliot. New York: New Directions, 1968. 361–70.

Pound, Ezra. "Swinburne Versus His Biographers." *Poetry* 11.6 (March 1918). Rpt. in *Literary Essays of Ezra Pound*. Ed. T. S. Eliot. New York: New Directions, 1968. 290–94.

Pound, Ezra. "Date Line." *Literary Essays of Ezra Pound*. 1934. Ed. T.S. Eliot. New York: New Directions, 1968. 74–87.

Pound, Ezra. *The Cantos of Ezra Pound*. 1970. New York: New Directions Publishing Corporation, 1996.

Pratt, William. "Introduction." *The Imagist Poem: Modern Poetry in Miniature*, Revised edition. 1963. Ed. William Pratt. Ashland, OR: Story Line Press, 2001. 19–46.

Pupin, Michael. *Romance of the Machine*. New York: Charles Scribner's Sons, 1930.
Raitt, Suzanne. "Lesbian Modernism?" *GLQ: A Journal of Lesbian and Gay Studies* 10.1 (2003): 111–21.
Reed, Brian M. *Hart Crane: After His Lights*. Tuscaloosa: University of Alabama Press, 2006.
Reed, John R. *Decadent Style*. Athens: Ohio University Press, 1985.
Riddel, Joseph. "Hart Crane's Poetics of Failure." *English Literary History* 33.4 (1966): 473–96. Rpt. in *Hart Crane*. Ed. Harold Bloom. New York: Chelsea House, 1986. 91–110.
Rimbaud, Arthur. *Collected Poems*. Trans. Martin Sorrell. Oxford: Oxford University Press, 2001.
Riordan, Maurice. "Introduction." *Hart Crane – Poems Selected by Maurice Riordan*. Ed. Maurice Riordan. London: Faber and Faber, 2008. vii–xiv.
Roberts, Neil, Ed. *A Companion to Twentieth-Century Poetry*. Oxford: Blackwell, 2011.
Robinson, William H. "Lost in Translation: American Modernists in Ohio." *Remapping the New: Modernism in the Midwest, 1893–1945*, symposium organized by the Terra Museum of American Art and the Union League Club of Chicago. September 18, 2004. <www.stage.terraamericanart.pairsite.com/wp-content/uploads/2012/05/sb_subpages_file_5_1470.pdf> [accessed June 15, 2010]
Rodensky, Lisa. "Introduction." *Decadent Poetry from Wilde to Naidu*. Ed. Lisa Rodensky. London: Penguin, 2006. xxiii–xlviii.
Rodensky, Lisa, Ed. *Decadent Poetry from Wilde to Naidu*. London: Penguin, 2006.
Roditi, Edouard. "Cruising with Hart Crane." *The Autobiographical Eye*. Ed. Daniel Halpern. Hopewell, NJ: Ecco, 1982. 2000–8.
Rowe, John Carlos. "The 'Super-Historical' Sense of Hart Crane's 'The Bridge.'" *Genre* 11.4 (1978): 597–625.
Salvato, Nick. *Uncloseting Drama: American Modernism and Queer Performance*. New Haven CT: Yale University Press, 2010.
Schleifer, Ronald. *Modernism and Time: The Logic of Abundance in Literature, Science, and Culture, 1880–1930*. Cambridge: Cambridge University Press, 2000.
Schmitt, Carl, Jr. "The Young Hart Crane's Friendship with Carl Schmitt." *CSF Bulletin* 1.2 (1998): 1–2.
Schmitt, Carl. "'Don't Make Theories, Just Look at It.'" *CSF Bulletin* 2.1 (2006): 1–2.
Schultz, Susan M. "The Success of Failure: Hart Crane's Revision of Whitman and Eliot in 'The Bridge.'" *South Atlantic Review* 54.1 (1989): 55–70.
Scruton, Roger. *Kant: A Very Short Introduction*. 1982. Oxford: Oxford University Press, 2001.
Sedgwick, Eve Kosofsky. *Between Men: English Literature and Male Homosexual Desire*. New York: Columbia University Press, 1985.
Sedgwick, Eve Kosofsky. *Epistemology of the Closet*. Berkeley: University of California Press, 1990.
Sedgwick, Eve Kosofsky. *Tendencies*. Durham: Duke University Press, 1993.
Sedgwick, Eve Kosofsky. *Touching Feeling: Affectivity, Pedagogy, Performativity*. Durham: Duke University Press, 2003.
Selby, Nick. "'Queer Shoulders to the Wheel': Whitman, Ginsberg and a Bisexual Poetics." *The Bisexual Imaginary: Representation, Identity and Desire*.

Eds. Bi Academic Intervention: Phoebe Davidson, Jo Eadie, Clare Hemmings, Ann Kaloski and Merl Storr. London: Cassell, 1997. 120–40.

Shapiro, Karl. "Study of 'Cape Hatteras' by Hart Crane." *Poets at Work*. Ed. Charles D. Abbott. New York: Harcourt, Brace & World, 1948. 111–18. Rpt. in *Studies in* The Bridge. Ed. David R. Clark. Columbus: Charles E. Merrill, 1970. 37–43.

Shapiro, Stephen. "Marx to the Rescue! Queer Theory and the Crisis of Prestige." *New Formations* 53 (Summer 2004): 77–90.

Sinfield, Alan. *The Wilde Century: Effeminacy, Oscar Wilde and the Queer Moment*. New York: Columbia University Press, 1994.

Smith, Ernest. *'The Imaged Word': The Infrastructure of Hart Crane's 'White Buildings.'* New York: Lang, 1990.

Smith, Ernest. "Spending out the Self: Homosexuality and the Poetry of Hart Crane." *Literature and Homosexuality*. Ed. Michael J. Meyer. Amsterdam: Rodopi, 2000. 161–82.

Snediker, Michael D. *Queer Optimism: Lyric Personhood and Other Felicitous Persuasions*. Minneapolis: University of Minnesota Press, 2009.

Spengler, Oswald. *The Decline of the West: An Abridged Edition*. 1932. Eds. Helmut Werner and Arthur Helps. Trans. Charles Francis Atkinson. Oxford: Oxford University Press, 1991.

Spengler, Oswald. *Man and Technics: A Contribution to a Philosophy of Life*. 1932. Trans. Charles Francis Atkinson. London: European Books Society, 1992.

Stockinger, Jacob. "Homotextuality: A Proposal." *The Gay Academic*. Ed. Louie Crew. Palm Springs: ETC, 1978. 135–51.

Stork, Charles Wharton, Ed. *Contemporary Verse* 5.1 (1918). <http://babel.hathitrust.org/cgi/pt?id=nyp.33433076018112;seq=13> [accessed October 13, 2014]

Sugg, Richard P. *Hart Crane's 'The Bridge': A Description of Its Life*. Tuscaloosa: University of Alabama Press, 1976.

Swinburne, Algernon Charles. *Selected Poems*. Ed. Catherine Maxwell. London: Dent, 1997.

Symons, Arthur. "The Decadent Movement in Literature." *Harpers New Monthly Magazine* 87.522 (1893): 858–69.

Symons, Arthur. *The Symbolist Movement in Literature*. 1919. London: Kessinger, 2004.

Tapper, Gordon A. *The Machine that Sings: Modernism, Hart Crane, and the Culture of the Body*. London: Routledge, 2006.

Tashjian, Dickran. *Skyscraper Primitives: Dada and the American Avant-Garde, 1910–1925*. Middletown, CT: Wesleyan University Press, 1975.

Tate, Allen. "Crane: The Poet as Hero." *Essays of Four Decades*. 1969. London: Oxford University Press, 1970. 324–28.

Tate, Allen. "Hart Crane." *Essays of Four Decades*. 1969. London: Oxford University Press, 1970. 310–23.

Thacker, Andrew. *Moving Through Modernity: Space and Geography in Modernism*. 2003. Manchester: Manchester University Press, 2009.

Toomer, Jean. "The Experience." *A Jean Toomer Reader: Selected Unpublished Writings*. Ed. Frederik L. Rusch. Oxford: Oxford University Press, 1993. 33–76.

Toomer, Jean. *The Letters of Jean Toomer*. Ed. Mark Whalan. Knoxville: University of Tennessee Press, 2006.

Trachtenberg, Alan, Ed. *Hart Crane: A Collection of Critical Essays*. Englewood Cliffs, NJ: Prentice-Hall, 1982.
Turner, Mark W. *Backward Glances: Cruising the Queer Streets of New York and London*. London: Reaktion, 2003.
Ulrick-Désert, Jan. "Queer Space." *Queers in Space: Communities/Public Spaces/Sites of Resistance*. Eds. Gordon Brent Ingram, Anne-Marie Bouthillette and Yolanda Retter. Seattle: Bay, 2007. 16–25.
Unterecker, John. *Voyager: A Life of Hart Crane*. New York: Anthony Blond, 1969.
Untermeyer, Louis. *American Poetry since 1900*. 1923. London: Grant Richards, 1924.
Van Hulle, Dirk. *Textual Awareness: A Genetic Study of Late Manuscripts by Joyce, Proust, and Mann*. Ann Arbor: University of Michigan Press, 2004.
Vincent, John Emil. *Queer Lyrics: Difficulty and Closure in American Poetry*. Basingstoke: Palgrave Macmillan, 2002.
Virgil [P. Vergili Maronis]. *Aenidos: Liber Sextus*. Ed. R. G. Austin. Oxford: Oxford University Press, 1986.
Weber, Brom. *Hart Crane: A Biographical and Critical Study*. New York: Bodley, 1948.
Webster, Noah, Ed. *Webster's Unabridged Dictionary: An American Dictionary of the English Language*. Rev. Chauncey A. Goodrich and Noah Porter. Albany: J. B. Lyon, 1909.
Weir, David. *Decadence and the Making of Modernism*. Amherst: University of Massachusetts Press, 1995.
Weir, David. *Decadent Culture in the United States: Art and Literature Against the American Grain, 1890–1926*. Albany: State University of New York Press, 2008.
Whalan, Mark. "Introduction." *The Letters of Jean Toomer*. Ed. Mark Whalan. Knoxville: University of Tennessee Press, 2006. xvii–xli.
White, Eric B. *Transatlantic Avant-Gardes: Little Magazines and Localist Modernism*. Edinburgh: Edinburgh University Press, 2013.
Whitman, Walt. *Walt Whitman: Complete Poetry and Collected Prose*. Ed. Justin Kaplan. New York: Library of America, 1982.
Wilde, Oscar. *The Complete Works of Oscar Wilde*. London: HarperCollins, 2003.
Williams, William Carlos. *In the American Grain*. 1925. London: Penguin, 1971.
Williams, William Carlos. *Selected Essays*. 1954. New Directions, 1969.
Williams, William Carlos. "Hart Crane [1899–1932]." *Hart Crane: A Collection of Critical Essays*. Ed. Alan Trachtenberg. Englewood Cliffs, NJ: Prentice-Hall, 1982. 32–34.
Williams, William Carlos. *Collected Poems I: 1909–1939*. 1987. Eds. A. Walton Litz and Christopher MacGowan. Manchester: Carcanet, 2000.
Williams, William Carlos. "Author's Introduction [to *The Wedge*]." *The Collected Poems of William Carlos Williams, Volume II, 1939–1962*. Ed. Christopher MacGowan. Manchester: Carcanet, 2001. 53–55.
Winnubst, Shannon. "Temporality in Queer Theory and Continental Philosophy." *Philosophy Compass* 5.2 (2010): 136–146.
Winters, Yvor. "The Progress of Hart Crane." *Poetry* 36 (1930): 153–65. Rpt. in *Hart Crane: A Collection of Critical Essays*. Ed. Alan Trachtenberg. Englewood Cliffs, NJ: Prentice-Hall, 1982. 23–31.
Witchey, Holly Rarick. "The Battle of the Early Moderns: The Kokoon Club [sic] and the Cleveland Society of Artists." *Cleveland as a Center of Regional Art*.

Proceedings from a symposium presented by the Cleveland Artists Foundation at the Cleveland Museum of Art. November 13–14, 1993. Ed. Sandy Richert. Cleveland: Cleveland Artists Foundation, 1993. 37-47. <http://academic.csuohio.edu/tah/regional_arts/Cleveland_as_a_Center/p37thebattle.pdf> [accessed October 13, 2014]

Yingling, Thomas E. *Hart Crane and the Homosexual Text: New Thresholds, New Anatomies.* Chicago: University of Chicago Press, 1990.

Index

Note: "n" after a page reference denotes a note number on that page.

abstraction, 42, 50, 52, 181; *see also* Chapter 2 *passim*
Ahmed, Sara, 140–1, 162, 169
Anderson, Benedict, 197n3
Anderson, Sherwood, 44, 45, 73, 151–2, 153
anti-social thesis, 70
Armstrong, Tim, 169, 197n7
atopias, 71–2, 90

Barthes, Roland, 71, 72, 105–6, 113, 118, 119, 120
Baudelaire, Charles, 17, 29, 30, 73, 74–5, 79, 190n10
Bell, Clive, 43, 46–7, 188n8, 188n11
Bell, Ian F. A., 127, 139–40
Benjamin, Walter, 17, 73, 75, 190n10
Berlant, Lauren, 2–3
Bersani, Leo, 70
Bishop, Ryan, and John Phillips, *Modernist Avant-Garde Aesthetics and Contemporary Military Technology*, 196n5
Blackmur, R. P., 8, 156
body, the, 14, 15, 22, 60–2, 65, 68, 69, 72, 96, 104–10, 112–15, 125–6, 136, 140–9, 153, 158, 160, 166–7, 168–70, 176–7, 192n22, 197n7, 197n8; *see also* Chapter 4 *passim*
Boone, Joseph Allen, 7, 173, 179
Brunner, Edward, J., 183n4, 192n19
Butler, Judith, 142–3, 145, 146, 178; comments on Foucault's analysis of Herculine Barbin, 89–90

Certeau, Michel de, 63, 74, 79, 83, 84, 87; phatic aspect, 88–9
chiasmus, 59, 60–1, 62
Clark Doeren, Suzanne, 92, 96

Cowley, Malcolm, 9, 12, 13, 128, 129, 130, 183n6
Crane, Hart, and modernism, 3–7, 13–14, 15, 37, 44–5, 96, 98–9, 134, 139–40, 168, 170, 172–3, 175, 178–9, 181, 182, 197n1; relationship with T. S. Eliot, 4, 14, 15, 17, 31–2, 86, 92, 96, 100, 123, 134, 135, 136, 138–40, 147, 153, 179–80, 194n16, 194n17; theory of interior form, 44, 64, 73–4, 130; logic of metaphor, 8, 14, 56, 65, 84–90, 132, 137, 177–8; early poems: "Episode of Hands," 1, 2, 7, 9, 107, 171, 172; "In Shadow," 22, 30; "The Moth that God Made Blind," 20–3; *White Buildings*: "At Melville's Tomb," 84, 128, 148–9, 169; "Black Tambourine," 43, 73–4; "Legend," 55, 59, 61, 81–2, 107, 180; "My Grandmother's Love Letters," 80, 81; "October-November," 33–5; "Passage," 133–6; "Possessions," 75–9; "Recitative," 54–60, 189n19; "Voyages I," 12, 14, 62, 71–2, 91, 100, 101–2, 106, 108, 112, 113, 183n4, 191n1; "Voyages II," 12, 71–2, 101, 104–8, 112–15, 117, 118–20, 177; "Voyages III," 12, 71–2, 107, 114, 116–7, 118, 119, 120, 176; "Voyages IV," 12, 71–2, 128–9; "Voyages VI," 12, 71–2, 101, 122–3 (for "Voyages" sequence, *see also* unpublished poems below); "The Wine Menagerie," 65–71, 81; *The Bridge*, as epic poem, 12–13, 91–4, 95, 135, 153; and myth, 93, 94, 95, 122, 159, 164, 191n23;

Crane, Hart, and modernism, – *continued*
"Atlantis," 87–90, 93, 122, 123, 164–5, 168, 170, 197n8; "Ave Maria," 87–8, 109–10, 111, 185n12; "Cape Hatteras," 15, 84, 109–10, 115–16, 123, 154–6, 157–64, 165–7, 168–9, 195n2, 196n3, 196n4, 196n5; "Cutty Sark," 84, 109–10; "Indiana," 108–9; "Quaker Hill," 102, 112; "The Dance," 84, 102, 141; "The Harbor Dawn," 107; "The River," 111; "The Tunnel," 112; "To Brooklyn Bridge," 84, 145; "Van Winkle," 102–3, 110–11, 195n2; other poems: "Interludium," 44, 45, 46, 48, 49–50; "The Broken Tower," 12–13, 15, 142, 144–9; unpublished poems (including manuscript drafts): "A31a, The Bottom of the Sea is Cruel ["Voyages I,"]," 100–2, 191–2n4; "A32, "Notes for Voyages" ["Voyages II"]," 72, 104–8, 114–15, 118–19, 177, 190n9; "A33 ["Voyages II"]," 72, 107, 113–14, 119; "A35 ["Voyages II"]," 119; "A36 ["Voyages II"]," 72; "A37 ["Voyages II"]," 72, 114, 119; "A39 ["Voyages II"]," 72; "Voyages ["Voyages IV"]," 128–9; "B24, CAPE HATTERAS ["Cape Hatteras"]," 167; "B29, NOTES Cape Hatteras section – (the forge) ["Cape Hatteras"]," 160; "C45, The Broken Tower ["The Broken Tower"]," 145–6; "D102, SONNET ["The Broken Tower"]," 116–17; prose: "General Aims and Theories," 8, 9, 37–8, 56, 82, 86, 88, 128, 137, 139, 146; "Joyce and Ethics," 22, 28–30; "Modern Poetry," 63, 167; "Sherwood Anderson," 151–2, 153
crisis of perception, 52–9

Dean, Tim, 8, 9–10, 135, 137, 175–6
Decadence, 5, 14, 17–40, 41, 179, 183–4n1, 185n18, 185–6n21; *see also* Chapter 1 *passim*
deregulation of space, 14, 79–80, 83–5
Delany, Samuel R., 109–10
difficulty, 6, 7–11, 53, 56–57, 60, 62, 105, 126, 135, 172–3, 177, 189n19
dimensional aesthetic, 7–8, 39–40, 74, 127, 176
ding an sich, 43, 47–8, 51, 53
Doan, Laura, 3, 5, 6, 7
Donne, John, 73, 189n19
Doolittle, Hilda (H.D.), 5, 31, 34–6, 178–82, 184n7, 197n4

ecstasy, 51, 82, 120–3, 131, 136–7, 138, 191n1
Edelman, Lee, 2, 56–7, 59–60, 61, 70–1, 86–7, 99–100, 104–5, 106, 120, 122, 146, 148–9, 170, 192n18
ekphrasis, 9, 14, 42, 44–50, 51–2, 74
Eliot, T. S., 5, 8, 15, 17, 30, 31–2, 33, 86, 92, 100, 135, 136, 138–40, 168, 179, 191n3, 194n16, 194n17; *The Waste Land*, 4, 100, 123, 134, 136, 138, 147, 153
encoded homosexuality, 6, 9, 26, 175–6, 177, 181–2
epistemology, *see* knowledge
Evans, Walker, 1, 2, 61, 107

failure, *see* queer failure *and* Chapter 6 *passim*
flâneur, *see* queer flâneur
Foucault, Michel, 10, 178; panopticism, 67, 189n5; analysis of Herculine Barbin, 89–90; *The Will to Knowledge*, 173, 193n7
fourth dimension, and higher consciousness, 126, 136–7, 138
Frank, Waldo, 4, 19, 52, 60, 117, 137, 152, 164, 193n2, 195n1, 195n2; *Our America*, "The Machine and Metaphysics," 160; view of *The Bridge* as something to be used, 170
French Symbolists, 5, 184n3
Futurism, 153, 154–6; "The Founding and Manifesto of Futurism 1909," 155
futurity, 3, 14, 70–1, 72, 96, 99–104, 108–9, 112–13, 121–2, 177, 182; *see also* Chapter 4 *passim*

Gabriel, Daniel, 11–12, 93–4
Garrity, Jane, 3, 5, 6, 7
genetic criticism, 12, 91, 176–7
geometry, 138, 179–80
Giles, Paul, 13, 183n5
Grossman, Allen, 96, 142, 177, 178

Hammer, Langdon, 6, 17, 26, 32, 51–2, 99, 134–5, 139, 146, 186n24
handiness, 15, 157, 161–2, 171, 60–1; *see also* Chapter 6 *passim*
hands, 1–2, 7, 15, 21, 22, 49, 54, 72, 76, 80, 82, 107, 109, 112, 117, 123, 153, 157, 161–3, 166–7, 168, 170–1, 172; *see also* Chapter 6 *passim*
hauntology of the body, 147–9
heteronormativity, 11, 14, 48–50, 64, 67, 83–4, 90, 95, 101–2, 143, 148–9, 176, 182
Heidegger, Martin, 14, 15, 96, 98–9, 106, 114, 120–2, 147, 170, 171, 196–7n5; *Being and Time*, 120–2, 161–3; "The Question Concerning Technology," 163–5, 168
Hellenism, 6, 17, 35–40, 186n29
Hickman, Miranda, B., 179–80, 197n4
history, 14, 63, 74, 88, 89, 91–7, 98, 107–8, 111, 121–3, 130, 136, 146, 163–5, 183–4n1, 191n23
Hocquenghem, Guy, 101–2, 106–7
homographesis, 148–9
homotextual space, 64, 189n2

Imagism, 5, 17, 32–5, 41, 47, 179, 186n29
immateriality, 14–15, 124, 126–9, 133–6, 140–2, 149, 179
intersubjectivity, 7, 9, 14, 50, 52, 53–4, 58, 68, 171, 178, 181; *see also* Chapter 2 *passim*
Irwin, John T., 12–13, 184n3, 187n34, 187n36

James, William, radical empiricism, 132–3
Johnson, Lionel, 4, 17, 19, 22–3, 31, 32
Joyce, James, 168, 187n34; *Ulysses* 28–30, 38, 134–5, 140; *A Portrait of the Artist as a Young Man*, 167

Kern, Stephen, 190n13
Kling, Joseph, 5, 16, 22
knowledge, 6–7, 21, 23, 48, 56, 66, 94, 105, 170, 196n4; in opposition to experience, 12, 14–15, 100, 124, 126, 127–36, 138–9; *see also* Chapter 5 *passim*
Kokoon Arts Klub (Cleveland), 43, 187n3
Kramer, Lawrence, 12, 111, 191n26, 192n14

Lachaise, Gaston, 42, 51, 188n13; *La Montagne*, 46, 49–50
Laity, Cassandra, 6, 17, 31
Laukhuff's bookstore (Cleveland), 17, 184n2
Lefebvre, Henri, 11, 65–7
lesbian modernism *see* Sapphic modernism
literary impressionism, 17, 18, 32–5, 42, 53–4
little magazines, 4, 5, 15, 17, 19, 36, 150, 183n2, 183n3, 191–2n4
Little Review, The, 5, 17, 19, 22, 28, 30, 32, 43–4, 167, 185n19, 185–6n21, 188n5, 188n8, 191–2n4
logic of metaphor, *see* Crane, Hart
Lohf, Kenneth, A., 186–7n33, 190n9
Love, Heather K., 39, 40, 54, 173

Machine, the, 15, 150–71, 196n3
Mack, Stephen John, 110
Marinetti, F. T., *see* Futurism
Martin, Robert K., 2, 46, 76, 115, 188n11
Marx, Leo, *The Machine in the Garden*, 165–7
masculine language, 5, 30–2
materiality, 15, 123, 126–7, 135–6, 143–50, 164, 194–5n19; new materiality, 127, 136–42
McM, R., 28–30
Merleau-Ponty, Maurice, 11, 60–2, 107
modernism, 2–17; *see also* queer modernism *and* Introduction *and* Conclusion
Modernist Moment, 97–9
Monroe, Harriet, 9, 11, 56, 65, 84–7, 128, 169–70

movement, 7, 10–11, 14, 34, 61, 65, 74, 76, 79–82, 83–4, 85–6, 88–9, 97, 109, 111, 114, 116, 117–18, 121, 123, 153, 174; *see also* spatial practices *and* Chapter 3 *passim*
Mumford, Lewis, 171
Muñoz, José Esteban, 11, 69–70, 71, 88, 170
Munson, Gorham, 4, 5, 31, 32, 43, 44, 52, 56, 77, 128, 129, 130–2, 134, 138, 152, 153, 185n19, 188n6, 190n12, 193n4, 193n5, 193n6, 193n7, 194n13, 195n2; *Waldo Frank*, 152, 153–4
mysticism, 4, 14–15, 124, 125–7, 136–42, 149, 180, 195n2, 197n4; *see also* Chapter 5 *passim*

Nealon, Christopher, 3–4, 55, 81, 92, 95, 97, 105, 121, 133
Nietzsche, Friedrich, 14, 96, 185–6n21; eternal return, 97–9, 106, 114
normativity, 10, 11, 14, 48, 64, 79, 86–7, 95, 101–2, 112, 118, 120, 168–9, 175, 183–4n1, 197n8

obscurity, *see* difficulty
Olson, Liesl, 168, 170
Opffer, Emil, 82, 117, 128–9
Ouspensky, P.D., 126–7, 137; *Tertium Organum*, 132, 137–9, 194n15

Pater, Walter, 4, 14, 17, 35–6, 37–40, 57, 63, 140, 144, 179, 187n34, 187n36, 188–9n18; the "impression," 10, 42, 53–4, 61, 72, 141; *The Renaissance*, 38–9, 54, 61, 187n34; "Diaphaneitè," 141–2
Pearce, Roy Harvey, 135; view of *The Bridge* as a machine, 170
Pease, Donald, 93
Peterson, Christopher, 147–8
phatic aspect, 88–9
Phillips, John, *see* Bishop, Ryan
Poe, Edgar Allan, 194–5n19
production of space, 64, 65–7, 74, 82, 89
Pupin, Michael, 151, 158

queer
community, 157–61, 172–3, 178–82; *see also* Conclusion
extension, 15, 168–71, 197n8
failure, 3, 150, 156–7, 162–3
flâneur, 73–9, 190n10
modernism, 2, 3–11, 13–15, 98–99, 172–6, 178–82, 197n1
negativity, 3, 64, 70–2, 81, 99–103, 120, 122, 177
space, 11, 63–74, 89–90, 112–15, 133, 140–1, 163, 173, 182; *see also* deregulation of space
spatial practices, 65, 74; cruising, 75–9; walking, 79–82, 84; *see also* logic of metaphor *and* phatic aspect *and* queer flâneur
temporality, 11, 14, 90, 91, 95–7, 98–9, 101–2; and temporal gaps, 104–10
temporal blur, 110–12; recurrence and sameness, 112–15
reparative reading, 172, 174–6, 177–8, 181
self-consciousness, 18, 68, 69–70, 95, 115–18, 122
utopias, 14, 61–2, 65, 67–71, 120, 121, 197n8

Raitt, Suzanne, 6
Reed, Brian M., 5, 17, 21–2, 33, 178, 184n8, 191n1
relationality, 2–3, 7, 8, 53, 55, 88, 144, 172, 178–9; *see also* Introduction
Riddel, Joseph, 92, 93, 94, 95
Rosenfeld, Paul, 41, 44–5, 188n8

Salvato, Nick, 10
Sapphic modernism, 6, 172, 173
Sappho, 5, 35–6, 37
Schleifer, Ronald, 98
Schmitt, Carl, 42–3, 45
Sedgwick, Eve Kosofsky, 40, 116, 131, 142, 174–6, 177, 181
Sinfield, Alan, 25, 26, 185n14, 185n18
Sommer, William, 14, 41–2, 43–9, 50–1, 52–3, 152, 187–8n4, 188n16

space, *see* queer space *and* Chapter 3 *passim*
spatial practices, *see* queer spatial practices
Spengler, Oswald, 151, 163, 165, 195n1
Stanley Lee, Gerald, 151, 152, 163
sterility, 29, 80, 99, 108
Stieglitz, Alfred, 4, 41, 44, 51–2, 54, 79, 181, 188n15
Swinburne, Algernon Charles, 4, 20–2, 29, 30, 33, 184n7
Symons, Arthur, *Symbolist Movement in Literature, The*, 17–19, 22, 23, 28

Tapper, Gordon A., 12, 67, 78, 190n7
Tate, Allen, 55, 56, 92, 93, 100, 130, 134, 138, 142, 156, 157, 179, 189n19, 191n3, 194n15
technology and failure, 15, 154–61, 162–3; *see also* Chapter 6 *passim*
temporality, *see* queer temporality *and* Chapter 4 *passim*
Toomer, Jean, 4, 41, 76, 77, 78–9, 125–6, 127, 128–9, 133, 136, 137, 149, 193n2, 193n3, 194n12, 194n13, 195n2
transgression of space, 11, 27–8, 62, 65, 79–82, 83
twelve blank pages in the *Little Review*, 19

unexpectedness, 1–4, 7, 113, 140, 172–3, 177–8
Unterecker, John, 16, 43, 184n2, 188n16
Untermeyer, Louis, 36–7, 38, 186n32

Van Hulle, Dirk, 91, 176
Vincent, John Emil, 13, 189n3

Webster's Unabridged Dictionary, 13, 118, 134, 135, 144, 146, 183n5, 183n6
Weir, David, 5, 19
White Buildings, see Crane, Hart
White, Eric B., 183n2, 195n2
Whitman, Walt, 2, 4, 5, 84, 92, 93, 103, 109–10, 123, 154, 156, 158–161, 162, 164, 165–7, 168, 194n14, 196n3
Wilde, Oscar, 4, 5, 14, 16–19, 22, 25–30, 31, 32–5, 37, 54, 81, 105, 173, 179, 185n14, 186n25
Williams, William Carlos, 4, 5, 52, 93, 128, 129, 130, 131, 132, 135, 170, 194n11

Yingling, Thomas E., 8–10, 17, 24, 27, 68, 83, 85, 94, 95, 121, 133, 135, 136, 175, 176

Printed and bound by CPI Group (UK) Ltd, Croydon, CR0 4YY